Library of Congress Cataloging-in-Publication Data

Marich, Jamie.

EMDR made simple : 4 approaches to using EMDR with every client / Jamie Marich. p. cm.

Includes bibliographical references.

ISBN-13: 978-1-936128-06-8

ISBN-10: 1-936128-06-3

1. Eye movement desensitization and reprocessing.
2. Psychic trauma--Treatment. I. Title. II. Title: Eye movement desensitization and reprocessing made simple.

RC489.E98M37 2011

616.89'17--dc23

2011024807

www.pesi.com

When I began reading *EMDR Made Simple*, I couldn't put it down. With her four faces of EMDR, Marich has broken out of the EMDR orthodoxy representing a fresh new voice and perspective that is intelligent, clinically sound, and an important contribution to the evolution of EMDR. This well-written, engaging book is full helpful, easy-to-digest practical information that will be an important aid to EMDR therapists seeking to integrate EMDR into their clinical practices. Marich has the rare talent of being able to break down complex ideas into guiding principles that therapists can easily grasp, and weave research studies into the text providing the work substance, while still maintaining a relationship with the reader that is personal and collegial. I will be sure to recommend *EMDR Made Simple* to my EMDR trainees and consultees.

Laurel Parnell, Ph.D. is an EMDRIA-approved trainer and consultant, author of *A Therapist's Guide to EMDR, Tapping In: A Step-by Step Guide to Activating Your Healing Resources Through Bilateral Stimulation, Transforming Trauma: EMDR* and *EMDR in the Treatment of Adults Abused as Children.*

After completing both Part I and II EMDR training I felt somewhat lost in how to tailor my personal approach with clients while maintaining the integrity of the EMDR method. Dr. Marich's book not only illuminated the way for me but gave me the confidence I needed to expand my private practice using EMDR. Her vast clinical experience, directed resources and practical hands on examples demonstrated to me the usefulness of EMDR for a range of clients. *EMDR Made Simple* is an easy to read guide to EMDR greatly influenced by Dr. Marich's friendly and very personable style. Her 4 approaches to EMDR allow the reader to find a mode that works for them while not compromising the best practices efficacy of the EMDR protocol.

Karen Anderson, M.S., LMFT
Private Practice, Las Vegas, NV

I am convinced that eye-movement desensitization and reprocessing (EMDR) is the most important psychological discovery since Freud. The only problem seems to be that early EMDR researchers, who were very successful in terms of demonstrating the clinical efficacy of EMDR, may have prematurely "locked into" a rather strict protocol that could have benefited from some improvements along the way. Dr. Marich provides a very thoughtful analysis of this issue. Her work will do much to help us evaluate both the future of EMDR, and many of its various derivatives.

Allan Botkin, Psy.D.
Induced After Death Communication: A New Therapy for Healing Grief and Trauma

Unlike many authors and EMDR practitioners who have attempted to –and for decades have succeeded in– shrouding this efficient, effective trauma modality in secrecy and mystique– imbuing fear and doubt in many trauma-competent clinicians, Marich clarifies, simplifies and sheds much needed light on this heretofore esoteric process. Thank you for a well-written, common sense, hands-on elucidation of EMDR. If *EMDR Made Simple* was the first book on this subject a clinician were to read, it is close to a guarantee that it will be the first of many.

Linda Curran, BCPC, LPC, CACD, CCPD
Trauma Competency: A Clinician's Guide

As a self identified Protocol-Oriented EMDR Therapist, I applaud Dr. Marich for expanding the accessibility of the EMDR Approach even further. *EMDR Made Simple*...provides an inclusive scope sending a clear messages of mutual respect while supporting an understanding of the EMDR Approach uniting the therapeutic community. A must read for all clinicians!

Earl Grey, Ph.D.
Unify Your Mind: Connecting the Feelers, Thinkers, and Doers of Your Brain

Kudos to Dr. Marich for cutting through the dogma and ideology that so often surrounds new approaches and creating a a practical, how-to volume on EMDR. Her thoughtful and ecumenical approach insures that clinicians of all stripes will be able to benefit from the important material in her book.

Scott D. Miller, Ph.D.
The Heart and Soul of Change: Delivering What Works in Therapy
Founder, International Center for Clinical Excellence

Dr. Marich has shown her years of wisdom and professional experience to write a captivating book on EMDR. Her touching stories about her own recovery from trauma will inspire the reader to empathize with the struggles of their patients. Dr. Marich uses her struggles as metaphors to help the reader understand complex treatment protocols while encouraging readers to adapt theory and protocol to their own personal style of therapy. This is a must read book for both beginning and experienced therapists.

Douglas Darnall, Ph.D.
Divorce Casualities and Beyond Divorce Casualties

EMDR

Made Simple

4 Approaches to Using EMDR with Every Client

Jamie Marich
P.h.D., LPCC-S, LICDC

To Mom and Dad—

Thanks for doing the best you could with what you had. Everything turned out just fine.

Acknowledgments

I struggled over whether or not to write this book. Although I had many experiences and insights to share with my fellow clinicians, I was aware that it was a risk to go against the grain of what many in established EMDR circles asserted as truth. At the risk of being labeled unpopular by people I respect, I trudged on and decided to present my view of EMDR, thanks to the encouragement of many people. Thank you for helping me believe that I have something new and fresh to share for the benefit of ordinary clinicians working in the clinical trenches around the world.

Thank you most especially to colleagues and friends Dr. Earl Grey, Dr. Laurel Parnell, Dr. Amy Donovan, Dr. Scott Miller, Dr. Howard Lipke, Robin Shapiro, Dr. Erica Matthews, Mike Olson, Linda Curran, Joel Wood, Bill Aley, Janet Thornton, Rev. Betsy Schenk, Bruce Merkin, Amber Stiles-Bodnar, Dr. Doug Darnall, Mary Riley, Jason Glaspell, Claire Taylor, Ellen DeCarlo, Adam Guerrieri, and Thom Williams. Each of you in your own special way led me to find my inner Galileo. You helped me see that my relative youth and quirky sense of humor are assets rather than detriments when it comes to sharing knowledge. I love you for your encouragement. Thanks to many of you in the EMDRIA community as well for your indirect, but very powerful influence on developing my voice and encouraging me to speak.

Thank you to Janet Leff, the American social worker who mentored me in Bosnia; the children of Majcino Selo in Bosnia-Hercegovina who taught me the vast majority of my clinical skills; and my clients, who have been my greatest instructors over the years. I am indebted to all of you who touched my life in your special way...

Lastly, I would be remiss if I did not extend my sincere thanks to Dr. Francine Shapiro, founder of EMDR. Although I may not agree with many of your positions, Dr. Shapiro, my respect for you and what you have given us is profound. Many thanks!

Table of Contents

Part I : Foundations

Chapter 1: Simplifying My Complex Perspective

"The older I get, the more wisdom I find in the ancient rule of taking first things first—a process which often reduces the most complex human problems to manageable proportions."

—Dwight David Eisenhower

In a 1999 documentary on Eye Movement Desensitization and Reprocessing (EMDR), world-renowned trauma expert Bessel van der Kolk remarked that, "EMDR is so simple, it should have been invented thousands of years ago" (Donovan & Nalepinski, 1999). Some might accuse me of taking van der Kolk's comments out of context, since it is only one in the vast catalogue of neurological perspectives that he has contributed to elucidate EMDR's efficacy. However, after reading all that he has written on EMDR, that statement made a lasting impression because I have learned in my own recovery and professional development that complex problems often have simple solutions. As a clinician, I have learned that working with the most complex clients does not have to be as complicated as we often make it. Just as the Occam's razor principle (entities must not be multiplied beyond necessity) implies, the simplest solution is usually the right one. Yet time and time again I have seen people get tripped up by EMDR because they overcomplicate it. Often, this is not their fault. It happens because they are going to trainings or reading books that present EMDR in academic language that is out of touch with the ordinary clinician's world. Before I go on any further, perhaps I should begin by sharing my own story.

Jamie's Professional Journey

Like many therapists, I entered the helping professions as a result of my own experiences with healing. I saw my first cognitive-behavioral counselor at the age of 18 and entered addiction recovery at the age of 21 to address a myriad of issues including chemical dependency, depression, and coping with past wounds from a dysfunctional family. These traditional methods helped me a great deal. These methods allowed me to attain my initial sobriety and put me on the path toward mental wellness. A significant amount of my own healing occurred when I worked in post-war Bosnia-Hercegovina as an English teacher, language assistant, and aid worker. I spent 3 years working in the country after college, my interest in the area sparked by my Croatian heritage. What I ended up getting was an immersion course in the realities of trauma and its impact on the human experience.

When I returned from Bosnia, having built up some quality sober time, I returned to the States and entered a graduate program in counseling. What I encountered at my first practicum site blind-sided me; in many ways, it was worse than anything I saw in Bosnia. I interned at a child and adolescent inpatient treatment facility and felt very triggered by the way staff members treated the children—they were retraumatizing them! I was powerless to do anything about it and would literally freeze, even dissociate, at the hospital. Old memories surfaced. I even felt suicidal at times. I continued my recovery program and wanted to stay sober, but I was miserable. A wise friend suggested I enter therapy again to address these surfacing issues. Deep down, I knew he was probably right, but I was resistant.

"I know everything that the therapist is going to say," I argued. "I know I'm good enough, I know that the past is the past, I know that my beliefs are irrational, but I just can't get it to really sink in."

Chapter 1: Simplifying My Complex Perspective

Clearly, I was "treatment smart" and cynical about whether traditional cognitive methods would continue to help me. They had gotten me far, but not far enough. I still felt like I was just functioning in life with a big black cloud hanging over me. Desperate for solutions, I was willing to try anything alternative, even anything that I had dismissed in the past, like hypnosis or Reiki, if it demonstrated some potential of helping. One of my graduate school professors, having listened to my dilemma, referred me to a therapist in my Ohio town who was known to utilize some different techniques and approaches. I scheduled an appointment and soon met with my new therapist. I immediately felt as though she understood my plight. During our first session she suggested EMDR and sent me home with a pamphlet about it. Like many a desperate client I have since treated, I said to myself, "Sure, why not." The fact that it was something different from the cognitive-behavioral, rational-emotive, reality therapy norm convinced me to give it a try. At the time, I had no idea what I was in for!

I engaged in EMDR sessions with my therapist at intermittent intervals over a 2-year period. The EMDR helped me finish graduate school, guided me through a difficult transition into life as a professional, and relieved me, finally, of destructive suicidal thoughts. In one of my early EMDR sessions, I was able to encounter a memory of my first suicidal impulse at the age of 9. By confronting the memory, feeling the feelings I'd repressed about the incident at the level of my body, mind, and soul, I was freed from the torture, released from the mental anguish. The EMDR helped me confront, emote, and ultimately address many of the negative feelings I had about my parents and the mixed messages I received growing up. By honoring what I expressed and having that experience validated by my therapist, I was able to let go of the distress that these memories caused. Since receiving EMDR, my relationship with my parents has improved because I was finally able to genuinely forgive them. For me, catharsis was essential before I could truly forgive, and EMDR helped with this process.

I could probably write an entire book solely on my EMDR experience. My 2004 folk music CD *Under My Roof* chronicles many of the touchstone memories that emerged during my EMDR treatment. The memories and issues that I confronted with EMDR were numerous—everything from being bullied on a Catholic school playground as a child to dealing with romantic relationship roadblocks as an adult. EMDR helped me address my whole package of issues, and for the first time in my life, my heart and soul were able to accept positive messages, such as "I am good enough." It helped me put responsibility for past abuse in its proper place, and it confirmed my perspective on events. I maintain that EMDR was effective for me because it validated every aspect of my selfhood—my thoughts, my body, my emotions, my creativity, my spirituality, and my intuition. For me, the bilateral stimulation that essentially defines the EMDR process seemed to tie it all together. I'm not suggesting that EMDR works this fantastically for everyone, but I am confident that it can produce results for many people, especially those who have grown frustrated with traditional therapy.

Within 2 years of becoming a therapist, I chose to get trained in EMDR because I wanted to offer it to my own clients. As a therapist, I seemed to best click with clients who were chronic substance relapsers or who were therapy smart in an intellectual sense but unable to internalize and apply what they learned in treatment. EMDR seemed like a good fit for these clients. I often joke that some of my clients know so much about therapy and recovery, I would probably trust them to run one of my treatment groups. However, with these types of clients, there often exists an inability to sustain long-term growth.

My desire to help the stuck, complicated clients led me to invest in a full training through the EMDR Institute based in Watsonville, California. I began implementing EMDR into my clinical repertoire after my training, and I elected to pursue additional training and individual consultation through providers approved by the EMDR International Association (EMDRIA) out of Austin, Texas. I had the privilege of working with several consultants and EMDR experts to obtain this rich continuing education. I eventually became a Certified Therapist and Approved Consultant, and I have been involved as a volunteer consultant and training organizer with the EMDR Humanitarian Assistance Programs (HAP). As a post-training consultant for HAP, I have had the privilege of working with hundreds of clinicians around the country following their basic trainings, and I feel that this experience has given me a unique perspective on the needs of such clinicians.

I have been trained by the best in EMDR and consider myself to have a solid understanding of the various protocols and procedures that are officially endorsed by EMDRIA. However, as I learned about and applied EMDR, my approach and perspective began to shift. As previously mentioned, I began my human services career in Bosnia-Hercegovina following the civil war that paralyzed that country in the 1990s. It was there, while working under an American social worker and a wise Croatian priest, that I was schooled in the value of the human relationship as the foundation for all healing. My two mentors sent me back to graduate school in the States to learn the "science" of the helping professions, believing that the 3 years I spent working with people throughout Bosnia-Hercegovina provided enough of an education on the "art" of how healers relate to clients in healing relationships. Although I acknowledge the necessity of good science and technique, as I scrambled to learn everything I could about EMDR, my experience of doing EMDR became so much more enriching (and my client outcomes improved) when I allowed the relational imperative, not theory and technique, to drive my EMDR treatment. The essential premise of this book is that if you put the therapeutic relationship in the metaphorical front seat of the car and keep the theory and technique close by as backseat navigators, you will optimize your chances of succeeding in complex cases. In this front seat, the client drives and the therapist guides, with the therapist needing to take the wheel at times when the journey gets too overwhelming for the client.

My view on the relational imperative, which will be explained more thoroughly in Chapter 4, differs from EMDR founder Francine Shapiro's position that execution of EMDR should be a fusion between client, method, and clinician (Dworkin, 2005; Shapiro,

2001). My interpretation of her position is that all three are essentially equal; I maintain that the relational factors should take precedence, especially in work with complex clients. I must clearly explain that although I maintain my EMDRIA credentials, my work that you are now reading does not represent EMDRIA's view of EMDR, nor does it represent the views of Shapiro, the EMDR Institute, or EMDR HAP. Although my perspective was influenced by many of the great minds in the EMDR community, what I am sharing with you in this book is a synthesis of my clinical experiences, research, teaching, and consulting experiences. Take what you like and leave the rest. Throughout the book, I clarify which information is based in research that is not my own, and which information results from my practice and research knowledge.

I consider myself to be a second-generation EMDR therapist. In other words, I was still experiencing my childhood trauma when Shapiro developed EMDR in 1987. Many of the books currently on the market about EMDR have been written by people who are close to Shapiro or who have consulted with her extensively. I can claim no such allegiance, but as a result, I feel that my perspective is fresh. I am merely a clinician who learned this therapy after having an amazing experience with it myself, and I have developed my own ideas, based on my general clinical training and experiences, about how EMDR can be simply, elegantly implemented into daily practice even with the most difficult clients. When I cite major research studies or other works in this book, I make every attempt to do so in a manner that is relevant to the clinical setting. I am simply a clinician, writing for other clinicians.

At present, I work primarily as an EMDR therapist out of PsyCare, Inc., a group counseling practice in Youngstown, Ohio. I offer consultation to new EMDR trainees, and I travel around the country training counselors on a variety of clinical topics. I am a part-time and adjunct faculty member at several universities, having taught undergraduate courses in psychology, ethnicity studies, and human services, as well as graduate courses in psychology (general and organizational) and mental health counseling. I have had the privilege of bringing the gift of EMDR to many clients who have crossed my path in various settings. Throughout this book I share many stories about my joys and struggles using EMDR in both public and private practice.

The reason I opened this book by sharing my story was so you know where I am coming from. I believe in genuine, appropriate disclosure in the therapeutic relationship as well as in the professional relationships that I forge. You will learn more about me throughout this book, as I am full of stories. In the spirit of one of my clinical role models, Irvin Yalom, storytelling is one of the mechanisms that I use to teach. For me, storytelling is one of the best ways to simplify the complex—even the problems surrounding the complex client.

So, What Is a "Complex" Client Anyway?

Throughout this book, I frequently use the phrase "complex client," or "complicated client." Let me take a moment here to explain myself. I know what you might be thinking: Aren't all clients complex? On one hand, you are exactly right. Etymologically, the word complex first surfaced in 1652 (a Latin derivation) meaning composed of several parts. Indeed, there are biopsychosocial (and often spiritual) factors that comprise a human being, and it is a great wonder of creation is that no two people are created equally. So yes, every human being is complex, and I acknowledge that uniqueness in each client.

There is, however, another hand. In 1715, an alternate usage of the word complex emerged, with the word complexity meaning something that is not easily analyzed. Some of the clients we are asked to assess and treat, although unique in their own way, have a more cut and dry presentation. These are the types of clients who are relatively easy to diagnose, and conceptualizing a treatment plan with them seems almost second nature to the experienced clinician. Let's be honest, you may even call some of these the "easy clients" on your caseload (I'll 'fess up, I know I do). But then you have those clients who are a real challenge, those who may be more difficult to assess, more complicated to treat, and, despite your best efforts and their best attempts, may not get better. I'm not even talking about the clients who are a nightmare because of their belligerence or blatant noncompliance. Although complex clients may include these types of people, not all complex clients are this overtly challenging.

In my own experiences with EMDR, the process goes much more smoothly and quickly when you use it on clients who do not bring as many complexities into the treatment setting. Indeed, most of the research that EMDR advocates use to validate the therapy was conducted with clients with post-traumatic stress disorder (PTSD) caused by a single traumatic incident. In many of these studies, potential confounding variables, such as other severe Axis I disorders (in other words, the complexities we often encounter in clinical settings), were weeded out. Sure, I can take one of my higher-functioning clients or a client with single-incident PTSD, do a few sessions of traditional EMDR to clear up a problem, see this therapy work in a near textbook manner, and be awestruck. However, I quickly learned that EMDR does not go as smoothly with clients who present with multiple complexities in addition to the trauma-related concerns that would warrant the EMDR. These complications can include addiction, other mental illnesses (e.g., bipolar spectrum disorders, psychotic disorders, attention deficit hyperactivity disorder), learning disorders, angry and aggressive behaviors, low motivation, lifestyle issues, and deficits in basic needs (e.g., food, shelter, positive social support). Moreover, there is the entire notion of single-incident versus complex PTSD to consider, a diagnostic caveat that will be explored more fully in Chapter 7.

Yes, it is not easy to do EMDR while addressing one or more of these complexities; however, clients with these complications are typically the ones who can benefit most from EMDR. This book gives you the tools and the guidance you will need to deal with complex clients, clients whose cases cannot be easily conceptualized due to one or more complicating factors aside from the trauma. From my experience with consultation, clinicians often emerge from EMDR trainings very confused. As one of my consultees recently expressed after a Part I training:

> At first I heard the trainer going on and on about how wonderful EMDR is and how it's not just a trauma therapy and can be used with just about anybody. And then the next day, she scared me into thinking that I couldn't do it with the tricky clients—the addicts, those on psychotropic medications. I felt so confused because I work in community mental health and I only have the "hard" clients on my caseload, so how am I supposed to do the recommended number of practice sessions before the Part II training?

Rest assured, you can do EMDR with the more complex clients, provided that safety for the client is your priority and that you carefully prepare the client for the experience of reprocessing, using a variety of methods if needed. Preparation, which is officially Phase 2 of 8 in Shapiro's traditional protocol (2001) is, in my opinion, the most important and often most overlooked phase in EMDR. Many of the guidelines and suggestions that I provide in the book are designed to bolster the preparation phase of EMDR. Preparation is essential in doing EMDR with any client, but it takes on even greater significance in doing EMDR with the complex client.

Preparation also encompasses your personal development as a clinician. The importance of building your personal trauma competency and looking at your own issues with trauma and certain client populations is explored later in this book. As Linda Curran (2010) articulated in her book *Trauma Competency*, EMDR is not a dangerous process; it becomes dangerous when it is placed into the hands of the wrong people—those who are not prepared to address trauma issues in a manner that honors safety. Appreciating the importance of the therapeutic alliance in trauma therapy and EMDR, especially in work with complex clients, is stressed throughout these pages. Above all, it is my hope that after reading this book, you will feel more comfortable with the intricacies of using EMDR in your clinical setting. Although evaluating these intricacies sometimes means that EMDR may not be the therapy of choice for certain clients (I do not believe EMDR is for everyone), I hope that after reading this book you will be less afraid to use it with the people who can most benefit from it. Wherever possible, I have tried to include tools throughout the book that you can copy and use with clients. However, my overall mission is to provide some guidance about how to conceptualize cases and to pass along some of my suggestions for what can work with complex clients, especially when EMDR isn't going as smoothly as you would like.

A Note About Training and a Disclaimer

I have been a high school speech coach and consultant for 14 years. Although I typically teach the speaking and dramatic facets of the activity, I have learned a thing or two from my colleagues who coach debate. In most debate tournaments across the country, students are given a monthly topic of social importance that they debate at tournaments throughout that month. Some students go into debate rounds with pre-written cases their coaches prepared for them and are prepped with specific responses they should use if they are attacked with point X, Y, or Z. Very often, these students are successful, but in my view, they never really learn how to debate if they are just spouting off what their coaches are telling them to say. A coaching colleague of mine is well respected in our region because he does not do this. As another coach told me, "Ric doesn't just tell them what to say, he teaches them how to debate." He teaches them the simple philosophical underpinnings of what they are arguing, and he fosters in them solid critical thinking in the process.

I will admit my personal bias up front: I am not a fan of scripted EMDR protocols and textbook EMDR. If you are the type of person who needs scripted protocols to learn, I respect that, but you will not find those in this book. Instead, I try to parallel what my colleague Ric does with his debaters. In other words, I want to teach you to think critically about how to best use EMDR in the most difficult of situations. Trust me—at debate tournaments, the rounds get harder and harder as the event goes on. As they do, the students who rely on their scripts usually do not hold up against the kids who really know how to debate. Similarly, when the going gets tough with clients, those of you who can conceptualize EMDR within the broader context of your clinical experience will shine.

This book is written primarily for individuals who have completed a training course in EMDR. As many of you are aware, there are a variety of training course options available on the market today. In this text, I do not endorse any specific training program; rather, be assured that you can benefit from this book regardless of which training program you have taken. There is a place for various styles of training programs, especially because there is no current research connecting length and style of a clinician's EMDR training with client outcomes.[1] We are in the process of discovering what works best when it comes to the training of clinicians in EMDR, and the answer may be that different clinicians will benefit from different styles of instruction. In this book, I encourage you to see EMDR within the larger framework of the psychotherapeutic disciplines, a challenge from which I feel all new EMDR trainees can benefit.

The first six chapters of this book are foundational in nature. After reading these chapters, you should be well on your way to grasping the fundamentals of advanced conceptualization. Chapter 2 explains my concept called the Four Faces of EMDR, or the various ways that EMDR is used in today's professional settings. In this chapter, I discuss why there is a time and a place for different applications of (or approaches to) EMDR, especially because the solutions I propose throughout the book come from all four faces. Chapter 3 gives readers a general primer on trauma competency, and it explains

---

[1] Preliminary evidence suggests that training programs in evidence-based practices employing multiple components (e.g., live instruction, reading, guided practice, follow-up consultation) produce better training outcomes than single-component trainings or self-study (Herschell, Kolko, Baumann, & Davis, 2010). However, even the authors of this large meta-analysis acknowledge that there is very little research available that actually connects any therapist training to client outcomes.

several models that will help you to conceptualize the most difficult EMDR cases. Chapter 4 reviews the importance of relational issues in the counseling relationship and presents a case for why these often-overlooked issues can be a ticket to success for your work with complex clients. Chapter 5 addresses general stabilization issues that need to be addressed, such as safety, lifestyle, secondary gains, motivation, and learning styles, when working with complex clients. This chapter also includes several best practice guidelines for knowing when and how to use EMDR. Chapter 6 offers specific strategies for using EMDR to help unstick the stuck client once EMDR has been deemed appropriate. This chapter also offers strategies for blocked EMDR processing and how to handle EMDR sessions that do not go as planned.

The second part of the book goes into specific suggestions and guidelines for the various types of complex clients. Chapter 7 overviews strategies for using EMDR with complex PTSD, Chapter 8 covers addictions, Chapter 9 addresses violent and acting out behaviors, Chapter 10 focuses on other Axis I disorders (including eating disorders and dissociative issues), and Chapter 11 evaluates grief, loss, and spiritual concerns. Finally, Chapter 12 reviews uses of EMDR with other conditions that sometimes contribute to a client being stymied in their progress towards wellness, including chronic pain, somatization, phobias, lifestyle choices, developmental disabilities, and performance enhancement issues. Although the principles I will be addressing in this book may have some applicability to children and adolescents, this book is mostly geared for use with adult clients.

My goal is to present many of the latest research findings and academic concepts in a manner that is readable and enjoyable for ordinary clinicians. I blend my own writing and storytelling together with case studies and, in some cases, have even included direct sharing from former clients themselves. Most of these cases are from my own clinical practice; in some instances to protect confidentiality I have used composites of two clients with similar outcomes. My intention is to facilitate in the reader a sense of connection to the material, since several of these cases are likely to remind you of your own clientele.

You may be able to derive some benefit from this book even if you are not trained in EMDR. For instance, you may be encouraged to use EMDR as a collaborative referral for one of your long-standing complex clients who is not making progress. Some of my most treasured professional moments have been when my colleagues and I have worked collaboratively with a client. I have been engaged in several collaborative relationships in which a colleague has worked with the client on present issues and I have done EMDR with the client every other session on past issues that are affecting present functioning. I have jokingly told a colleague with whom I frequently collaborate that he should just go and get trained in EMDR already; however, he feels the clients benefit from our arrangement because they obtain multiple perspectives. You may or may not be inspired to receive EMDR training after reading this book.

It is important for me to caution you, however, that this book is not intended to be a substitute for an actual, live training course in EMDR. Moreover, this book is not intended to be a substitute for a professional assessment or clinical care. Please approach this book as suggestive only. I don't think that any one book can tout itself as the bible of EMDR or as a definitive source, and I certainly do not attempt to do that. My book is, in fact, the opposite of a textbook. When I was learning EMDR and presented complex cases from my practice to more experienced colleagues, they would often say, "Well, this is what the [2001 Shapiro] textbook would tell you to do, but this is what I actually do." Then, they proceeded to offer me clinically-informed consultation.

I don't believe that this sentiment is unique to EMDR. With so many therapeutic approaches, the manuals or textbooks may tell us to do one thing, but we find, through practice knowledge, that there are often slightly different paths to get to the same goal, paths that may tread easier for specific clients. In this book, I am going out on a limb and sharing with you what I actually do with EMDR in my ordinary practice in Youngstown, Ohio. Some of what I do corresponds exactly to the Shapiro text, and different facets of my clinical training have informed other strategies. As you will see in Chapter 2, EMDR has many faces, and there are many ways of beholding those faces. My work offers but one perspective.

Chapter 2: The Four Faces of EMDR

"Four towns join each other in Ohio somewhere,
A traffic light brings them together, and some businesses
here and there.
And I live on the corner of them all.
And I want to bring them all together somehow,
For I live on the corner of them all."
  — From the song "Cornersburg" by Jamie Marich
       (*Under My Roof,* 2004)

As my song "Cornersburg" metaphorically expresses, I am a unifier. I have always been known for trying to persuade people of different intellectual orientations to at least consider the other sides of a story or different approaches to a problem. Before I fully explain the Four Faces of EMDR, I feel it is important to tell more of my story, which helps explain how the environment into which I was born made me constantly evaluate and honor the other's perspective. My intention is for the reader to understand why I believe that such a multi-faceted concept is essential in discussions about EMDR and how to best practice it in real-life clinical settings.

There is a picture of me that was taken when I was 9 months old. In this photo, I am wearing a Cleveland Browns sweatshirt and a Pittsburgh Steelers hat. For those of you who know football, you know that this wacky combination epitomizes a mixed message. For those of you who don't follow football, the Cleveland Browns and the Pittsburgh Steelers are the fiercest of rivals, and I was born to a Cleveland Browns–loving father and a Pittsburgh Steelers–worshipping mother. This picture is the perfect symbol of the discord between my parents. My father was a Republican evangelical Christian, and my mother was a Democratic Roman Catholic. Although legend has it that they really loved each other at one point and got married, my father's joining a fundamentalist church when I was 5 years old ushered in years of disputes between my parents over practically everything. As the oldest child, I was often placed in the middle of their heated debates, and I had to perfect the art of answering them in such a way that wouldn't offend either.

At the time, it was hell. I remember when I was 8 years old being asked for my theological opinion about the Catholic solemnity of the Immaculate Conception. I just wanted to enjoy my chicken nuggets at dinner, and here I was, being invited into a debate in which I had to diplomatically maneuver. This was just one example of what life was like for me in my family. Although I had to do many EMDR sessions to get over the trauma of being put in the middle of my parents' disagreements, I look back on the experiences with no regrets, because over time I developed the skill of being able to honor differing perspectives on complex issues.

Defining EMDR

Eye Movement Desensitization and Reprocessing and controversy seem to go hand in hand. Shapiro published her first study on the forerunner of EMDR, EMD (eye movement desensitization) in 1989, and spent the next 20-plus years putting EMDR on the map in the clinical community. However, criticisms came from many angles. Some denounced EMDR because it seemed too good to be true, others felt that EMDR was dangerous because it could possibly destabilize traumatized clients, and still others criticized Shapiro herself, calling her a spin doctor who knew how to cleverly package several existing therapies into a specialized protocol that she could market at multi-day trainings (Devilly, 2005). When a variety of clinical bodies including, but not limited to, the American Psychiatric Association (2004), the American Psychological Association (Chambless et al., 1998), the Department of Veterans Affairs/Department of Defense (2004), and the International Society of Traumatic Stress Studies (Foa, Keane, & Friedman, 2000) endorsed EMDR's efficacy on some level, the therapy obtained greater credibility in the clinical community at large. It is important to note that these validations flowed largely from the first decade of research on EMDR and its application in clinical settings.[2] However, it is also important to note that critics of EMDR still exist (Institute of Medicine of the National Academies, 2008), which is to be expected, considering that no major school of therapy is without its critics (Lee, 2008).

Interestingly, controversy and disagreement even takes place among EMDR practitioners about what exactly constitutes EMDR. Shapiro has made her case clear in various writings, talks, and interviews (Luber & Shapiro, 2009; Shapiro & Forrest, 1997; Shapiro, 2001; Shapiro & Solomon, 2008), yet many EMDR practitioners have challenged or added to Shapiro's work based on their clinical experiences with using her discovery in diverse settings. The EMDR International Association (2009) has attempted to establish uniformity in a definition over the years, but others see this definition as too protocol-centered, not allowing for sufficient adaptation by the clinician. Others see the EMDRIA definition as not strict enough. Like with many aspects of EMDR, it all depends on who you ask. Shapiro has acknowledged the need to continually evaluate the balance between rigid orthodoxy and an anything-goes approach to EMDR (Luber & Shapiro, 2009); however, negotiating this balance has sparked much debate (Lipke, 2009; Marich, 2010).

I have read just about everything that is out there on EMDR by writers with varied perspectives and opinions. Moreover, through networking, I have talked to a plethora of clinicians who identify as using EMDR, some of them associated with EMDRIA and others not.

---

[2] For a full listing of all published research articles on EMDR, please visit the Francine Shapiro Library at: http://emdr.nku.edu/emdr_data.php.

I completed my doctoral research on an EMDR topic, and this process challenged me to think critically about EMDR—not simply act as its cheerleader. Through these experiences, I developed the Four Faces of EMDR. I took the name from a concept called the four faces of God, attributed to St. Augustine (Groeschel, 1984). Augustine contended that God manifests himself in a variety of ways, and that there are four main spiritual personality types among people: God as truth, God as beauty, God as good, and God as passion. One's spiritual personality type is the greatest indicator of how he or she will receive and manifest God, and each spiritual personality can encounter unique pitfalls. Most importantly, Augustine believed that there is a place for all four faces; although all four faces are different, none is superior. If you wish to read more about this idea, I refer you to Fr. Benedict Groeschel's (1984) *Spiritual Passages: The Psychology of Spiritual Development.*

You may be wondering why I am talking about a Catholic saint's theory of spirituality in a book about EMDR. Amusing, I know, and I fully recognize that I am going out on an even bigger limb with my academic reputation by proposing such a concept. What I have found is that debate in the psychotherapeutic professions can sometimes be reminiscent of that in religious circles. Each school of thought has the potential to think that its way is the "best way" to help people, and within each school of thought, like within each major religious group or denomination, you have people with different degrees of rigidity or fundamentalism to their tenets. Every time I hear major figures in the psychotherapeutic professions talk about "the research" or "the literature" (Box 1), I am often reminded of religious fundamentalists using phrases like, "The Bible says ...," "The Torah says ...," or "The Koran says ..." Something I concluded long ago is that it's all a matter of how you interpret what those sources say, and your individual spiritual personality type (a la Augustine's *four faces of God*) provides the lens through which you will interpret the literature.

This happens with every major therapeutic approach, including EMDR. In current clinical settings, I see EMDR being used in one of four ways, which reflect the Four Faces of EMDR that I will be referencing throughout the book:

1) Protocol-Oriented EMDR:

Strict adherence to the current EMDRIA definition of EMDR (EMDR International Association, 2009), influenced largely by the protocols and procedures as developed by founder Dr. Francine Shapiro. In this "face," EMDR is clearly viewed as an approach to psychotherapy, and Shapiro's adaptive information model (2001) is regarded as the sole theoretical guide. Many practitioners described by this face use EMDR alongside other interventions but only if fidelity to the Shapiro protocols is maintained for the EMDR component. Within this face, as with all of the faces, there are different degrees of flexibility (e.g., some practitioners believe that eye movements are the only form of bilateral stimulation that should be used, and others are more open to the other forms; some insist on 90-minute sessions as Shapiro recommends, and others are willing to work within the 50-minute clinical hour).

2) Flexible EMDR:

Use of Shapiro's original protocols and procedures with modifications made by the clinician to better suit the clinician's personal style or to better accommodate the client's learning/ processing styles and other unique needs. With this face, EMDR is still largely regarded as an approach to psychotherapy. However, many who practice flexible EMDR choose to incorporate other models of treatment conceptualization aside from Shapiro's adaptive information processing model (2001). People who practice flexible EMDR are more likely than Face 1 practitioners to use the general EMDR approach to psychotherapy alongside of another approach to psychotherapy (e.g., 12 Step facilitation, ego state therapy).

3) EMDR as Technique:

Same as Number 2 in terms of using the original Shapiro protocols and procedures with necessary modifications; however, with this face, EMDR is simply used as an adjunctive technique or procedure to another psychotherapeutic orientation (e.g., Gestalt, 12 Step, client-centered therapy, choice theory, psychoanalysis). With this face, EMDR does not dominate or guide the treatment. Some Face 3 practitioners stay true to Shapiro's eight-phase main protocol, whereas others jump around as it suits their main orientation.

4) EMDR-Informed Interventions:
Use of EMDR-informed interventions or evolutions of original EMDR elements into a new technique or approach to therapy. May also include the use of bilateral stimulation as a desensitization process, similar to the original EMD.

I will go into a more detailed explanation of each face of EMDR in this chapter. These four faces are meant to be general classifications; of course I realize there are overlaps and some practitioners may find themselves meeting criteria for two or more of the faces. That's okay. In fact, I feel that is healthy because it shows adaptability, an essential trait when it comes to working with the complex or oft-labeled "impossible" client (Duncan, Hubble, & Miller, 1997). Many don't realize this, but adaptability is an essential part of what constitutes an evidence-based practice as defined by the American Psychological Association as of 2006.

I recently did an audit of my charts from 2009, paying special attention to the clients I treated with EMDR. This audit confirmed what I have known all along: I use all four faces of EMDR in my practice based on client need. With the four faces of God concept, Augustine believed that an individual predominantly identifies with one of the faces, and the same holds true for me as when it comes to my use of EMDR. I most connect with Face 2—Flexible EMDR, and that is what I am most likely to use in my clinical practice, especially when I treat complex clients. In fact, the only time I used

Chapter 2: The Four Faces of EMDR

Face 1 EMDR was with high-functioning clients who came into treatment with few complications.

I believe there is a place for all four faces of EMDR in today's clinical world. I hope that by the time you have finished this chapter, you will be able to identify which face of EMDR best defines your use of it. I hope you will also see that when it comes to conceptualizing a complex client's case, using an alternate face (aside from the one you're most comfortable with) may be more appropriate. The personal challenge for clinicians then becomes, "Am I open minded enough to consider another face of EMDR when my face doesn't seem to be helping the client reach his or her goals?"

The Four Faces of EMDR: Results from a Pilot Survey

In late 2010, I distributed a survey on EMDR training, use, and implementation to Master's level helping professionals in the state of Ohio using a combination of mailing lists that were available to me from clinical organizations and training. Of the 28 professionals who responded to the survey, 20 reported being trained by an EMDRIA-approved provider. Of that number: 10 reported being Certified EMDR Therapists through EMDRIA, 9 reported that they were not certified by EMDRIA, and 1 respondent was unsure. The respondents were asked to read the Four Faces of EMDR taxonomy and asked how they would best describe how they identify their EMDR practice. The results from the 20 respondents trained by an EMDRIA-approved provider are presented here, suggesting diversity of practice, even amongst those who have completed approved trainings.

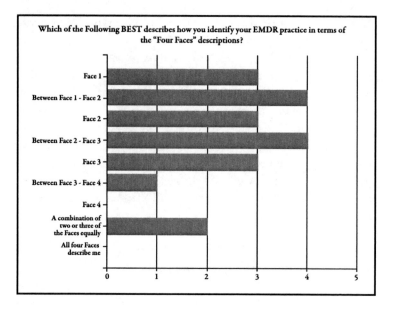

The breakdown of responses amongst the 10 Certified Therapists, who are more likely to be regarded as "purists," also suggest diversity of practice and are not overwhelmingly represented by protocol-oriented, Face 1 responses.

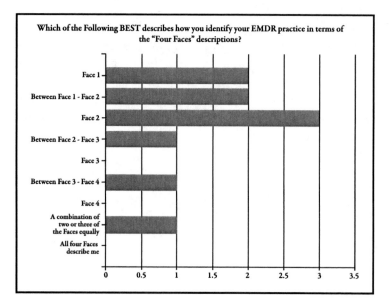

A larger pilot study article is currently in preparation, which will hopefully lead into a full-scale study on investigating how EMDR has been implemented nationally and globally.

Demystifying Bilateral Stimulation

The use of bilateral stimulation (which some prefer to describe as dual attention stimulus) is the major, common factor that runs throughout the four faces of EMDR. Within each face, what the clinician does with it may differ. Thus, it is important to explain the notion of bilateral stimulation before I go into a more thorough explanation of each face of EMDR.

The use of EMDR as a formal process of psychotherapy traces back to Shapiro's famous walk in the park in 1987. As she tells the story, Shapiro (a cancer survivor well attuned to intricate healing connections between mind and body) was on a walk, and she stopped for a rest by a lake. She recounts that her eyes began moving in a rapid, diagonal fashion when she was disturbed by a particular thought. After her series of spontaneous eye movements, she recalled the thought and noticed that it didn't have the same charge as before. This ushered in a process of experimenting on herself, her colleagues, and willing volunteers; what emerged were the initial procedures of EMD (Donovan & Nalepinski, 1999; Shapiro & Forrest, 1997). If you are interested in more of the history behind how EMD evolved into EMDR, including the identification of bilateral stimulation forms (e.g., tactile, audio) as being viable alternatives to eye movements, several sources go into various levels of detail (see Box 1).

Box 1. Resources on the History of EMDR.

The EMDR Institute (n.d.). *History of EMDR*. Retrieved April 17, 2010, from http://www.emdr.com/history.htm.

Greenwald, R. (2006). The peanut butter and jelly problem: In search of a better EMDR training model. *EMDR Practitioner*. Retrieved April 7, 2008, from http://www.emdr-practitioner.net.

Shapiro, F., & Forrest, M. (1997). *EMDR: The breakthrough "eye movement" therapy for overcoming stress, anxiety, and trauma*. New York: Basic Books.

Shapiro, F., & Maxfield, L. (2002). Eye movement desensitization and reprocessing (EMDR): Information processing in the treatment of trauma. *Journal of Clinical Psychology/In Session: Psychotherapy In Practice*, 58(8), 933–946.

Shapiro, F. (2001). *Eye Movement Desensitization and Reprocessing: Basic principles, protocols, and procedures* (2nd ed.). New York: The Guilford Press.

There is evidence in world literature, history, and anthropology indicating that others before Shapiro noticed the effects of bilateral stimulation, especially in cultures where dancing and drumming have been used for centuries as a way to release pent-up distress (Parnell, 2007). Following are some thoughts I presented in an editorial in the *Journal of EMDR Practice and Research* (Marich, 2010):

In Isaac Bashevis Singer's prolific Holocaust novel, *Enemies: A Love Story* (1972), the main character, Herman Broder, sets his eyes into an oscillating motion whenever he needs to deal with stress or anxiety. The books and poems of Native American author Sherman Alexie (1992, 2009) beautifully document how centuries of tribes have utilized the dance, an activity of tactile bilateral stimulation, to cope with distress and heighten performance. Kyra Gaunt (2006) documented how generations of African American girls have used clapping games, double-dutch jump rope, and other bilateral rhythmic activities to transition into adulthood (p. 97).

These are just a few examples. Think critically about all the ways we see bilateral stimulation manifested in society. Have you ever driven down an interstate and seen one of those flashing warning signs? Something to the effect of "Check Your Brakes," "Toll Plaza 500 Feet," or "Construction Ahead." It is not uncommon to see these warning signs accompanied by alternating bilateral flashing lights to get your attention. I grew up in Ohio and still live in this very snowy state, so I have followed my share of salt trucks on highways during the winter. Salt trucks also use rear alternating bilateral flashing lights to keep you alert and attentive on the road.

I often go to a massage therapist as part of my self-care regimen, and between my own massage therapist at home and others with whom I have worked at spas around the world, I have observed that they use bilateral stimulation quite a bit. For instance, a massage therapist will often alternate pressure from shoulder to shoulder or from hip to hip. Curious, I asked my massage therapist why she did that, and she told me that it helps to enhance relaxation because it can cause sensory confusion. Indeed, confusion is often an important component of inducing deeper hypnotic states, and when I get massages, I typically enter a state of light to medium hypnosis. I often experience reflective consolidation of my thoughts, stressors, and experiences when I'm on the massage table.

The most loving, simple forms of bilateral stimulation I have experienced have major imprints on my memory. My mother and I often played patty-cake just before she read to me in the evening, certainly a positive experience that yielded some of the healthy bonding I formed with my mother. For any of you who have cats, you know that certain felines will take their paws and do an alternating back-forth, back-forth, back-forth motion on your bare skin. My 7-year-old cat, Joy, has done this to me ever since I adopted her when she was just a few months old. This alternation mimics the motion cats make when they nurse from their mother. When cats use this motion on their human companion, it typically represents their desire to be close. I know that whenever Joy engages in about 30 seconds of alternating paw movements, she begins to purr very loudly, a sign of contentment.

Bilateral stimulation is everywhere. Walking is bilateral stimulation, as is running, swimming, and dancing. As Linda Curran accurately observed in *Trauma Competency* (2010):

> Bilateral stimulation is not dangerous, nor is EMDR as a modality. If it were, wouldn't it follow that we should all abreact when walking, snapping our fingers, or playing Miss Mary Mac? However, when administered by clinicians without prerequisite knowledge to effectively address and treat trauma's sequelae, the EMDR protocol proves challenging, fear-inducing and, oftentimes, traumatizing for clinicians and re-traumatizing for clients.

My observation is that many new EMDR trainees are scared of bilateral stimulation. My general feeling echoes that of Linda Curran. Bilateral stimulation is not dangerous. In fact, I believe that it is the inherent healing gift that Shapiro tapped in to and systematized.

Several of my clients had never heard of EMDR yet shared with me some bilateral "techniques" they've come up with to help alleviate stress. One client told me that whenever he feels stressed at work, he goes outside and takes a cigarette lighter and tosses it back and forth from one hand to another. Interestingly, he doesn't smoke cigarettes anymore; he just uses this self-created technique with the lighter. Another client (see the Case of Marta in Chapter 10) was intrigued when I first pitched EMDR to her because it seemed like a process she has used to help her calm down over the years. She told me that someone gave her a ring on which a bejeweled bumblebee is set on a spring hinge. When you touch the bee, it rapidly moves back and forth horizontally. Marta would stare at the back-and-forth motion of the bee to calm herself down whenever she felt agitated or triggered.

Clearly, my clients had experiences similar to Shapiro's walk in the park, the major difference being that Shapiro had the psychological knowledge, drive, and curiosity to harness this discovery into a process that can be purposely used for therapeutic reasons. I tell you these stories not to impugn Shapiro's amazing work in creating EMDR. Rather, I share these stories to diffuse your fear about the use of eye movements or other bilateral stimulation. It is not the bilateral stimulation that is dangerous. What is potentially dangerous is when it is not properly applied. This happens for a variety of reasons, the most obvious being when clinicians do not adequately prepare the client for EMDR, especially the component that involves the processing of traumatic memories. As I noted earlier, a major, often overlooked part of preparation is for the clinician to prepare himself or herself for encountering the traumatic energy that will emerge in EMDR sessions. When the therapist does not adequately prepare in this way, it can lead to unproductive or even harmful EMDR sessions. (See Chapter 4 for more information)

New trainees also worry that if they deviate slightly from the protocols they learned in training, major damage will result. My experience has suggested that trainers who most strongly identify with Face 1, protocol-oriented EMDR, instill much of this fear. As a senior EMDR facilitator shared with me once, "These trainees need to learn that if they stay within the protocol, they have nothing to worry about, even with these difficult clients." Obviously, as a Face 2 person, I respectfully disagree. In fact, I have even seen sessions go bad because clinicians were so worried about staying within the protocol that they ignored more intuitive factors, such as attending to the therapeutic relationship or honoring the need to pull back from the processing. (See Chapter 4 for more information.)

In the next section of this chapter, I go into more detail about what defines each face of EMDR: protocol-oriented EMDR (Face 1), flexible EMDR (Face 2), EMDR as technique (Face 3), and EMDR-informed interventions (Face 4). How each face is used when working with complex clients is also addressed. As you read each description, note which one makes the most sense to you and fits with your personal style.

Face 1: Protocol-Oriented EMDR

When we discuss "protocol-oriented EMDR," it is important to make some critical distinctions. In her 2001 book, *Eye Movement Desensitization and Reprocessing: Principles, Protocols, and Procedures* (2nd edition), an academic text that is required reading for any EMDRIA-approved training, Shapiro discussed several different types of protocols. Protocol, in the broadest sense, refers to her eight-phase model of EMDR treatment: (1) client history, (2) preparation, (3) assessment, (4) desensitization, (5) installation, (6) body scan, (7) closure, and (8) re-evaluation. Shapiro also described EMDR as being a *three-pronged protocol*, meaning that it was designed to:

(1) Clear out *past* disturbance so as to improve ...
(2) Present and...
(3) Future functioning.

Protocol (n.d.), as Shapiro uses the term, closely matches the medical definition: "the plan for a course of medical treatment or a scientific experiment."

The third usage of *protocol* relates to how a clinician sets up and executes an EMDR session. For instance, the script that trainees are given to complete phases 3 through 6, which includes elements like measuring the subjective units of distress (SUDs) and validity of cognition (VoC) scale, would be a part of the protocol. The prescribed, sequenced steps for phases 3 through 6, as originally produced by Shapiro (2001), are also referred to as the 11-step procedure. The EMDRIA definition of EMDR (Box 2) honors this 11-step procedure and establishes stringent guidelines cautioning against deviation from the spelled-out phases 3 through 6. Prescribed usage of the SUDs and VoC scales is a major part of this protocol. Several books have been published on how to use these standard EMDR protocols in special situations (Leeds, 2009; Luber, 2009, 2010), and if you are a Face 1 type of EMDR practitioner who learns best through scripted protocols, these resources may be helpful to you when working with complex clients. There are many spin-off protocols available in these sources, some of which were developed by Shapiro (e.g., the Recent Events Protocol) and many that other clinicians developed. Some of these spin-off protocols have formal research validation, but most do not. When Face 1 practitioners are faced with the prospect of working with a complex client, they typically consult one of the sources that I am recommending for a specialized protocol.

Box 2. Resources on Protocol-Oriented EMDR.

The EMDR International Association (2009). Definition of EMDR. In *What is EMDR?* Retrieved April 18, 2010, from http://www.emdria.org/displaycommon.cfm?an=1&subarticlenbr=56.

Hensley, B. J. (2009). *An EMDR primer: From practicum to practice.* New York: Springer Publishing Company.

Leeds, A. (2009). *A guide to the standard EMDR protocols for clinicians, supervisors, and consultants.* New York: Springer Publishing Company.

Luber, M. (2009). *Eye movement desensitization and reprocessing (EMDR) scripted protocols: Basics and special situations.* New York: Springer Publishing Company.

Luber, M. (2010). *Eye movement desensitization and reprocessing (EMDR) scripted protocols: Basics and special populations.* New York: Springer Publishing Company.

Shapiro, F. (2001). *Eye Movement Desensitization and Reprocessing: Basic principles, protocols, and procedures* (2nd ed.). New York: The Guilford Press.

Another major facet of the EMDR International Association (2009) definition of EMDR (which essentially corresponds with Face 1, protocol-oriented EMDR in my proposed system) is that EMDR treatment ought to be guided by Shapiro's adaptive information processing (AIP) model, the working hypothesis she formulated to explain how psychopathology develops and how EMDR works to resolve it. One of the early criticisms of EMDR is that it was atheoretical. Shapiro proposed the AIP model, which evolved into the adaptive information processing model, as foundational support for her discovery. Although there are eleven tenets of the AIP, this is different from the 11-step sequence; these tenets include (Shapiro, 2008; Shapiro & Solomon, 2008):

1. Memory targets are the basis of perception, attitude, and behavior.

2. The information processing system moves disturbance to an adaptive resolution.

3. Disturbing events (Large "T" and small "t" trauma) are a primary basis of pathology.

4. Disruption of the information processing system causes information (e.g., seen, heard, felt) to be unprocessed and inappropriately stored as it was perceived.

5. As the perceptions of the present link to the memory networks, various components of the previous unprocessed memories are experienced (e.g., emotions, physical sensations, thoughts/beliefs).

6. Accessing information allows a link between consciousness and where information is stored.

7. The physical information processing system is like other body systems—a cut closes and heals unless blocked—physiologically geared to go toward health.

8. The unprocessed components/manifestations of memory (image, thought, sound, emotions, physical sensations, beliefs) change/transmute during processing to an adaptive resolution.

9. Processing is metaphorically like moving down a train track. (Each stop = linkage of adaptive networks)

10. Byproducts of reprocessing include desensitization (lessening of disturbance), insights, and changes in physical and emotional responses.

11. Information processing transmutes information through all accessed channels of memory network.

Neurological evidence continues to support the validity of AIP as a model for explaining how and why EMDR works (for review, see Grey, 2008). For people who most readily identify with Face 1, protocol-oriented EMDR, AIP is also called on to help with the conceptualization of treatment.

Proponents of protocol-oriented EMDR continue to cite a variety of studies, meta-analyses, and reviews (Maxfield & Hyer, 2002; Shapiro, 1999) to show that adherence to the protocol yields better treatment outcomes. Shapiro has consistently advocated fidelity to established EMDR protocols (see the various forms of protocol earlier in this section) in both research and practice (Shapiro, 2001; Shapiro & Luber, 2009). However, an important comment must be made in this discussion. As Korn (2009) so aptly expressed in her review on using EMDR with complex PTSD, "While EMDR and other trauma treatments have been proven efficacious in the treatment of simpler cases of PTSD, the effectiveness of treatments for more complex cases has been less widely studied" (p. 264). Indeed, the studies that protocol advocates generally cite to support the efficacy of established EMDR approaches do not often apply to the complex clients that we are addressing in this book. In the randomized controlled studies that support EMDR, participants/clients with complex issues (e.g., substance abuse, psychosis) were typically excluded due to concerns with confounding variables. In other words, these are the clients we are likely to see in our offices, especially if we work in settings more geared toward public practice! Confounding variables exist in real-world clinical settings, and that is a reality to which we must be attuned when working with the complex client.

Presently, the protocols so widely advocated by Face 1 individuals only apply to single-incident PTSD, if we are using a strict interpretation of the research. Moreover, an argument can be made that several methodological limitations exist in the major studies (e.g., failure to consistently control for researcher allegiance and the common factors of therapy that are discussed in Chapter 4). Granted, several case studies and clinical position papers demonstrate that the standard EMDR protocols can work with more complex cases of trauma-related pathology (for reviews, see Korn, 2009 and Maxfield, 2007).

In fairness to EMDRIA, some provisions are made for flexibility and creativity in a clinician's execution of the protocol, but within limits. For instance, wider openness to interpretation is allowed in phases 1 to 2 and 7 to 8, which is significant in working with the complex client because proper preparation (Phase 2) and ensuring safety in the closure process (Phase 7) is absolutely vital. Also, creativity in presenting the protocol can be incorporated in phases 3 through 6 for the purposes of meeting the unique developmental needs of an individual (e.g., children, the developmentally disabled). If you are a Face 1 practitioner, this represents a major strength of the standard definition when it comes to working with the complex client, but the degree of malleability allowed often depends on whom you ask.

Face 2: Flexible EMDR

Protocol is a word that I have heard a lot around my house. My former husband was once the medical director of an addiction treatment center, and he was on call four or five nights a week, giving orders for the new admissions. In order to safely detoxify patients, he ordered Valium protocol for alcoholics, opiate protocol for heroin addicts, and Phenobarbital protocols for those addicted to benzodiazepines, just to list a few examples. Several times in any given week, I heard him issue a standard protocol but with some significant alterations due to a variety of special medical conditions. I decided to pick his brain one day about what exactly constitutes a protocol. He described a protocol as a series of set evidenced-based instructions for medical care. When I played devil's advocate and asked him why he often changed the protocol to a certain degree, he responded, "to accommodate for the vicissitudes of individual differences between human beings."

His use of the word *vicissitude* was right on. Human beings are prone to change, alteration, and variation. People are like snowflakes: No two are alike. Although, in psychology and the helping professions, we can formulate general patterns, standards, theories, and protocols, it is important to realize that ethical treatment often means deviating from a protocol. People who practice Face 2, flexible EMDR, typically embrace this idea, and they find it especially useful in working with the complex client.

There are a few major traits that characterize those who practice Face 2 EMDR. For clinicians who most readily identify with Face 1, protocol-oriented EMDR, AIP is the primary, and often the only, theoretical model they will accept to understand EMDR. In contrast, people who are more Face 2 might still view EMDR as an approach to psychotherapy but may find other models of conceptualization more useful. One such model, The Four Activity Model (Lipke, 2000, 2004) is presented in greater depth in Chapter 3.

Another major distinction is that for those who practice mostly Face 2 and Face 3 EMDR, the execution of phases 3 through 6 is open to interpretation. For instance, Parnell (2007) proposed a modified EMDR protocol that aims to achieve the same purpose as a standard EMDR protocol but with less emphasis on quantification (e.g., SUDs and VoC scale) and more emphasis on the flow of the session. Face 2 EMDR therapists also know when to step back from EMDR processing within the standard or modified protocol and meet a client with another therapeutic strategy if needed.

Face 2 EMDR therapists are also much more likely to use all available forms of bilateral stimulation (tactile, audio, and eye movements), not just eye movements. Even if they stay true to the original protocol, Face 2 therapists are much more likely to integrate EMDR with other therapies and philosophies if this integration will optimally serve the client. I have compiled a list of books and other sources that typify the Face 2 EMDR therapist (Box 3). **Please keep in mind that my inclusion of these resources does not imply their endorsement of my "Four Faces of EMDR" concept.**

Box 3. Resources on Flexible EMDR.

DiGiorgio, K. E., Arnkoff, D. B., Glass, C. R., Lyhus, K. E., & Walter, R. C. (2004). EMDR and theoretical orientation: A qualitative study of how therapists integrate eye movement desensitization and reprocessing into their approach to psychotherapy. *Journal of Psychotherapy Integration*, 14(3), 227–252.

Forgash, C., & Copeley, M. (2008). *Healing the heart of trauma and dissociation with EMDR and ego state therapy.* New York: Springer Publishing.

Greenwald, R. (2007). *EMDR within a phase model of trauma-informed treatment.* Binghamton, NY: The Haworth Press.

Lipke, H. (2000). *EMDR and psychotherapy integration: Theoretical and clinical suggestions with focus on traumatic stress.* Boca Raton, FL: CRC Press.

Manfield, P. (2003). *EMDR casebook: Expanded second edition.* New York: W. W. Norton & Company.

Parnell, L. (2007). *A therapist's guide to EMDR: Tools and techniques for successful treatment.* New York: W. W. Norton & Company.

Shapiro, R. (2005). *EMDR solutions: Pathways to healing.* New York: W. W. Norton & Company.

Shapiro, R. (2009) *EMDR solutions II: For depression, eating disorders, performance, & more.* New York: W. W. Norton & Company.

I was very grateful to be treated by an EMDR therapist who was, in my estimation, a Face 2 EMDR clinician. Institute trained and EMDRIA certified, I sensed right away that she was using some type of standard procedure with numbers and formulas to set up this very heavy emotional work. But she also knew how to leave the numbers alone when I needed to just cry and talk at the end of a session, or within a session. She had a high comfort level with intense affect and was able to just sit and be with me calmly before proceeding. She knew how to skillfully use other strategies, such as imagery and a little bit of hypnosis, whenever my processing became blocked or I came into a session too resistant to use EMDR. More importantly, she knew when I needed just to talk and was open to discussions about my addiction recovery using other measures, such as motivational interviewing and 12-Step Facilitation. From my perspective as a client, my therapist was a true eclectic who specialized primarily in EMDR, and she artfully helped me to achieve my treatment goals. Interestingly, an EMDR fidelity specialist probably would have had a field day with the way my therapist executed the EMDR protocol with me. Clearly, none of that mattered to me because I got better in a way that honored my complexity, and for that, I am eternally grateful.

Face 3: EMDR as Technique

When I began my involvement with EMDRIA, I was having a casual discussion with a senior member of the community about how wonderfully EMDR has impacted my practice. I said something to the effect of, "It's amazing to have this technique in my toolbox of trauma treatment." He quickly corrected me, saying, "EMDR's not a technique anymore. It's an approach to psychotherapy." I respectfully listened to his position and saw where he was coming from. EMDR has its own hypothetical model for explaining the emergence of psychopathology and its own series of protocols for assessing, conceptualizing, and executing treatment. When I first started reading about EMDR, I encountered more material about using EMDR as an integrative psychotherapy approach or as a therapy that can be elegantly applied alongside other therapeutic approaches. However, the phrase I have heard more often over the past several years has been that *EMDR is an approach to psychotherapy*, just as my colleague said.

Ever the devil's advocate: I couldn't help but wonder, "What if a clinician is interested in EMDR, but only as a technique?" Carrying the religion metaphor I offered at the beginning of this chapter a step further, "What if someone believes in God but doesn't want to go to church? Does that make the person any less spiritual?" Today, when it comes to religious issues, it often depends on whom you ask. The same applies to EMDR.

My EMDR therapist once told me that for her, EMDR defines her practice. However, for the other clinicians in her office who also went through EMDR training, it is simply an "event," something that they use to complement or augment their primary therapeutic orientations. One of my coworkers is a man who was trained in EMDR many years ago, and he shared with me that he uses it, "Only when needed, with about 10% of my clients." Indeed, many of the consultees with whom I have worked following EMDR training have expressed that they only see themselves using EMDR in this Face 3 manner.

A prime example of a Face 3 EMDR clinician is Linda Curran, developer of the PESI EMDR training. In an interview I conducted with Curran in 2009, she shared the following thoughts that encapsulate Face 3 EMDR:

I believe that EMDR is a modality that has proved efficacious in both internal resourcing and reprocessing traumatic material. There should be no need for me, or any other clinician, to renounce his/her chosen discipline to utilize EMDR as a modality .... I completely identify with old-school trauma therapy, a.k.a. Gestalt therapy. Gestalt therapy is a humanistic, present-centered, relational psychotherapy with an emphasis on contact, body/somatic awareness, and the working through of unfinished business. As PTSD (both simple and complex) is the quintessential disorder of unfinished physiologic, emotional, and cognitive business, Gestalt therapy lends itself perfectly. In terms of EMDR, I do EMDR, but I am not an EMDR therapist.

The training Curran developed for PESI reflects her personal paradigm and it teaches clinicians how to use EMDR in a Face 3 manner. EMDRIA-approved trainings seem to better serve those individuals who intend to use EMDR in a Face 1 or Face 2 manner. See Box 4 for further resources.

Box 4. Resources on EMDR as Technique.

Curran, L. (2010). *Trauma competency: A clinician's guide.* Eau Claire, WI: PESI, STET.

DiGiorgio, K. E., Arnkoff, D. B., Glass, C. R., Lyhus, K. E., & Walter, R. C. (2004). EMDR and theoretical orientation: A qualitative study of how therapists integrate eye movement desensitization and reprocessing into their approach to psychotherapy. *Journal of Psychotherapy Integration,* 14(3), 227–252.

Marich, J. (2010). EMDR in addiction continuing care: A phenomenological study of women in early recovery. *Psychology of Addictive Behaviors,* 24(3), 498-507.

Face 4: EMDR-Informed Interventions

In her 1997 book on EMDR explaining the evolution of the therapy to that point, Shapiro seemed most concerned that a "cottage industry" of eye movement therapies would crop up in the wake of EMDR's validation. Indeed, there are numerous therapies and techniques practiced by a wide variety of people (from therapists to ministers to fly-by-night hypnotists) that utilize eye movements or bilateral stimulation. Some of these methods may be more credible than others, which is why it is important to evaluate them with a critical eye (pun intended). However, seeing with this critical eye does not mean dismissing everything that is not approved by EMDRIA.

There are several high-quality approaches and techniques available to clients today that have been influenced by EMDR but do not incorporate the reprocessing elements of EMDR as defined by Shapiro. Some may appear more "fringe" than others to clinicians and consumers. There are notable examples of books on the market that clearly fall into this Face 4 usage of EMDR; for example, Laurel Parnell's *Tapping In* (2008) and Alan Botkin's *Induced After-Death Communication: A New Therapy for Healing Grief and Trauma* (2005). Both of these approaches were developed by credible EMDR therapists. David Grand, an EMDR therapist and former chairman of the EMDR Humanitarian Assistance Program, has taken his inquiry to another level by developing a powerful technique called Brainspotting. First introduced in 2003, Brainspotting is different from EMDR, but there are similarities, and many clinicians use Brainspotting in conjunction with traditional EMDR for both preparation and processing.

Shapiro (2001, 2006, 2008) has continually noted that "preparation [for EMDR] is not processing" and thus does not constitute EMDR in and of itself. However, many clinicians and clients have found value in using only the preparation strategies of EMDR, with or without bilateral stimulation. The value of preparation took on a new level of importance in 2002 when Korn and Leeds officially wrote up the process of Resource Development and Installation (RDI). RDI is now taught by many EMDRIA-approved training courses as part of Phase 2 preparation.

But what if RDI alone can be therapeutic to a client? As a colleague shared with me, she once had a client who came to her for EMDR. After my colleague did the RDI with her in preparation for trauma processing, the client was so satisfied, she no longer wanted to go through with full-scale EMDR trauma processing. She had achieved her goals and considered treatment to be a success. For a clinician who honors Face 4 manifestations of EMDR, what happened with this woman is completely acceptable.

Tapping In (Parnell, 2008) teaches clients and casual readers how to use their own slow sets of alternating bilateral stimulation to build and secure helping resources. What Parnell essentially did in this book was to describe a variety of helpful imagery and sensory strategies, demystifying the processing of tactile bilateral stimulation in the process. This is the type of book a therapist can use to engage in exercises with clients, or it can also be used as a self-help book. It's controversial to some but helpful to others.

Botkin's (2005) *Induced After-Death Communication* describes his journey with serendipitously realizing that a client could correspond, either literally or figuratively, with a deceased individual during an EMDR session. Interestingly, Botkin had already been modifying some of the standard EMDR procedures, opting for a process he developed and called "core-focused EMDR." With this approach, he found out he was able to induce after-death communication. In Botkin's book, he is careful to describe that his use of EMDR is not how it is taught by the EMDR Institute, yet he never denies his immense respect for the richness of Shapiro's discovery. For Botkin, his process was about taking her work to another level, using the same heuristic process that Shapiro herself once used following her serendipitous discovery.

There are many who are fascinated with Botkin's process and others who are skeptical. When I spoke with a Face 1 acquaintance about Botkin's work, she was concerned. She asserted that "it's not EMDR" and expressed a fear that others would get the idea that we communicate with the dead in EMDR, adding to EMDR's wacky reputation in certain circles. For those who see Botkin's work as just another face of EMDR, there is no problem. It's one more tool that can be used with clients.

Perhaps through trial and error you have stumbled on a technique or two that has worked. Not all of you will have the ambition, time, or money to conduct formal research on it, and that's okay. If the modified EMDR interventions you come up with are related to a broader tradition of psychotherapy and do no harm to your clients, go ahead and use them. Some of the strategies that I describe throughout this book are my own techniques that spontaneously emerged from the flow in a session, and I am more than willing to share them. See Box 5 for more resources.

Box 5. Resources on EMDR-Informed Interventions.

Barbieri, J. (2008). The URGES approach: Urge reduction by growing ego strength (URGES) for trauma/addiction treatment using alternate bilateral stimulation, hypnotherapy, ego state therapy and energy psychology. *Sexual Addiction & Compulsivity*, 15, 116-138.

Botkin, A. (2005). *Induced after-death communication: A new therapy for healing grief and trauma*. Charlottesville, VA: Hampton Roads Publishing Company.

Grand, D. (2010). Brainspotting BSP. Accessed April 21, 2010, from http://www.brainspotting.pro/.

Parnell, L. (2008). *Tapping in: A step-by-step guide to activating your healing resources through bilateral stimulation*. Boulder, CO: Sounds True Books.

Schmidt, S. J. (2009). *The Developmental Needs Meeting Strategy: An ego state therapy for healing adults with childhood trauma and attachment wounds*. San Antonio, TX: DNMS Institute.

So Which Faces Are Clearest to You?

In this chapter, I presented my original concept, "The Four Faces of EMDR," which illustrates how EMDR and EMDR-informed interventions are being used in a variety of fashions. As with religion or politics, there are many clinicians who believe with fervency that their way is the right way, and they are not open to negotiation. Yet there are others, especially those who identify with or utilize more than one of the faces of EMDR, who see the beauty in each face. Personally, I think that there is a place for all four faces and that greater cooperation among clinicians in sharing ideas and working cooperatively would benefit our clients, especially the complex ones. For instance, if you are treating a client with serious complications, and your primary face of EMDR isn't working, are you willing to consult with someone who primarily identifies with another face? My hope is that, for the sake of your clients, your answer to this question is "yes."

Practical Issues: What Research Means to Me

Some clinicians working in the trenches of Main Street America are skeptical of research published in academic journals, mainly because they perceive it to be out of touch with the realities of day-to-day practice. Research takes all forms—qualitative, quantitative, experimental, quasi-experimental, in vitro, and in vivo. High-level academics and policy makers continue to embrace such concepts as randomized controlled research and manual-driven treatment as the gold standard of research and care. However, many of us who see the limitations of randomized controlled research and recipe-like manuals are often accused of adopting an anything-goes approach to treatment.

There is a middle ground. The CEO of my group practice advocates that his clinicians read academic journals, as long as we can critically apply that knowledge to what we are doing clinically. I think this approach is logical. However, many of my colleagues are resistant to reading research, not only because of the time commitment, but also because they see it as being conducted and reported in a way that is out of touch with their actual experience with clients. Experience, practice knowledge, and the age-old trial-and-error process are all legitimate forms of inquiry. Yet clinicians who learn only through trial and error can be easily misguided. There needs to be a balance.

One of the best ways I have found to scrutinize one's own work, to conduct research, so to speak, is to track outcomes with clients, an approach advocated by the International Center for Clinical Excellence (www.centerforclinicalexcellence.com), founded by Scott Miller and his colleagues. Outcome studies are often implemented as forms of research, but what's great is that anyone can research the work of their individual or agency practice by tracking outcomes. For instance, one way that I do this is to have my clients periodically fill out our company's *Problem Severity Rating Scale*, a tool we give all of our clients on admission and at various points throughout treatment. I also engage in regular treatment plan review with my clients. A major approach advocated by Miller's team is to have clients regularly (every session, if possible) fill out a feedback form so that clinician and client can gauge progress in a collaborative manner. Such a process has been dubbed the *Client-Directed Outcomes Initiative (CDOI)*. This is practice-based evidence, and it is research that can potentially validate one's personal style with clients. Furthermore, copies of session rating scales and outcome rating scales used by the International Center for Clinical Excellence can be accessed through Miller's website, www.scottdmiller.com.

Then, the ultimate practical issue arises: What role does research and policy play in influencing third-party payers? A fear-based question that comes up for many of my clinical peers is: 1) Is insurance going to pay for EMDR? and 2) If I combine EMDR with other interventions and "get creative" here and there, will third-party payers cover it? Without going into a lengthy discussion on the interconnections among research, policy, and payment, let me simply answer these two questions based on my experience. Most insurance panels with whom I work are presently covering EMDR. There are still exceptions, and my advice to those who are concerned about this is to check with the individual panels. In terms of the second question, I suggest finding out how third party payers, state accreditation/licensure bodies, and individual agencies prefer progress notes and treatment plans to be written. When combining EMDR with strategies that come from another major, validated approach to psychotherapy, it actually may be better to list the other intervention as the primary one. Those with concerns about this matter should consider consulting with another clinician who has been using any of the faces of EMDR and regularly bills third-party payers.

Evidenced-Based Practice Defined

According to a task force of the American Psychological Association(2006), an *evidence-based practice* in psychology is "the best available research with clinical expertise in the context of patient characteristics, culture, and preferences."

Sounds like common sense, right?

Chapter 3: A Crash Course on Trauma

"When we honestly ask ourselves which person in our lives means the most to us, we often find that it is those who, instead of giving advice, solutions, or cures, have chosen rather to share our pain and touch our wounds with a warm and tender hand."

—Henri Nouwen

Whenever I watch a movie, medical show, or documentary that might have the slightest bit of blood, guts, or gore, you can pretty much guarantee that I will be practicing my "turn-the-head-away-from-the-screen-as-quickly-as-I-can" maneuver. As much as I love watching wartime dramas like *Band of Brothers* and *Pearl Harbor*, I am bound to give myself a mild case of whiplash because I turn my head away so much. I know I am not alone in this; a lot of people get squeamish.

Well, I certainly hope that my medical doctor's not one of them! Think about that for a minute. How would you feel if you were being treated, especially in an emergency room situation, by a squeamish doctor? Don't get me wrong, I know that all doctors are human and that they are entitled to get shocked every once in a while. But by and large, one should have the capacity to tolerate the sight of serious physical wounds to be able to treat people medically.

Wound is the literal English translation of the Greek word trauma. As we embark on our discussion of trauma competency and why it is so important to EMDR professionals, we must start with this basic lesson in etymology. Helping professionals who are not prepared to look at and address wounds in the emotional sense are like medical doctors who have no tolerance for physical wounds. There are so many parallels here that are worth exploring, parallels that are relevant for helping professionals struggling to grasp the concept of trauma and why it matters. It is vital for therapists who are looking to add EMDR to their clinical repertoire or who want to enhance their effectiveness with EMDR to have an essential understanding of the principles of trauma (Greenwald, 2006; Curran, 2010). Some of you may already have a solid grounding in the principles of trauma, and this chapter may largely be review. Even if it is, I hope you will obtain a few different perspectives. In the spirit of my prismatic sense of inquiry, I believe that examining a problem from as many different angles as possible is vital; even though you may ultimately find one model that helps you best understand the problem. This chapter presents several models for conceptualizing trauma and the role that it plays in mental health. To fully understand these models, we must continue our discussion on wounding. Understanding the parallels between physical wounds and how they heal, and emotional wounds and how they heal is a vital part of any crash course on trauma.

Wounds, Scars, and Everything in Between

Let's consider some elementary principles regarding wounds:

- They come in all shapes and sizes.
- Open wounds are usually visible to others and include incisions (e.g., from knives), lacerations (tears), abrasions (grazes), punctures, penetration wounds, and gunshot wounds.
- Closed wounds are usually not obvious to others and include contusions (bruises), hematomas

(blood tumors), internal scar tissue, crush injuries, and slowly forming chronic wounds that can develop from conditions such as diabetic ulcers.
- They can form due to a variety of causes.
- Different wounds can affect different people in different ways, depending on other variables (e.g., medical issues, genetics, environmental factors, psychosocial considerations, economic issues, access to treatment).
- They heal from the inside out.
- They are usually obtained quickly but take time to thoroughly heal.
- Before wounds can begin their internal healing, steps must be taken to stop the initial bleeding (e.g., using bandages, gauze, stitches, sutures).
- Failure to receive the proper treatment after a wounding can complicate the healing process.
- They can leave a variety of scars (e.g., some are permanent, others are temporary; many no longer hurt after the scarring has taken place; some scarring can cause ongoing irritation).
- The skin around a healed scar is tougher than the rest of a person's skin.

One of the first lessons I remember learning in preschool is that no two individuals are created exactly the same. We are all different at the levels of body, mind, and soul. Apply this basic, preschool lesson to the notion of wounding, and we can see that no two people wound in the same way, even if they experienced similar injuries.

To explain these characteristics in more personal terms, let's look at an example of two rival teenage soccer players, Rhonda and Erin. During a game one evening, Rhonda and Erin collided on the field during an aggressive play. Both hit the ground hard in a similar, although not identical way. Each girl acquired a pretty significant laceration on her respective shin (Rhonda on her right, Erin on her left). Both girls were physically fit, but Rhonda's white blood cell production had always been poor and her overall vitamin C levels were low. The coaches attended to Rhonda and Erin with the same first aid procedures, and both girls sat out the rest of the game. By the next game, Erin was up and ready to play again, but Rhonda was still experiencing a significant amount of pain from the laceration, and it would ultimately take 2 weeks for her cut to fully heal, whereas Erin's healed in only a few days. White blood cell production and vitamin C levels are just two variables that can impact physical healing. There are so many other components that can affect healing: age, other health conditions, overall skin plasticity, genetic disorders (e.g., hemophilia), location of the wound, and how soon the appropriate treatment was received.

Failure to receive the proper treatment after a wounding can have disastrous consequences on the healing process. Certain wounds (especially minor ones) can heal on their own with little or no treatment. If a healthy man nicked himself cutting a bag of carrots, it would be no big deal. He would simply need to wash out the wound and put a Band-Aid® on it. But what if a hemophiliac got that same cut? Treatment is a life-or-death matter for the hemophiliac, even with minor wounds. For more significant wounds, sutures, stitches, and a prescribed dose of precautionary antibiotics are often in order. The most severe wounds, such as gunshot wounds, or those sustained in major industrial accidents require immediate medical attention. Otherwise, the wounded person can experience severe long-term consequences, especially if infection sets in. In worst-case scenarios, death can result.

When wounds go untreated, complications are common, especially if the wound gets worse. What if Rhonda, the soccer player who had a difficult time healing, went right back out, played soccer the next night, and got kicked in the same spot by another player's spikes? Clearly, Rhonda would get injured again, and not only would she have the new injury to contend with, but the healing of the original laceration would be further contaminated. **If this physical wound knowledge makes sense to you, simply transfer the logic to the emotional realm.**

Emotional traumas also come in various shapes and sizes, resulting from many possible causes. For some, simple traumas (wounds) can clear on their own, but for others with more complex emotional variables, the healing process may take longer. If a traumatized individual doesn't obtain the proper conditions to heal, it will likely take longer for the trauma to resolve. In the mean time, other symptoms can manifest. When drawing the parallels between physical and emotional trauma, understanding the concept of re-wounding is imperative. It is bad enough when a person experiences a traumatic event and is not given the optimal conditions in which to heal. But what if other people keep prodding the wound with their insensitive comments and potentially re-traumatizing actions? The wound will not get better. In all likelihood, it will get worse.

Let's look at a classic case example from the realms of popular culture. Imagine growing up with an alcoholic, verbally abusive father after the Great Depression in the rural South. Although she was what we now call a prototypical codependent, your mother provided you with one of the few means of coping that you had growing up: music. Imagine that your older brother, your best friend and companion in the misery of this home life, died suddenly in a work accident, cut by a saw, at the age of 14. Imagine that you sat by his bedside for a week while he suffered, and all the while your alcoholic father cursed that you, the 12-year-old little brother, should be the one who was dying.

From this traumatic upbringing rose one of the greatest figures in popular music, Johnny Cash. Minimized by his father throughout his life, Cash took the coping skill that his mother taught him in the fields of Arkansas, combined it with his unique perspective on life, and made millions in the music industry. But when music became his job and consumed his life, he had little else to help him cope with decades of unresolved emotional trauma, leading him into a notorious battle with addiction.

Johnny Cash spent his whole life trying to heal from the pain of his brother's death. In the 2005 movie *Walk the Line*, there is a tender scene in which Cash (played by Joaquin Phoenix) finds himself talking about his brother (Jack) to his future wife, June Carter (played by Reese Witherspoon). Johnny shares, "I ain't talked about Jack in a long time. It's funny, after he died, I used to talk about him all the time, but I guess people grew tired of it. So I just stopped." Clearly, Johnny's story is a prime example of a traumatized, wounded child who was never given the space he needed to heal and was re-wounded by his father's harsh comments. The wound ultimately festered.

There are many models used to explain trauma. Different models tend to develop over time and sometimes independently of each other, even though they all attempt to explain the effects of traumatic sequelae and the implications for more effective treatment. My intention in first explaining the parallels between physical and emotional wounds is because it is the simplest ways to understand trauma and *how it affects different people in different ways*. I get upset when I hear stories of therapists minimizing a client's trauma because he or she didn't "have it as bad" as someone else in the same treatment group or because he or she was not perceived to have suffered as badly as another client. Family and friends of the traumatized person are frequently guilty of this secondary trauma as well.

My personal axiom is that *if an experience was traumatic for the client, then it is worthy of addressing clinically*. This is a belief forged through my own experience and one that I have embraced from the beginning of my career. It has helped to promote positive, healing relationships between me and my clients. I am grateful that the people who worked with me in therapy embraced this approach; otherwise, I may have denied myself the emotional wound care I so desperately needed. I believe that honoring a client's struggle, regardless of how we as therapists may perceive it, is the cornerstone of quality EMDR treatment. Fortunately, the idea of honoring trauma and its subjective nature was acknowledged by Shapiro in her explanation of Large "T" and small "t" trauma as she developed EMDR (Shapiro & Forrest, 1997).

As a review, Large "T" traumas are those that would be overwhelming to almost anyone, and for diagnostic purposes, they involve the life-threatening or perceived life-threatening component that is needed to warrant a formal, DSM-IV-TR (*Diagnostic and Statistical Manual*, 4th edition, text revision; American Psychiatric Association, 2000) diagnosis of PTSD. In addition to life-threatening events, those that involve major injury (or the perceived threat of major injury) can also be covered by this formal diagnosis. Small "t" traumas are the upsetting experiences that life sends our way that we are not able to integrate into our system of understanding (Shapiro & Forrest, 1997). If small "t" traumas remain unprocessed (commensurate to the small wounds that don't receive the treatment that they need), they can end up being just as clinically significant as Large "T" traumas, especially if there are complicating variables, or if small "t" traumas continue to build one on top of another.

Interestingly, Shapiro has also employed the wound comparison in her AIP model. One of the tenets of her model purports that our brain's inherent information processing system is like other bodily systems—it is "geared to go toward health" (Shapiro, 2008; p. 7), and when this doesn't happen, it is like a cut that wants to close and heal but somehow gets blocked.

I have chosen not to go into much more detail on the AIP model in this chapter on trauma for several reasons. First, I overviewed AIP in Chapter 2 as I explained Face 1 (protocol-oriented EMDR), and I address the principle of processing in a general sense later in this chapter. Second, there are already a number of available sources that go into depth about the intricacies of AIP (Box 6). Third and most importantly, although I feel that AIP is an excellent model, especially when it comes to explaining how trauma and its sequelae affect a person, I think there are simpler, more elegant models available that can better guide the clinical execution of EMDR treatment. The models I explore in greater depth are the three-phase consensus model of post-trauma treatment (Briere & Scott, 2006; Courtis & Ford,

2009; Curran, 2010; Korn, 2009), Parnell's (2007) four essential elements of an EMDR protocol, and the four-activity model (Lipke, 2000; 2004). All of these models fall into the "simple solutions for complex problems" philosophy that I espouse throughout this book. Before we explore these models, it is important for us to cover our bases on two more of the essential elements of a trauma crash course: Examining the formal PTSD diagnosis and evaluating the fundamentals of processing.

Box 6. Resources on the Adaptive Information Processing (AIP) Model.

The EMDR Institute. (n.d.). Theory: The adaptive information processing model. In *EMDR Institute, Inc.* Retrieved April 23, 2010, from http://www.emdr.com/theory.htm.

Shapiro, F. (2001). *Eye Movement Desensitization and Reprocessing: Basic principles, protocols, and procedures* (2nd ed.). New York: The Guilford Press.

Shapiro, F., & Forrest, M. (1997). *EMDR: The breakthrough "eye movement" therapy for overcoming stress, anxiety, and trauma.* New York: Basic Books.

Shapiro, F., & Maxfield, L. (2002). Eye Movement Desensitization and Reprocessing (EMDR): Information processing in the treatment of trauma. *Journal of Clinical Psychology/In Session: Psychotherapy In Practice, 58*(8), 933–946.

Shapiro, F., & Solomon, R. (2008). EMDR and the adaptive information processing model: Potential mechanisms of change. *Journal of EMDR Practice and Research, 2*(4), 315–325.

Chapter 3: A Crash Course on Trauma

Oh No, Not the DSM!: Examining the Formal PTSD Diagnosis

The DSM-IV-TR (American Psychiatric Association, 2000) often gets a bad rap for being too cut and dry. I have heard many of my colleagues describe it as insufficient in addressing the complexities of clinical presentation. I, for one, am not without my criticisms of the DSM-IV-TR, but I think it is important to examine the existing definition of PTSD in the chapter on trauma competency (Box 7). The main reason that this definition needs to be examined is that many clinicians miss what is contained within the diagnosis, and this has direct implications for the care of complex clients. For instance, I have heard clinicians express their concern that patients with certain problems (e.g., anger issues, substance use disorders, psychosis) are not candidates for trauma work. By taking a closer look at the diagnosis, we see that many of these "problems," which often get slapped with other diagnostic labels, may be better explained by trauma.

The PTSD diagnosis first appeared in the DSM-III (American Psychiatric Association) in 1980, following a series of political maneuvers stemming from the Vietnam War (Scott, 1993). According to the DSM-IV-TR (American Psychiatric Association, 2000), an individual must have experienced a Criterion A trauma (or Large "T" trauma in Shapiro nomenclature) for PTSD to be officially diagnosed. Criterion A traumas are those that involved experiencing or witnessing an event that was life-threatening or perceived to be life threatening, resulting in a response of helplessness or horror. Bear in mind, a non-life-threatening event can be perceived to be life-threatening and it can still qualify as Criterion A. Thus, we can honor the subjective nature of trauma.

For example, think about a 4-year-old child growing up in a home full of domestic violence. This child routinely watches his alcoholic father beat his mother. If that child perceives that his mother's life is in danger and his life may be next, that would qualify as a Criterion A trauma. Once again, it is subjective. For a variety of reasons, the child's 7-year-old sister may be disturbed by the behavior, but for her it may not seem life-threatening. In conducting assessments, it is vital to get a sense of what these traumatic or wounding experiences meant to a client. *Meaning* is a powerful construct in assessment.

Box 7. PTSD in a Nutshell.*

- Actual or perceived threat of injury or death with response of hopelessness or horror (Criterion A)
- Re-experiencing of the trauma (Criterion B)
- Avoidance of stimuli associated with the trauma (Criterion C)
- Heightened arousal symptoms (Criterion D)
- Duration of symptoms longer than 1 month (anything less than a month can fall under the category of *acute stress disorder*)
- Functional impairment due to disturbances

* Please consult the DSM-IV-TR (American Psychiatric Association, 2000) for full diagnostic criteria.

Criterion B – The Case of Jim

Criterion B encompasses symptoms that mark the re-experiencing of the trauma. The classic examples include flashbacks, vivid dreams, and nightmares. However, what clinicians often do not realize is that hallucinations can also be a part of Criterion B. I am reminded of a client whom a consultee of mine once treated. This man, whom we'll call Jim, had a severe cocaine addiction and a wide spectrum of mental health symptoms, including hallucinations. Jim, who had intermittent sobriety over a period of several years, was nonresponsive to any medication that he was given for his hallucinatory symptoms. My consultee explored the content of his auditory hallucinations further and found out that the "voice" telling Jim to kill himself was that of his abusive mother. I truly believe that my colleague's ability to identify the root cause of the voices helped enhance Jim's overall treatment experience. My consultee used some Face 4 EMDR with this client, encouraging him to develop resources and containers with bilateral simulation when the voices began. When I last heard about Jim's progress, he had over 4 years of sobriety. My main message here is this: When a client talks about hearing or seeing things, don't automatically classify these symptoms as psychotic. Ask about the content of the voices and how they may be a part of the client's larger trauma history. You may find out that getting these issues out on the table will enhance the treatment experience.

Criterion C – The Case of Rachel

Criterion C refers to avoidance of stimuli associated with the trauma. The major symptoms that clinicians associate with this criterion include behaviors such as not driving near the location where the trauma took place and not wanting to talk about anything connected to the trauma. However, there are many more potential manifestations of Criterion C, including

- Isolation
- Withdrawal from activities that used to be important
- Having a sense of a foreshortened future
- Restrictive range of affect
- Fear of feelings

There are some clear parallels here to substance use disorders and other acting out behaviors. As noted in the literature, when an individual has a sense of a foreshortened future, instant gratification becomes more appealing (Fletcher, 1996; Terr, 1991). Secondly, if a person is afraid of feeling or showing emotion related to traumatic etiology, drugs and/or alcohol may be employed to suppress those feelings. Although substances are not directly mentioned in Criterion C, the connection is obvious. A participant observed during one of my live trainings, "Isn't drug or alcohol use a form of avoidance?" Let's take a closer look.

Consider the case of a girl we'll call Rachel. She was sexually abused by an uncle during her elementary school years and was never able to tell anybody. Although the abuse stopped by the time she was 8 years old, during her teenage years and early adulthood, her family still required her to go to holiday gatherings at her grandmother's house, where she had to see her uncle. Sometimes, she was forced into the position of making small talk with him. After Rachel tried marijuana for the first time at age 14, she surmised that if she had to go to these family affairs, smoking a joint before she went (and after she returned helped her avoid feeling the overwhelming sense of anxiety that emerged from having contact with her abuser. These experiences with smoking a joint to avoid the pain crystallized within her, and it was a strategy that she carried into her adult life for dealing with uncomfortable emotion. As we will examine further in our chapters on addiction (Chapter 8) and violent/acting out behaviors (Chapter 9), clearing out the negative cognition of "It's not okay to show my emotions" is often the vital first step in trauma processing with EMDR.

Criterion D – It Explains A Lot

Many traumatized individuals have also used drugs and alcohol for dealing with symptoms associated with Criterion D, heighted arousal symptoms. The two major symptoms associated with this category are hypervigilance (e.g., always being on guard for something bad to happen) and the exaggerated startle response (i.e. a person is more "jumpy" than what would be considered normal). **Yet clinicians tend to overlook that there are three other major avoidance symptoms that often get lumped into other diagnostic categories without the trauma ever being examined.**

One of the DSM-IV-TR listed symptoms that can fall under Criterion D is problems focusing or paying attention. However, when people come into treatment (either addiction or mental health), such a symptom is typically dismissed as being part of an attention-deficit disorder. Sleep disturbance, which includes problems falling or staying asleep (without nightmares), is also a valid symptom under Criterion D. Yet how many times have you seen clients with sleeping difficulties just given medication by a medical provider without the root issues being explored? Other possible symptoms listed under Criterion D are increased irritability and outbursts of anger. Often, when clients present with these symptoms, I see one of two things happen: Mental health traditionalists may lump these symptoms into the bipolar spectrum, and addiction traditionalists may write off these symptoms as part of the addiction. Once again, can these symptoms better be explained by trauma? Please hear me carefully: I'm not discounting the existence of attention deficit or bipolar disorders, nor am I refuting the notion that a person's anger difficulties can be a part of their addiction manifestation. What I am advocating here is for individuals to look deeper because that can enhance the treatment process. **Trauma can explain a lot, yet many clinicians are too afraid or ill prepared to look for it.**

In this next section of the chapter, I describe how trauma does not necessarily need to be Criterion A for it to be clinically significant. This is where a lot of clients get tripped up, believing that if they didn't survive a major disaster, than their trauma is somehow less legitimate. Sadly, as noted earlier, I have seen many professionals and family members further reinforce this devastating belief. A useful concept for further illustrating that trauma that does not meet criteria for PTSD comes from Shapiro. As mentioned previously, she introduced the notion of small "t" traumas—the upsetting events that life sends our way (Shapiro & Forrest, 1997). Despite being "small," if these traumas are not resolved or processed, a person can stay stuck in the resulting disturbance. Perhaps this idea can best be explained by looking at a case.

Other DSM Issues and the Case of Jane

Although many professionals do not feel that the DSM-IV-TR (American Psychiatric Association, 2000) sufficiently handles trauma that is not single incident, it is hoped that other types of trauma will be more comprehensively addressed in the upcoming DSM-5. The other issue to consider with the DSM-IV-TR (as it relates to EMDR therapists) is how to address small "t" trauma that does not meet Criterion A magnitude. For those of us who bill third-party payers, it is important to have a specified DSM-IV-TR diagnosis. The reality is that many of the diagnoses we treat—depressive disorders, anxiety disorders, adjustment disorders, and according to some, addictive disorders—are the manifestations of small "t" trauma. Hence, we can remain compliant with our diagnoses but conceptualize the etiology and progression of the diagnosed disorder using our understanding of small "t" trauma. Let's take a look at the case of Jane.

Jane entered treatment for crack cocaine addiction in her early forties. On assessment, she was diagnosed with cocaine dependence and dysthymic disorder. Jane indicated that the first time she ever remembered feeling like she was worthless and not good enough was in the first grade. She reported that she had a very small bladder (a condition that was later verified medically), and as a result, she required frequent trips to the restroom. One day, Jane asked her teacher if she could go to the bathroom, and the teacher refused. Jane continued to plead, but it was fruitless. After several minutes, Jane was no longer able to physically contain her need to urinate, and she wet her pants. This got her into even more trouble with the teacher, who labeled Jane as "no good." Needless to say, Jane became the butt of her peers' cruel jokes, and it became an experience that she was never able to live down throughout her school years.

Jane told me this story with a great deal of shame, crying the deep tears typically associated with someone who had been physically or sexually assaulted. Clearly, Jane had been profoundly wounded, and because she was never able to talk about or make sense of the experience (i.e., process it), she remained stuck in the message that the experience gave her: "Jane, you are worthless and not good enough. You can't even wait to go to the bathroom."

So What Does Processing Really Mean?

When I do live trainings, I love nothing more than asking a room full of clinicians, "So, what does *processing* really mean?" *Processing* is a term that gets thrown around mental health and other treatment centers very casually (i.e., "I pulled the client aside, and we processed what happened when he acted out" or "We had a process group to start the day"). I remember when I interned at my first mental health facility, *process* was one of the primary buzzwords in the clinical culture, and even the patients made jokes about it. But do we *really* know what it means?

Processing is just a fancy psychological term for making sense of an experience or learning. It can also include the ability to achieve the resolution needed to move on from a traumatic experience or series of experiences. Processing has been equated to *digesting* an unsettling event. If we go back to the wound parallel, processing is when proper treatment is given to the wound within an appropriate time frame, and the individual is allowed the space that he or she needs to heal. In a biological sense, processing occurs when the emotional material in the limbic system is allowed to link up with the more cognitively-oriented functions of the frontal lobe.

The simplest way I can explain the biological phenomenon of processing is to present MacLean's model of the triune brain (1990). This model acknowledges that the human brain really operates as three separate brains, each with its own special role, including respective senses of time, space, and memory. These three regions of the whole brain are:

- The R-complex brain (reptilian brain):
Includes the brainstem and cerebellum; controls reflex behaviors, muscle control, balance, breathing, and heartbeat; and is very reactive to direct stimulation.

- The limbic brain:
Contains the amygdala, hypothalamus, and hippocampus; is the source of emotions and instincts within the brain, including attachment and survival. When this part of the brain is activated, emotion is activated. According to MacLean, everything in the limbic system is either agreeable (pleasure) or disagreeable (pain/distress), and survival is based on the avoidance of pain and the reoccurrence of pleasure.

- The neocortex (or cerebral cortex):
Contains the frontal lobe and is unique to primates; the more evolved brain that regulates our executive functioning, which can include higher-order thinking skills, reason, speech, meaning, and sapience (e.g., wisdom, calling on experience).

The human being relies on all three brains to function. Thus, the human being depends on all three brains to optimally process.

Many cognitive therapies are primarily designed to activate and work with the frontal lobe; yet for a person who has unprocessed trauma symptoms, the three brains are not fully communicating. Indeed, during periods of intense emotional disturbance, the functions of the frontal lobe cannot be optimally accessed because the limbic, or survival brain, is in control (Solomon & Siegel, 2003; van der Kolk, 2003). This is why the visceral experiences of triggers are R-complex activities triggered by the survival brain that cannot be addressed through the frontal lobe. Moreover, if a person is triggered into a fight, flight, or freeze to submission response at the limbic level, one of the quickest ways to alleviate that pain after the distress is to feed the pleasure potential in the R-complex. As many individuals have discovered, alcohol or drugs, food, sex, gambling, shopping, hoarding, or other reinforcing activities are particularly effective at managing the pain.

One way I conceptualize how traumatized people operate is that they are "stuck in limbic," in other words, stuck in the survival mode. The limbic region of the brain was activated during the original trauma to help the traumatized person survive (through flight, fight, or freeze to submission). Because the left frontal lobe turned off (no blood flow) and the right frontal lobe was abandoned (awareness but lack of ability to process), the individual was never able to link up that limbic activation to the frontal lobe during the experience.

There are a variety of reasons why trauma remains unprocessed, undigested, unresolved, or unhealed (pick whichever word makes the most sense to you). I explained one of the major reasons earlier in the chapter when I asked you to consider the case of musician Johnny Cash. The entire *don't talk, don't trust, don't feel* culture of the alcoholic home in which Cash was raised was completely antithetical to healthy processing, which made it easy for the traumatic memories of his brother's death to stay stuck in limbic or survival mode. Another reason trauma remains unprocessed is because we tend to automatically assume that talking is the only way to process trauma. In many mental health and addiction treatment settings, *talking* is synonymous with *processing*. Although talking can help a person process, it is primarily a function of the left frontal lobe. A person can talk about the trauma all he or she wants, but until the person can address it at the limbic level blockage, traumas will likely stay stuck. Other healthy modalities of processing can include exercise, breath work, imagery, journaling, drawing, prayer, or dreaming. These experiential modalities are more likely (than talk strategies) to address limbic-level activity.

If you are still confused about trauma and how it can affect people, I would like to recommend a few fantastic sources from popular culture that may put more of a human face on these concepts (Box 8). I am the type of person who connects with a story more readily than with anything too academic or esoteric. However, in case you prefer brain studies to pop culture, I am also listing some recommendations in that realm. I hope that this brief primer, together with one or two of these resources, will put you on solid ground when it comes to understanding trauma. Having this understanding is a critical prerequisite for grasping the models of trauma work that I explain in the next section of this chapter.

Box 8. Resources on PTSD and Other Trauma.
From Popular Culture.

Burana, L. (2009). *I love a man in uniform: A memoir of love, war, and other battles*. New York: Weinstein Books. (*A memoir by a former stripper/Playboy model married to an Army officer and both of their struggles with PTSD*.)

Haggis, P. (Director & Producer). (2007). *In the Valley of Elah* [Motion picture]. United States: Warner Independent Pictures. (*A haunting film about the role of untreated PTSD in a soldier's murder*.)

Joplin, L. (2005). *Love, Janis*. New York: Harper Collins. (*Biography of rock star Janis Joplin by her sister, Laura; an excellent study in compounded small "t" trauma and addictive disorders*.)

Kotlowitz, A. (1991). *There are no children here*. New York: Anchor Books. (*Biography of two inner-city brothers, Lafayette and Pharaoh, over the course of several summers in their Chicago housing project*.)

Mangold, J. (Director), Keach, J. (Producer), & Conrad, K. (Producer). (2005). *Walk the line* [Motion picture]. United States: 20th Century Fox. (*The Johnny Cash biopic referenced in this chapter; also check out Johnny's autobiography "Cash: The Autobiography."*)

Shortridge, J. (2009). *When she flew*. New York: NAL Accent (Penguin Group). (*A novel about a former soldier with a severe case of PTSD found living in the woods with his pre-teen daughter*.)

Singer, I. B. (1972). *Enemies: A love story*. New York: Farrar, Straus, and Giroux. (*A novel in the classic style of Singer that tells the tale of a convoluted love triangle depressingly complicated by the aftereffects of Holocaust trauma. Also available as a movie [available through Warner Home Video, 1989].*)

Van Sant, G. (Director), & Bender, L. (Producer). (1997). *Good Will Hunting* [Motion picture]. United States: Miramax. (*Academy-award nominated film about a genius [played by Matt Damon] who grows up in a culture of trauma. In the film, he undergoes therapy with a Vietnam veteran [played by Robin Williams] also struggling with his own issues.*)

Winterbottom, M. (Director), Broadbent, G. (Producer), & Jones, D. (Producer). (1997). *Welcome to Sarajevo* [Motion picture]. Channel 4/Miramax. (*A war movie that focuses on the human side of each character and how each is affected by the siege of Sarajevo.*)

"Brainiac" Recommendations: The Neuroscience of PTSD

Grey, E. (n.d.). Your brain. In *Chrysalis Mental Health and Wellness, Inc.* Retrieved April 25, 2010, from http://www.rtpgh.com/YourBrain.html.

Grey, E. (2010). *Unify your mind: Connecting the feelers, thinkers, & doers of your brain*. Pittsburgh, PA: CMH&W, Inc.

Levine, P. (1997). *Waking the tiger—Healing trauma*. Berkeley, CA: North Atlantic Books.

MacLean, P. D. (1990). *The triune brain in evolution: Role in paleocerebral functions*. New York: Plenum Press.

Rothschild, B. (2000). *The body remembers: The psychophysiology of trauma treatment*. New York: W. W. Norton & Company.

Scaer, R. (2005). *The trauma spectrum: Hidden wounds and human resiliency*. New York: W. W. Norton & Company.

Solomon, M. F., & Siegel, D. (2003). *Healing trauma: Attachment, mind, body, and brain*. New York: W. W. Norton & Company.

Stickgold, R. (2002). EMDR: A putative neurobiological mechanism of action. *Journal of Clinical Psychology*, 58(1), 61–75.

van der Kolk, B., McFarlane, A., & Weisaeth, L. (Eds.). (1996). *Traumatic stress: The effects of overwhelming experience on mind, body, and society*. New York: The Guilford Press.

Conceptualization Made Simple: Models of Trauma Work

Three-Stage Consensus Model

When a patient enters a hospital with a major injury, he or she is rarely, if ever, rushed immediately into major surgery. Certain steps need to take place before this happens. Some of these steps are so basic, their importance is often overlooked: Reading vital signs, cleaning up the wound, assessing for the presence of allergies, and screening for other medical conditions or factors that may be a contraindication to surgical treatment. Surgeries are typically planned events, even in some of the most severe medical emergencies. Even when patients are "rushed to surgery, STAT," the medical team has already taken the steps needed to get a patient into surgery.

After a patient has surgery to address a significant illness or to treat a major wound, it would be pretty irresponsible just to throw him or her out on the street to fend for himself or herself, right? Typically, the wound needs to be properly cared for to prevent infection, and physical therapy or other medication is often needed to help a patient get back to functioning. These medical procedures seem like common sense, yet so often we lose sight of the need for such steps when it comes to conceptualizing emotional trauma work, even in EMDR.

There is a general consensus in the literature that clinically addressing trauma should occur in three stages[3] (Briere & Scott, 2006; Courtis & Ford, 2009; Curran, 2010; Korn, 2009):

1.) stabilization;
2.) working through of the trauma; and
3.) reintegration/reconnection with society.

There is a clear parallel here to the medical model that I described at the beginning of the section: Stabilize a patient, perform surgery, and then rehabilitate the patient to return to functioning. Yet, too often I have seen mental health practitioners struggle with this model. Many are able to handle a bit of the stabilization work, but if the client clearly needs emotional surgery, he or she may get shut down or sent to a psychiatrist to be prescribed medication to quell the symptoms. Alternatively, I have seen overly eager clinicians (including many new trainees in EMDR), who are excited about the method, rush through stabilization and jump right into the "working through." **This is the jump where the greatest damage can result.** A third major error is when clinicians work the first two stages and then assume that the client is healed and everything is alright; however, in many cases, help is still needed to assist the client in getting back on his or her feet in a functional sense.

Shapiro's eight-phased EMDR protocol (2001) actually fits nicely within this three-stage consensus model. However, this three-stage

[3] I use the term stages in referring to the consensus model to avoid any confusion with the use of the term *phases* that I employ when referring to the eight phases of the traditional Shapiro EMDR protocol (2001).

model can be simpler, more compact, and easier for EMDR clinicians (especially those who struggle with learning standard protocol) to grasp the big picture of trauma treatment and where EMDR can fit into it. Let's take a look at how all of this fits:

1.) Stabilization (EMDR Phases 1 and 2)
2.) Working through the trauma (EMDR phases 3–7; some of the Phase 7 work calls for the stabilization skills built in Phase 2)
3.) Reintegration/reconnection with society (EMDR Phase 8)

It is important to consider that there is never a "perfect" model for explaining the intricacies of human behavior, so there is going to be some overlap among models. For instance, you may be doing reintegration work with a client (EMDR Phase 8) when he or she notices that something else from the past is coming up when he or she is trying to positively reconnect with life. Thus, you may need to go back and work collaboratively through some more of the trauma to assist with reintegration. This is why it is vital to stay involved with a client through all three stages of the consensus model, just as it is critical for medical professionals to follow a patient through rehabilitation.

All of the current EMDR training programs of which I am aware have a practicum component that allows participants to do some of their own work with another trainee. Typically, targets of low to moderate disturbance are selected for this work. Thus, many clinicians going through EMDR trainings have a healthy amount of stabilization (in the form of coping skills, positive life experiences) to be able to integrate this brief work at the training into their life experiences. What I see happen too frequently is that trainees carry the optimism that results from their experiences with EMDR back to their clinical work and then expect similar results when they use EMDR with their complex clients. Positive results will not occur if the client is not adequately stabilized. Many training programs in EMDR teach Phase 1 and Phase 2 of the traditional Shapiro protocol as the stabilization piece, but in my professional opinion, the importance of stabilization is not adequately emphasized. When trainees go back to their work with clients, many are prone to rushing through Phases 1 and 2. More high-functioning clients may require only minimal stabilization, but for the complex client, doing one guided imagery, like a calm safe place exercise, isn't going to cut it.

If a trainer or consultant has done his or her job correctly, he or she will typically advise a trainee to try EMDR with a higher-functioning client first—one with whom he or she has already established a relationship. This is for good reason: EMDR can be a tricky process to master, and your first attempts with it ideally should be with a client who is already stable. However, I have had trainees from community agencies tell me (in consultation) that they don't really have any high-functioning clients on their caseload. My advice to them is to work on stabilization. If you can adequately stabilize a client and *prepare* that person for trauma processing, you may find that you will be able to do EMDR with some success, even if the client has a complex presentation. But to do that, the preparation cannot be rushed, and it may require that you bring in other modalities of treatment to assist. (See discussions in Chapter 2 on Face 2 and Face 3 EMDR.)

Stabilization and preparation are so important that I have devoted an entire chapter to these connected constructs (see Chapter 5). A research participant whom I interviewed once shared with me, "I think that EMDR can help just about anyone, as long as they're not coming unglued" (Marich, 2009b). I loved her use of the term *unglued*, for indeed, we need to assess for this factor and make sure that clients have just enough emotional "glue" to hold themselves together during the working through of the trauma. The damage is done when we try to do active, stage-two trauma work with a person who is coming unglued.

There are two worksheet tools provided in this book to help you better understand how the three-stage consensus model can guide your decision-making in all trauma work, including EMDR. The worksheet called "Mapping Out Your Treatment" is already filled out to reflect my treatment process with a former EMDR client. I have also included a clean copy of this worksheet that you can use with clients. Sometimes I have clients take this worksheet home to reflect on independently. With other clients, I work on it with them as part of our treatment planning process. For clients who may require a simpler approach, I have also included another worksheet called "Wound Care 101: All About Your Treatment." Feel free to copy and use this handout in your clinical settings.

Mapping Out Your Treatment

POINT A: Where I Am At Now

What are the main problems that brought you to treatment in the first place?

How would you like these problems to be different?

What are you willing to do to help yourself solve these problems?

STEP 1 of the JOURNEY:
Getting Yourself Ready to Make the Trip

Travel is often a very difficult process, especially on a journey that can be as tough as change, and especially when that journey requires that you may need to do some traveling through your past. If you were driving a long distance, you would need to put gas in your car and have a plan for how to acquire food, water, and other basic needs along the way. If you were taking a rough trip across a dark, rugged forest, you would need to have ample supplies in your backpack to help you survive along the way. Sometimes, you need to make sure that you are feeling well enough to make the trip in the first place.

What are some emotional skills that I will need to develop to be ready for travel on this journey of change?

How will I know that I am stable enough to begin traveling on the roughest parts of my journey?

STEP 2 of the JOURNEY:
Traveling Through the Dark Forest of the Unresolved Past

What are some of the issues from your past that you know you will need to address in order to reach your "Point B" wellness goals? (You *do not* need to get into a lot of detail here, just write down in general terms what issues or negative beliefs have been your sticking points.)

What conditions will need to be in place for me to travel back to the past like this and still know that I am safe here in the present?

STEP 3 of the JOURNEY:
Arrival at "Point B"

After I have gained the stability that I need to look at all of my issues, I will need to take steps to really put my goals into action in my life. This is what I believe my "Point B" will look like:

Mapping Out Your Treatment

POINT A: Where I Am At Now

What are the main problems that brought you to treatment in the first place?

addiction/chronic relapsing, nightmares about sexual abuse, problems with saying "no" to others

How would you like these problems to be different?

to stay sober for longer than 6 months at a time, to be able to sleep through the night without a nightmare/put my abuse in the past, be able to say "no" to people when it's the right choice for me

What are you willing to do to help yourself solve these problems?

continue working with my A.A. sponsor, come to counseling once a week, write in my journal more regularly

STEP 1 of the JOURNEY:
Getting Yourself Ready to Make the Trip

Travel is often a very difficult process, especially on a journey that can be as tough as change, and especially when that journey requires that you may need to do some traveling through your past. If you were driving a long distance, you would need to put gas in your car and have a plan for how to acquire food, water, and other basic needs along the way. If you were taking a rough trip across a dark, rugged forest, you would need to have ample supplies in your backpack to help you survive along the way. Sometimes, you need to make sure that you are feeling well enough to make the trip in the first place.

What are some emotional skills that I will need to develop to be ready for travel on this journey of change?

to ask others for help/use the phone when my feelings are overwhelming

use the coping skills that I know can work: prayer, journaling, listening to music

How will I know that I am stable enough to begin traveling on the roughest parts of my journey?

when my sponsor and counselor suggest to me that I am ready

when I can use coping skills on most days of the week to deal with my feelings

when I have worked A.A. steps 1–3

STEP 2 of the JOURNEY:
Traveling Through the Dark Forest of the Unresolved Past

What are some of the issues from your past that you know you will need to address in order to reach your "Point B" wellness goals? (You do not need to get into a lot of detail here, just write down in general terms what issues or negative believes have been your sticking points.)

to no longer believe "I'm in danger" and "I'm not good enough;" these are things that my abuser made me believe about myself

to forgive myself for relapsing three times when I tried to get sober; one of those times, I missed my daughter's graduation and she's never forgiven me

sick romantic relationships...I always get into them

What conditions will need to be in place for me to travel back to the past like this and still know that I am safe here in the present?

having my counselor remind me of my coping skills

being available to talk to my sponsor or A.A. support group on the phone at night when I get lonely

STEP 3 of the JOURNEY:
Arrival at "Point B"

After I have gained the stability that I need to look at all of my issues, I will need to take steps to really put my goals into action in my life. This is what I believe my "Point B" will look like:

I will stay clean and sober for longer than 6 months, one day at a time, and no longer experience the consequences of my addiction (e.g., legal issues, missing too much work, improved relationship with my family)

I will be able to sleep in peace without any nightmares

I will be able to have healthy relationships with people and stay away from men who take advantage of me

I will be able to say "no" and mean it to the unhealthy people in my life

I will hold down a job for more than a year and eventually go back to school for what I really want to do (nursing)

Wound Care 101: All About Your Treatment

STEP 1: Bandaging the Wounds

<u>Useful Coping Skills</u>   <u>When to Use This Skill</u>

STEP 2: Looking Beneath the Surface

<u>Issues I Will Need to Work on to Reach My Goals</u>

STEP 3: Total Healing

<u>What My Life Will Look Like After I've Done the Healing Work</u>

Wound Care 101: All About Your Treatment

STEP 1: Bandaging the Wounds

Useful Coping Skills	When to Use This Skill
drawing	when my "inner child" acts up
taking a hot bath	when I start to get shaky
deep "ocean" breathing	when someone gets on my nerves
praying	when I start to miss my mother (deceased)

STEP 2: Looking Beneath the Surface

Issues I Will Need to Work on to Reach My Goals
all of the deaths in my family
being teased at school for not learning as fast as the other kids
anger management problems/hitting people too easily
bad beliefs about myself: "I'm stupid," "I'm ugly," "I can't speak up for myself"

STEP 3: Total Healing

What My Life Will Look Like After I've Done the Healing Work
I won't hit people anymore or be tempted to hit them
I will be able to think about my mother and brother without crying so much & losing sleep
I will be able to finish my G.E.D.
I will no longer have to go to court for trouble I get into for hitting others

Chapter 3: A Crash Course on Trauma

The Four Essential Elements of EMDR

Well-respected EMDR practitioner Laurel Parnell, who has published several books on the use of EMDR in clinical settings, is known for simplifying the complex. In her 2007 book, *A Therapist's Guide to EMDR*, she discussed how using a very simple formula as a guideline can help any EMDR practitioner with his or her conceptualization of a case or session:

1.) Create safety
2.) Stimulate traumatic neural network
3.) Add alternating bilateral stimulation
4.) End with safety

As one can easily see by looking at Parnell's guidelines, safety must "bookend" the EMDR experience and the each session. Creating safety for the client is critical. Often, it involves more than just having a predetermined safe place visualization exercise. Rather, the environment you create in your office, the rapport you build with your client (which is covered further in the next chapter), and the procedures you and your client have discussed to provide safety outside your office are all part of the larger context of safety. Former EMDR clients have shared that safety is absolutely critical for EMDR to work effectively (Marich, 2009b; 2010).

When you stimulate the traumatic neural network and add bilateral stimulation, what happens happens: Trauma work is unpredictable. However, if you have a safety plan in place to end each session and bring the client back to the here and now, the trauma work does not have to be as scary as clinicians fear it may be. People tend to believe that EMDR can bring up too much or get dangerous, but I have consistently seen that it is not the processing that is dangerous. It's dangerous when the client has processed the trauma, has possibly abreacted, and does not have a safe space to which to return at the end of the session.

Let's examine the case of Julie. Julie is a recovering opiate addict in her early twenties who came for EMDR to work on early childhood issues so that she would not relapse. Julie and her counselor immediately clicked, and because of that rapport, Julie expressed that she was willing to do anything that her counselor might attempt with the EMDR, even if that meant looking at scary places from her past. Julie and her counselor went through some basic guided imagery exercises that helped the client feel calm and safe. When Julie's counselor oriented her to the EMDR process, Julie expressed, "Well, that sounds good, but when it's all over at the end of a session, will we be able to just talk?"

That sounds like a simple enough question, right? However, many clinicians who use EMDR see it as a "better" alternative to talk therapy. Therefore, they forget that sometimes "just talking" is a vital part of the therapeutic relationship. For Julie, *talking* was a significant part of what helped her to feel safe at the end of her EMDR sessions. Julie's counselor always made sure she left 5 to 10 minutes at the end of the session to talk about what came up that day. Sometimes, the intensity was so great that Julie needed to use one of her guided imagery activities, but overall, talking was a sufficient closure.

A word of clarification here about the Parnell model: I do not interpret Step 1, "Start with safety," to mean that you need to begin every EMDR session with a positive or safe activity, although you certainly could if it is clinically appropriate and you feel it is necessary to get the client in a good place before processing. Step 1 in Parnell's model is like Stage 1 in the consensus model of EMDR: Safety needs to be established from the start, even if it takes several sessions. However, by simply talking to a client and making him or her feel at ease, we are, in essence, starting each session with safety. It is also good practice to remind clients of the safety plan you have collaboratively developed in the stabilization stage before beginning active processing with EMDR (i.e., stimulating the traumatic neural network and adding alternating bilateral stimulation).

And of course, *end with safety*. If you make *end with safety* your mantra as an EMDR therapist, you will be in good shape!

Chapter 3: A Crash Course on Trauma

The Four Activity Model

First published by Howard Lipke in 1996, the Four Activity Model is a general model of psychotherapy into which EMDR work can easily fit. The four activities Lipke addressed in his model are:

1.) Access existing information
2.) Introduce new information
3.) Facilitate information processing
4.) Inhibition of information accessing

Interestingly, these four activities appear in EMDRIA's (2009) clinical definition of EMDR. According to EMDRIA, the methods that composed the standard EMDR protocols were designed to reach these four activities as an end product. Lipke (2000, 2004), however, contended that the Four Activity model alone can guide EMDR treatment.

Although I don't believe that the Four Activity model is quite as simple as Parnell's Four Essential Elements model for conceptualization, I do see the Four Activity model as a useful guide for clinicians. The Four Activity model looks similar to other schools of psychotherapy with which new trainees are familiar. In all of the major cognitive approaches of psychotherapy that I studied in graduate school, interventions similar to Lipke's activities 1 and 2 were taught. For instance, in rational emotive behavioral therapy (REBT) or Reality Therapy, the clinician assesses what the client knows to be true (Activity 1) and then challenges the client with new information (Activity 2). Activity 3, processing of the information, allows the client to link old, dysfunctional cognitions with his or her healthier potential. Lipke (2004) defined processing as *the active communication, or sharing, among information networks, resulting in adaptive transformation of the information*. He indicated that processing can come in degrees and that there are different ways of doing it. Indeed, processing can be achieved at cognitive, emotional, biological, and spiritual levels. Many current therapies, including EMDR, are capable of holistically processing at multiple levels (i.e., physically, mentally, spiritually, emotionally). Activity 4 in Lipke's model is similar to the fourth function in Parnell's model ("End with safety"), further emphasizing the importance of having a mechanism to shut down active processing.

There are multiple ways to interpret and utilize the Four Activity model. If you feel that it would be useful to increasing your understanding of how to use EMDR, I encourage you to go to Lipke's website and download the free article that explains his model at: *http://www.howardlipke.com/articles/Four_Activity.pdf* . One of the most useful elements I have taken from the Four Activity model (as it relates to all of my trauma work, both with and without EMDR) is the importance of ending sessions with the fourth activity, inhibiting information accessing. It has been well documented in the traumatic stress literature that asking a client just to talk about traumatic experiences can often do more harm than good. Of course, one of the reasons this happens is that clients are encouraged to talk about their memories before adequate stabilization has been achieved. Secondly, talking about those memories can activate an enormous amount of limbic level activity (or *information*, using Lipke's terminology). If the client does not have a method to calm down from that limbic level activity, further damage can result. This is why I always take great care to wrap up sessions, especially early assessment and orientation sessions, with strategies designed to inhibit the accessing of new information. When you meet a client for the first session, especially if you get into a great deal of history, leave him or her with something: a breath strategy, a quick guided imagery, or a muscle tension release technique (I cover more of these in Chapter 5) to help inhibit the flurry of information processing in a healthy way.

There's a Time and a Place

A good way to wrap up this chapter is to reinforce that in clinical trauma work, there is a time and a place for everything. This logic goes for EMDR as well. Although we would eventually love to see all of our traumatized clients dig deep and process the negative material from their past in order to restore health and wholeness, rushing them into the process can do more harm than good. Making them deal with the trauma without having adequate limbic-level soothing strategies in place to create a sense of calmness and safety can cause damage. Ignoring that sometimes tedious processing of stabilization and safety planning can be disastrous. On the other end of the spectrum, dismissing the need to treat trauma, which, unfortunately, occurs all too often in mental health and addiction treatment settings, can be equally devastating for a growing population that needs trauma care.

This chapter has provided you with a crash course on some of the basics of trauma. Although hopefully, many of you have already learned these basics coming into your EMDR training, the unfortunate truth is that trauma competency often is ignored in graduate-level curricula. This lack of training in trauma can cause new trainees to have trouble understanding EMDR (Greenwald, 2006). We have covered some fundamentals of trauma at the etymologic, cultural, psychological, and biological levels. It is my hope that one of these avenues will resonate with your learning style and that you have gained some of the knowledge needed to comprehend the goals of EMDR treatment. This chapter also covered three models other than Shapiro AIP model (2001) that may be helpful in clarifying how EMDR fits into the bigger picture of trauma treatment.

There is a time and a place for every function of the trauma treatment process that was explained in this chapter. Clinicians are challenged to navigate the intricacies of how much stabilization a client needs before trauma processing can begin and when to segue from the resolutions of trauma processing into reintegration. The ability of a clinician to make these critical decisions is often impacted by skill and personal ease with trauma work. Who we are—what we bring to the counseling setting—is an important part of our effectiveness with all trauma work, including EMDR. Many of these issues are woven into the discussion of the therapeutic alliance that follows.

Chapter 4: It's the Relationship that Heals

"Therapy is simply self-change that is professionally coached."
—Arthur C. Bohart and Karen Tallman

When I was in graduate school, Carl Rogers really got a bad rap. Of course, the professors requisitely covered client-centered therapy as we went through the many theories and techniques of counseling, but Rogers was regarded as too "non-directive." His three central skills of unconditional positive regard, empathy, and congruence were labeled "important." However, if we really wanted to see changes in our clients, we needed to get in there and *do* something. When a colleague interviewed for her first job after graduate school, the interviewer asked her which theoretical orientations best described her. She replied that even though she believed in direct intervention, she most strongly resonated with the theories of Carl Rogers. Shocked, the interviewer rolled his eyes and said, "Well, we're really very cognitive-behavioral around here." My colleague was not called back for a second interview.

In this age of evidence-based medicine, gold standards in research and practice, and adoption of the medical model into in the helping professions, the critical importance of the therapeutic relationship has often been placed on the back burner. It's true that even with the emphasis on manual-driven therapies and the advent of more and more therapeutic techniques in the past several decades, the value of the therapeutic relationship was never forgotten. I am pleased to say that research backs up those of us who have continued to declare that a quality therapeutic relationship rests at the heart of what we do in our field. Honoring the therapeutic relationship and taking the necessary steps to building a quality working alliance between you and your client are absolutely essential when using EMDR as an intervention. Respecting the therapeutic relationship is one simple factor that enhances our work with clients.

This chapter includes a brief literature review on the therapeutic relationship and alliance, especially in the treatment of complex PTSD and other tricky clinical presentations. Following the literature review is an explanation of what all of this information means for you as a therapist using EMDR with complex clients. I also address the all-important notion of working on your own interpersonal issues as a vital part of ensuring a solid therapeutic alliance. I provide some detail on the importance of empowerment in the therapeutic alliance, the logistics of doing EMDR with another clinician's client, and honoring the individual needs of the client. As always, I include resources throughout the chapter if you would like to investigate certain aspects of the relational concept further.

The Gift of Therapy

Several years ago, after emerging from many years of clinical formation and advanced training and consultation in EMDR, a fellow clinician in recovery made a potent recommendation to me: Read *The Gift of Therapy* by Irving Yalom (2001).

"Yalom?" I questioned, "Isn't he the guy who wrote the thousand-page text on group therapy?"

"Yes," responded my colleague, "But *The Gift of Therapy* is different. It's written by a much older Yalom who has learned from his mistakes, declaring that despite all of his years writing about techniques, it really is the relationship that matters most."

Intrigued, I logged on to Amazon® and ordered myself a copy. To say that the book changed my clinical life is an understatement. Written in very readable prose, the book's essential premise is that *therapy should not be theory driven, but relationship driven.* In this and many of his other writings, Yalom contends that a heightened sensibility to existential issues deeply influences the nature of the therapeutic relationship and the therapy itself. Moreover, in Yalom's view, a therapist has no place forcing solutions, a piece of guidance I have found extremely helpful in doing EMDR work with the complex client. When I began applying many of Yalom's principles to my own clinical work (principles he clearly traces back to Carl Rogers), I noticed that my own effectiveness with EMDR improved tremendously, and the improvement was reflected in my client outcomes.

Yalom elucidated that my view of a therapy session may be drastically different from a client's view. When I started doing EMDR, I often felt elated when I saw a client go through the "textbook" protocol. The distress levels would come down to zero and the validity of cognition levels would rise significantly. Then one day, after such a textbook session, a client told me, "Just getting all that out and telling another human being I trust seems like it took a huge weight off of my shoulders." This phenomenon reminds me of another famous work of Yalom's, *Every Day Gets a Little Closer: A Twice-Told Therapy* (Yalom & Elkin, 1974). This book chronicled a year Yalom spent doing therapy with one particular client. After each session, Yalom would write his reflections of the session down, and the client would do the same. Yalom's reflections were focused on technique and all of the "brilliant" things he said and did in the session. For the client, the impact of the session was all in the relationship.

Although these relational ideas of Yalom's may be too flowery and non-directional for some, the research literature backs them up. Several scholar-practitioners at the forefront of investigating what works in psychotherapy have recently published massive meta-analyses (studies that statistically analyze the results of several studies) and literature reviews that confirm what people who think like Irving Yalom have believed all along: It's the relationship that heals.

These analyses and reviews are handily referenced in the new, second volume of *The Heart and Soul of Change: What Works in Psychotherapy*. In this volume, Duncan, Miller, Wampold, & Hubbard (2009) concluded that the collaborative, therapeutic alliance between client and clinician is a primary factor in determining successful therapy outcomes and is more important than the specific execution of therapeutic protocols. They also stressed that obtaining continuous client feedback throughout the therapeutic process is a critical element of enhancing client care. These conclusions were not made flippantly: This book, now in its second edition, represents the most complete complication of psychotherapy research and meta-analyses currently available. What the collective body of research shows is that little difference exists among the specific factors (e.g., technical elements) of *bona fide*, researched therapies that are intended to be therapeutic. Rather, there are a series of four *common factors* amongst these therapies that seem to be what's really contributing to change.

These common factors are the clients and their extra-therapeutic factors (e.g., what they bring to the table in therapy and situations out of the control of the clinician), models and techniques that work to engage and inspire the client, the therapeutic relationship/alliance, and therapist factors. It is noteworthy to explore how the editors explain models and techniques as a common factor:

"...We conclude that what happens (when a client is confronting negative schema, a dressing family boundaries, or interpreting transference) is less important than the degree to which any particular activity is consistent with the therapist's beliefs and values (allegiances) while concurrently fostering the client's hope (expectations). Allegiance and expectancy are two sides of the same coin: the faith of both the therapist and the client in the restorative power and credibility of the therapy's rationale and related rituals. Though rarely viewed this way, models and techniques work best when they engage and inspire the participants" (p. 37).

Interestingly, these four common factors were first proposed and published by psychiatrist Saul Rosenzweig in 1936, predating the work of Rogers and Yalom.

Norcross arrived at similar conclusions in *Psychotherapy Relationships that Work: Therapist Contributions and Responsiveness to Patients* (2002). Using a collection of empirical research studies and chapters from various psychotherapeutic professions that were gathered as part of an American Psychological Association Task Force, Norcross demonstrated that the therapy relationship, together with discrete method, influences treatment outcomes. Norcross further concluded that therapists can hone these relational elements, and that it is their responsibility to tailor these skills to the needs of individual patients. Thus, the relationship should drive the theory, not the other way around.

Norcross' work makes clear that we should not just throw theory and technique out the window—it is clearly important. However, if we are adhering to these technical elements at the expense of the relationship, then we're going to have a problem. Metaphorically speaking, if we put theory in the driver's seat and shove the relationship all the way back in the trunk of the car, the therapy isn't going to go anywhere. In my view, especially when it comes to doing EMDR and other advanced trauma work, the therapeutic relationship needs to take the front seat. Typically the client will steer the course of the treatment and the therapist will be the trusted front-seat navigator. At times, the client may need a rest, and the therapist will need to take the wheel for a while. The technique is like a navigating passenger in the backseat with a map or GPS system. It can give you good direction, especially when you're lost, but ultimately, the technique should never be the entity actually doing the driving. To carry the metaphor further, sometimes maps are hard to read and don't take into account the creative elements of a drive (e.g., point A to point B may look quicker, but if you've actually driven it before, you know there's a better way to go). For those of you who have used a GPS, you know its lack of artistry can be even worse!

This logic becomes especially important when conceptualizing how to best treat a complex client. The literature in general traumatic stress studies indicates that the therapeutic alliance is an important mechanism in facilitating meaningful change for clients with complex PTSD (Fosha, 2000; Fosha & Slowiaczek, 1997; Pearlman & Courtois, 2005). Recently, the EMDR community has paid greater attention to the role of the therapeutic alliance in EMDR treatment, especially after the publication of Dworkin's *EMDR and the Relational Imperative: The Therapeutic Relationship in EMDR Treatment* (2005). Dworkin contended that relational issues between client and clinician often impact whether EMDR results are positive or negative.

Dworkin's position challenged many long-standing beliefs about EMDR, one being that a client can have a couple of sessions without having much of an alliance in place because the therapy is so experiential. For instance, his work opposed the research findings of Edmond, Sloan, and McCarty (2004), who used client-centered, qualitative methods. In their study, sexually abused women receiving EMDR reported that the therapeutic alliance was secondary to perceived efficacy, compared with women receiving eclectic therapy, who stated that efficacy was secondary to the therapeutic alliance. Dworkin drew attention to a very important issue in his work when he noted that it is important not to rush through the EMDR process. Yes, EMDR can work more quickly than most conventional psychotherapies—even in a few sessions for some people. However, I have had many clients who heard of these fantastic results (e.g., on the news, on the Internet, by word of mouth) show up expecting EMDR to be a "quick fix." In fact, some of these clients are not even appropriate for EMDR. Those who come in seeking the quick fix are often resistant to doing any kind of advanced preparation, which can be detrimental to their wellness.

Although these issues are covered more fully in Chapter 5, they are worth mentioning here because establishing the all-important therapeutic alliance is a critical part of EMDR preparation. In its absence, EMDR may not be a positive experience at all, let alone the quick fix that many are seeking.

In my own phenomenological research on incorporating EMDR into addiction treatment with women, former EMDR clients (participants I studied who were not my own clients) identified the importance of the therapeutic relationship to their overall experience of safety (Marich, 2009b; Marich, 2010). According to these women, safety was an essential element that needed to be in place for them to experience good results with the EMDR. The experiences of two women from this larger research study offer fascinating case examples for review in our discussion of the therapeutic relationship in EMDR treatment.

The Case of Cindy and JoElle

Cindy and JoElle (pseudonyms were both recovering drug addicts who went through long-term treatment several years ago at the same facility in the rural Midwest (Marich, 2010). The facility Cindy and JoElle attended provided a month of stabilization after detox, followed by a halfway house program that each elected to attend while remaining in outpatient chemical dependency treatment. The facility offered many other programs and services for the women aside from traditional group treatment for addiction, one of which being EMDR therapy. At any given time since the mid-1990s, the facility has employed several EMDR Institute–trained therapists, and EMDR is worked into the treatment plan of each individual resident when the treatment team determines it is needed. Using the Four

Faces of EMDR model I proposed in Chapter 2, it is fair to say that this facility incorporates mostly Face 2 and Face 3 EMDR.

Cindy and JoElle were both referred to EMDR Therapist "A" around the same time. Cindy, a lesbian recovering from heroin addiction and having multiple mental health issues (PTSD, Bipolar Disorder, Borderline Personality Disorder), believed that she experienced virtually no progress with Therapist A, whom she described as rigid, scripted, and not comfortable with trauma work. Cindy indicated that Therapist A seemed overly concerned with getting scale readings throughout the session (e.g., SUDs, VoC), which inhibited her from forging a connection with the therapist. JoElle reported a similar experience with Therapist A, JoElle, a biracial woman who identifies as black developed a heroin addiction in her late thirties following 23 years of sobriety from marijuana. In speaking about her experiences with this therapist, JoElle remembered that "She didn't make it really clear to me that I could just do nothing, so I felt uncomfortable." JoElle further indicated that the therapist seemed overly anxious after each set of stimulation to see some kind of effect, and when nothing out of the ordinary happened, JoElle felt like she was doing something wrong.

Interestingly, both Cindy and JoElle were heroin addicts who went through multiple prior addiction treatments, and both grew up in homes where rigid religious beliefs impacted their experiences of shame. For both, having a solid connection with their therapist was an important part of their perceived progress. Both women did not have this with Therapist A, but as soon as they switched to EMDR Therapist B, they felt that the EMDR started to work. Looking back on her experience, Cindy viewed EMDR as "something that's very personal and very involved, and I think it takes a special kind of counselor to pull stuff out of you." She described the second therapist as intuitive, natural, and very comfortable with trauma work. Interestingly, Cindy was the only woman in the overall study who credited EMDR as being the reason why she was sober at the time of the interview (1 year of continuous sobriety), yet the EMDR was something that she believed did not initially work for her in the absence of a therapeutic connection. Like Cindy, JoElle began to experience immediate results with EMDR when she switched to Therapist B. JoElle shared:

She was a natural for this job. I could think something and she would say it. She was just amazing and she knew so much... she just knew a lot about me and she was really easy to talk to. She used, to me, a lot of common sense along with counseling. That's not always done. She was the greatest.

Like Cindy, JoElle indicated that Therapist B seemed to have a solid understanding of trauma that enhanced her overall comfort level. Moreover, the new counselor had a way of making JoElle feel empowered. "With her," JoElle stated, "I did not seem like just a number."

The cases of Cindy and JoElle are important to consider as we discuss what makes a good EMDR therapist, because they experienced EMDR as complex clients, not as trainees or research subjects. For all of the talk that has gone on in EMDR about technique and fidelity to the protocol, it is important that we continue to honor the therapeutic relationship. We should look to clients as being able to provide the best possible fidelity check about how well we are honoring the therapeutic alliance and important data about how this alliance is impacting their EMDR treatment.

What Makes a Good EMDR Therapist?

There are Face 1 EMDR therapists who would argue that allegiance to the Shapiro protocols is a prime element of what makes a good EMDR therapist. However, even with her emphasis on fidelity to the protocols of EMDR, Shapiro has acknowledged the importance of the therapeutic alliance in EMDR treatment. She has continually described the execution of EMDR as an essential interaction between client, method, and clinician (Dworkin, 2005; Shapiro, 2001). Her writing on the therapeutic relationship, including her instructions about it in her 2001 text, is very powerful. She has noted that because the potential for disturbance between sessions is high, the need for a strong therapeutic alliance becomes extremely important. She suggests that having truth-telling agreements in place is key and that the therapist must be able to impart safety, flexibility, and unconditional regard. One of her passages specifically highlights the importance of the therapeutic alliance when it comes to working with the complicated presentations on which we are focusing in this book:

> Clients with severe abuse backgrounds should be given careful consideration before proceeding with treatment, because they generally have difficulty around the issue of safety and trust. Until the client feels comfortable with the clinician in the common interactions of traditional therapy, EMDR should not be used (p. 94).

Laurel Parnell, whose work is compatible with the Face 2 EMDR approach described in Chapter 2, compiled a valuable list of qualities of a good EMDR therapist. I have cited the list from her 2007 book *A Therapist's Guide to EMDR* here and have rewritten each item as a question that you can use for self-review:

1. *Good clinical skills*
   - What abilities or special skills do I have going for me as a clinician outside of the EMDR realm?
   - How comfortable am I with implementing the

most basic clinical strategies for safety (e.g., risk assessment, contracting for safety, seeking outside help when necessary)?
- If an EMDR session did not go as planned, what other clinical skills do I have to work with so that I would not harm my client?

2. *Ability to develop rapport with clients*
- What strategies have worked for me so far in establishing rapport at the first meeting with a client?
- What are my struggles with forging a solid therapeutic relationship?
- Are there certain populations with which I find it especially difficult to connect?
- If it becomes clear that the client and I are not connecting after several sessions, am I willing to explore the potential problems and solutions? Would I be willing to make a referral?

3. *Comfort with trauma and intense affect*
- How do I feel when a client enters a state of extreme emotional catharsis in my office (which can include, but is not limited to, intense crying, screaming, lashing out at a figure from the past, who is not in the office, such as a past abuser)?
- What issues of my own do clients seem to provoke the most?
- What aspects of trauma and its sequelae might I still find hard to grasp clinically or personally?

4. *Spacious*
- Have I ever forced a client to work on an area that they might not be ready to handle?
- What might my motives be for pushing a client to work on traumatic material that they are not yet ready to address?

5. *Well-grounded*
- Have I worked on my own issues when it comes to trauma, addiction, and mental health?
- What were my motives for getting trained in EMDR?
- Do I let the client lead the session, or is it the other way around most times?

6. *Attuned to clients*
- What issues may keep me from staying present with my client during sessions?
- At what times might I find myself drifting off or distracted during sessions?
- Am I able to read my client's non-verbal and para-verbal cues?

The questions I presented under each Parnell quality are open-ended and merely there for your self-evaluation—this is not an inventory with "right" and "wrong" standardized scoring to indicate that if you get a certain number of questions wrong, you shouldn't be doing EMDR.

There are, however, some red flags to be aware of, which are explored in the following paragraphs. If you noticed any of these red flags come up during your self-evaluation, that doesn't necessarily mean you shouldn't be doing EMDR. It does, however, mean you may consider addressing these issues further with a clinical supervisor, peer consultant, personal therapist, or support group before proceeding with EMDR, especially with the complex client.

One red flag is failing to have an awareness of one's own clinical abilities. Shapiro (2001) was clear in her early work that a clinician should not treat a client with EMDR that he or she wouldn't feel qualified to treat with another therapy. This is excellent guidance, for if we go into a session thinking that EMDR is the only hope for a certain client and then it backfires, we have nothing left to ensure the client's safety. From my experience, those who enter EMDR training with solid clinical abilities usually turn out to be the best EMDR practitioners.

Another red flag is not being able to recognize one's ability to build rapport with clients. Ask yourself a couple questions and answer from your gut: Are people comfortable with you? From the first meeting, are you able to create a safe space for clients without coming across as phony? We often don't think of assessing for our phoniness as an exercise in evaluating our rapport-building strategies, yet it is so important. Respecting clients and making them feel safe does not mean that you should present yourself as an all-loving, saccharine angel of mercy, especially if that doesn't jive well with your personality type. Be the best version of yourself that meets people where they are in a manner that is respectful. Trust me, a traumatized person from any of the difficult populations discussed in this book can spot a phony a mile away.

As Yalom (2001) and others before him so aptly observed, the therapeutic relationship is not something that should be forced. Let it develop naturally, in an environment where the client and the clinician can test the waters with each other. Attaining and maintaining good rapport-building skills takes constant self-evaluation. If you have noticed that people are not clicking well with you, this may be a sign that you need to consult with a clinical supervisor about your approach. If you have noticed that clients only come to see you once or twice and never come back, are you at least willing to explore whether it may be something about the way that you're operating? More importantly, if it becomes clear to you after several sessions that the therapy isn't really going anywhere for a client, are you willing to consider that the client may not be comfortable with you? If you bring this up with the client and it becomes obvious that he or she feels uncomfortable, are you able to respectfully discuss the possibility of referral?

The bottom line is that some therapists are right for certain clients and others are not. I realize that some of you may work in agencies where you have to work with whomever is sent your way and referral is not an option. Others of you may fall on the other end of the spectrum: Your entire practice is based on client numbers, and referring a client out, especially during tough times, may have economic consequences for you. These are delicate issues that often require supervision, consultation, and putting your ego aside to navigate. However, I think taking an honest look is imperative. The more I have done EMDR, the more I have realized that the client must feel comfortable with me (especially the complex client) for the trauma processing aspect of EMDR (Stage 2 in the consensus model; phases 3–6 in the traditional Shapiro model) to work.

Just as clients must be comfortable with me, I, as the clinician, must be comfortable with what emerges from clients' psyches during EMDR sessions, which can be very intense, as can all trauma work. Another red flag is not being able to handle this intensity. Many of us were raised in traditions that taught how to confront irrational thoughts and behaviors, but not how to deal with lots of intense, often irrational (by our standards) material, which can come up during EMDR. Are you willing to engage in a paradigm shift and let the material simply flow, without judgment on your part? If a client starts whining and wailing and crying and gnashing his or her teeth (i.e., abreacting) when the processing brings out something subconscious, are you able to manage your own emotional reactions in an appropriate way? In short, can you handle the intensity that comes with trauma work?

I'll speak forthrightly on this issue: Doing Stage 2 trauma processing work is not for every clinician. It is my hope that someday every clinician will be able to at least assess for trauma and complete Stage 1 stabilization work as defined by the consensus model. If you can't take the heat that comes with doing trauma processing in Stage 2, this does not make you a bad clinician, but it may mean you need to refer out or get a great deal of supervision to handle yourself during the processing. I happen to be very comfortable working with trauma, so Stage 2 work and using EMDR comes naturally for me. However, there are many populations and presentations with which

I'm not comfortable working (e.g., children, couples), so I let the people who have greater skills in and comfort with these areas work with them. Again, it all boils down to knowing yourself, your strengths, and your weaknesses. If you can handle the intense affect that comes with trauma work, chances are that you will do great with EMDR.

Issues 4 through 6 on the Parnell (2007) list are all intricately connected with this notion of *clinician, know thyself.* Whole books have been written on this topic, and I am not attempting to summarize all of that knowledge here. However, one big red flag related to this concept is the clinician having unaddressed intrapersonal and interpersonal issues, especially with his or her own trauma history, because it will bleed out onto work with clients. This can be especially dangerous in EMDR, which requires your attunement to the client and his or her needs to be keen. Of course, no one can be completely self-actualized, and it would be unrealistic to think one must be to do EMDR. However, the reality is that many of us got into this field because of our own issues, and although that can be an asset in being able to relate to clients, it can also be a deficit if we have a tendency to work out our own *stuff* through our clinical work.

Probably the most significant way these issues can affect EMDR sessions is when an EMDR therapist pushes a client into the trauma processing stage before he or she is ready to go there or before he or she has attained the adequate regulation skills to venture into that area. This can happen for a variety of reasons, ranging from us being eager to see our clients get better to our memories of how well trauma therapy worked for us and wanting clients to have the same experience. I have included the questions about motives on the list for this reason. It is healthy in our personal and professional lives to check our motives, and if you are willing to answer these questions honestly, your will open the door to a world of insight about how you do therapy.

The reasons why therapists decide to add EMDR to their clinical repertoire are multifarious. Many, like me, get into doing EMDR because of personal experiences with it that make us want to share that gift with others. Many of my consultees have reported that EMDR is appealing because it offers such a holistic approach to processing trauma when talk therapy has proved to be insufficient. Others get trained in EMDR because colleagues or supervisors suggest it. Several have even come to EMDR trainings as curious skeptics. Whatever your reason was for getting trained in EMDR, my hope is that you are willing to continuously evaluate yourself. Never push clients into trauma processing before they are ready and prepared, even if *you* think that they are ready. The decision to proceed with Stage 2 trauma work must always be a collaborative one. If you work *with* the client and meet him or her where he or she is, EMDR can go very smoothly, even when the client is complex.

When I worked in the addiction field, I learned of a useful model of change by Prochaska and DiClemente (Prochaska, Norcross, & DiClemente, 1994). The stages are as follows:

1.) *Pre-contemplation*:
The person is not prepared to take any action at this time or in the foreseeable future.

2.) *Contemplation*:
The person is intending to change soon.

3.) *Preparation*:
The person is intending to make a change in the immediate future.

4.) *Action*:
The person is making significant changes in his or her lifestyle.

5.) *Maintenance*:
The person is working to prevent relapse.

6.) *Termination*:
The person has achieved 100% self-efficacy, and the relapse potential is near zero. (There are those in the drug and alcohol field who will, of course, argue that a recovering addict is always in maintenance.)

In Prochaska and DiClemente's model (1994), *relapse* is defined as a retread from action to an earlier stage. This model is used widely in the addiction field, but it also has great utility in conceptualizing a complex's case when doing EMDR. During my addiction training, I was taught the importance of offering stage-wise treatment, especially with dual diagnosis clients. In other words, meet the client where he or she *is*. It may sound simple, but it takes a therapist who is truly committed to putting the therapeutic alliance in the front seat to carry out this strategy.

Countless times in the addiction field, I saw clients enter treatment completely pre-contemplative (having no desire to change any time soon) and get barraged by well-meaning clinicians with action-oriented interventions, such as going to 90 Alcoholics Anonymous meetings in 90 days or enduring premature confrontation in group, when they were clearly not ready. The same thing can happen in EMDR treatment when we push a client into active processing before he or she is ready. It is important to gauge where the client *is* in the stages of change, regardless of whether he or she has an addiction problem. In terms of trauma, we can do Stage 1 stabilization work with clients who are pre-contemplative, contemplative, and in preparation; however, Stage 2 trauma processing work (phases 3–6 in the conventional Shapiro protocol [2001]) should be done only with clients who are in the action or maintenance stage of change.

This guideline becomes even clearer when we explore what *lifestyle* really means. In the Prochaska & DiClemente model (1994), a person in the action stage of change is making significant changes in his or her lifestyle. The term *lifestyle* is credited to Alfred Adler

(1931), who explained that the "life-style" is a series of patterns that develop in childhood to compensate for feelings of inferiority. Interestingly, a lot of what we do in EMDR therapy is to access the origin of many of these patterns and process them through to an adaptive resolution. Clearly, a person needs to be willing to change these patterns before we, as therapists, engage in any major unraveling of them with Stage 2 trauma stabilization work.

So what do clients have to say about what makes a good EMDR therapist? What is the client's view of the therapeutic alliance? These areas of research need further expansion. I find these questions personally fascinating, probably because I was an EMDR client before I was an EMDR therapist. In my research with EMDR and addicted women (Marich, 2009b; 2010), 10 women who had attained a period of extended addiction sobriety (1–6 years) reflected on their experiences with EMDR as a part of their recovery process. All 10 had things to share about their EMDR therapists. Cindy and JoElle, the women whose cases I shared previously, were the only two participants who had negative experiences with an EMDR therapist (which I shared earlier in the chapter). The list of positive qualities by the women far outweighed the negatives:

- Caring
- Intuitive
- Connected
- Skilled
- Wonderful
- Validating
- Nurturing
- Smart
- "The bomb" (a colloquial expression implying excellence)

- Trustworthy
- Natural
- Comfortable with trauma work
- Accommodating
- Commonsensical
- Gentle
- Facilitating
- Consoling
- Magical (the participant knew that the EMDR wasn't magic and the therapist wasn't a magician, but she indicated that the experience was so special, the therapist seemed magical to her)

Of course, this list is not all-inclusive and came from an all-female sample, which may not be representative of all EMDR clients. However, it is worth noting that these women qualify as the complex clients we are discussing here.

It may be helpful for you to reflect on this list and ask yourself which of these qualities you possess and which ones you may need to work on. If you are actively seeking consultation or have the guidance of a clinical supervisor for your EMDR work, it may also be a good idea to go through this list with your mentor and obtain his or her opinions about how you rate in terms of these skills. Working on your own issues continues to be an important part of being an excellent clinician and EMDR therapist, regardless of which face of EMDR you primarily practice. Dworkin's (2005) book on the relational imperative contains an excellent questionnaire on clinician self-awareness if you feel you are in need of further work on personal issues, especially any that may surface during an EMDR session.

Self-care for any clinician doing trauma work is vital. As prolific Israeli clinician Elisheva Kaftal (2008) once shared, self-care must be preemptive; it is not enough to take care of yourself when you notice that the weight of trauma work is taking its toll on you. Kaftal used the metaphor of traversing the desert: You must constantly hydrate yourself and not wait to drink only when you are feeling thirsty. Clinicians doing EMDR or any trauma work must constantly evaluate themselves and engage in self-care. There are many screening tools available online to assess for your own compassion fatigue and satisfaction, several of which are listed in Box 9. As Kaftal advised me, it is generally wise to engage in one of these self-evaluation measures every 3 to 4 months as a preventative self-care measure. Not only are you worth this measure of self-care, but you will find that the better that you take care of yourself, the more effective you will be in your clinical work.

Box 9. Resources on Self Care.

Baranowsky, A. (n.d.) *Compassion fatigue pre-workshop materials.*
Accessed June 1, 2009 from www.psychink.com/rfiles/
PrewkshpScales.doc.

Compassion fatigue awareness project. Accessed June 1, 2009 from
www.compassionfatigue.org.

Duncan, B., Miller, S., Wampold, B., & Hubble, M. (2010). *The
heart and soul of change: Delivering what works in
psychotherapy* (2nd ed.). Washington, D. C.: The
American Psychological Association.

Dworkin, M. (2005). *EMDR and the relational imperative: The
therapeutic relationship in EMDR treatment.* New York:
Brunner-Routledge.

Empowerment is Key

My experience of working with clinicians has been that those
who take the best care of themselves and practice what they
preach about healing and recovery do the best job at empowering clients. Many clients come for services crippled by an overwhelming sense of shame and powerlessness. Both can block out
any semblance of light at the end of the proverbial tunnel. Thus,
it can be difficult to be hopeful about healing, no matter how
sophisticated the interventions you use. This is why you need to
foster empowerment.

To understand why this is so important to complex clients, we must
explore the concept of shame. *Shame* refers to the belief that a person
is bad at his or her core. This belief permeates at the levels of body,
mind, and soul, informing a person that she struggles with addiction

because she is unworthy or that he is suffering from the effects of trauma because he did something wrong. Toxic shame is paralyzing, and the clinician is in a powerful position (whether he or she knows it) to further solidify a client's shame-based identity or to begin the process of alleviating some of the shame by meeting the client where he or she *is* (remember the stages of change cited earlier) with a sense of unconditional positive regard. For many complex clients, this unconditional positive regard is the first step toward creating an environment of safety.

The Case of Fadalia

Fadalia was one of the participants in the study on the use of EMDR with women in addiction continuing care (Marich, 2009b; 2010). I was first acquainted with her as one of my research subjects, but her story opened my eyes to how I relate to complex clients. When Fadalia, a woman of mixed ethnicity (European and Middle Eastern), entered the gender-specific, long-term addiction treatment facility that I researched, she had already been through approximately 25 addiction treatment programs over a 6-year period. Fadalia grew up in a strict, religiously fundamentalist home, where her shame-based identity was fostered. She began drinking alcohol and smoking marijuana while in high school, during which time she also battled an eating disorder. Fadalia reported that her drug use escalated to cocaine by the time that she was 18 and to heroin by the time she was 21. Despite a significant overdose that took her to the hospital following her second episode of using heroin, Fadalia progressed to using heroin daily.

Shortly after her heroin use began, Fadalia attempted to get clean andsober through a variety of treatment programs: hospital detoxification, inpatient, outpatient, long-term residential, methadone maintenance, and suboxone maintenance. Fadalia reported her longest period of sobriety (before entering the facility where I met her) was 6 months, while she was living in a controlled environment in a different long-term residential facility. Interestingly, when Fadalia came to the facility (where she received EMDR treatment), she expressed that it was the first time staff members conveyed to her a belief that she could get and stay sober.

Fadalia was interviewed 3 years after attaining her sobriety and in her estimation, the staff's unconditional acceptance and belief that she could get better made all the difference. As she shared, "Everywhere else I went, it was the old clichés: 'Sit down and shut up; your best thinking got you here,' or 'Take the cotton out of your ears and put it into your mouth.'" Fadalia felt empowered by the simple respect she was granted by the staff at the treatment facility where she ultimately attained her most lasting sobriety to date. There was no way she would have been open to doing EMDR if she had been greeted with the same level of cynicism she had encountered at other facilities. In Fadalia's estimation, she had to feel safe in order to open up in the deep way that EMDR requires, and the first way safety was achieved for her was through an empowering connection with the facility staff (including all of the therapists).

Fadalia began engaging in EMDR treatment after 1 to 2 months of sobriety, and she worked with the same EMDR therapist (as well as a non-EMDR individual counselor and several other group counselors) over the course of her first year of sobriety. The main issues that they addressed surrounded Fadalia's negative cognitions of "I have to be perfect," "I am a failure," and "I cannot trust anyone." She processed multiple small "t" traumas surrounding experiences with her fundamentalist mother, whom Fadalia described as a "rageful, untreated bipolar." This work segued into processing a Large "T" trauma she experienced during her active addiction: Being shot three times while cruising for drugs. The fact that her toddler son was in the back seat of the car at the time that she was shot further impacted her sense of shame. Fadalia felt as though she was a bad mother for taking her son into that situation. Through EMDR, Fadalia remembered that the last image she saw before losing consciousness after being shot was that of her son's shoe. This image reminded her that she turned around to check on her son. Although she was able to accept the responsibility of putting her son into that dangerous situation, remembering that clarifying image gave her some sense of peace because she knew that at least she had tried to make sure her son was okay. This helped to release a great deal of her toxic shame.

An Overview of EMDR-Specific Empowerment Strategies

Clearly, the basics of rapport building and therapeutic alliance (as a course in Humanistic Psychology 101 would teach us) have a place in EMDR treatment. As Fadalia's case demonstrates, showing basic human decency and respect to a client goes far in establishing your credibility, something that is crucial for successful EMDR treatment with complex clients. A number of issues are unique to EMDR and offer us chances to further empower clients.

One issue is that because EMDR may sound strange to uninformed clients, before you begin using EMDR, you should explain the approach and allow clients to decide whether they would like to try it. This should go without saying as part of an ethical preparation for and orientation to EMDR (Shapiro Phase 2; 2001). Present the therapy in a style that suits you and fits the client's level of understanding best, and be sure it is clear to the client that he or she does not *have* to do EMDR. Encourage him or her to go online and read about it, and invite the client to ask questions before he or she officially makes the decision to continue.

This is a simple strategy that may seem like common sense, but you'd be surprised how many clinicians miss it. I have encountered clinicians who are orthodox in their stance that EMDR is an approach to psychotherapy, yet they have made clients feel as though EMDR is the only option. A clinician may hand an EMDR pamphlet to a new referral saying, "This is what I do," and the client may not have sufficient ego strength to voice his or her potential discomfort with the therapy. Although we may *think* that EMDR is the best way to go for a client's problem, it is never ethical to pressure a client into doing EMDR.

When I work with a client whom I think would benefit from EMDR, I endorse it but always offer at least two other treatment options that I can employ to help the client reach his or her goals (which is one of the benefits of being an eclectic therapist). **A client is much more likely to feel better about EMDR when he or she has had the choice to do it.** Even if a client initially chooses another modality of therapy, I have found that many are more likely to reconsider EMDR if you gently bring it up again later in the treatment because you showed enough respect to provide a choice in the first place.

There is debate among EMDR clinicians regarding which form of bilateral stimulation works best. Therefore, it is good practice to provide clients with the choice of how EMDR treatment will be executed. There are many purists (mostly Face 1 and some Face 2 practitioners) who believe that because eye movements are the most widely researched bilateral modality, this is the only form of stimulation that should be used or, at very least, *strongly suggested* to clients. However, a great deal of case evidence, pilot research (Grey, 2008), and experiential clinical knowledge suggests that alternating tones or various forms of tactile stimulation can work just as well.

Chapter 4: It's the Relationship that Heals

Because there are three major forms of stimulation used in EMDR (i.e., eye movements, tactile stimulation, alternating tones) with multiple variants of each (e.g., eye movements can be created with a hand, wand, toy, or mechanical "light bar"; tactile stimulation can come in the form of direct touch, from a mechanical pulser machine, or through physical activities such as walking or drumming) you can turn this issue into an empowering choice for clients. I always let clients choose which form of stimulation they prefer for our EMDR sessions, and I let them know that they can choose to change the form of stimulation at any time. Although I may make suggestions (e.g., when processing seems to be stuck, I may propose that we switch stimulation forms), I am committed to leaving this choice in clients' hands (or eyes or ears). From my experience, providing this choice does wonders for allowing the client to feel empowered and respected. I discuss the issue of modality choice again in Chapter 5.

Doing EMDR with Other Therapist's Clients

When I began doing EMDR on a regular basis, I found myself inundated with a flurry of referrals from colleagues. Most of them had been working long term with a particular client and heard good things about EMDR. "Maybe EMDR will work for my client!," they heartily declared and quickly sent their clients to me for a collaborative consult. My general position is that I'll evaluate anyone once, and my first session with another clinician's client is classic Shapiro Phase I history-taking: Doing an evaluation about the presenting problem, assessing how unresolved Large "T" or small "t" trauma may be complicating that problem, and determining the client's appropriateness for EMDR. In my experience, about half of the clients referred to me are appropriate for EMDR in some capacity, and the other half are not appropriate, typically because of overmedication with central nervous system depressants and/or poor motives for wanting to do the EMDR work. I explore the reasons why certain clients are inappropriate for EMDR more fully in Chapter 5.

Preliminary research evidence suggests that an EMDR clinician can successfully do EMDR with another therapist's client (Borstein, 2009) or as part of a treatment team that includes several clinicians (Marich, 2009b; 2010). The question typically arises of how the all-important elements of relationship-building and therapeutic alliance can be honored under such an arrangement. My answer is that it all depends on your mindset. If you take the attitude of "I'm just doing EMDR, and the relational issues aren't that important," I do not believe the EMDR will be very successful. However, I think that you can take some practical steps to build the alliance in a short period of time by collaborating with the referring clinician.

As several of the women in my 2009 research project shared, because they had a good relationship with their primary therapist, they trusted the EMDR clinician to whom their therapist referred them. When I get referrals from other clinicians, I obtain a release of information so collaborative contact can occur. When I know that a long-term therapist is referring the client, I spend some time in the history-taking session exploring that therapeutic relationship. Typical questions that I ask are, "How does working with Jeff [the original clinician] help you?" and "What can you tell me about your relationship with Jeff?" The responses are usually positive, and I typically make some comments about my connection with the original therapist, such as, "I respect Jeff a lot, and we work together with many of our clients." I find that statements in this vein create an effective bridge of trust and rapport from the original therapist to the EMDR practitioner and save time in terms of number of sessions, which may be a practical issue for many of you (see Practical Issues: Number of Sessions).

Practical Issues: Number of Sessions

Let's be practical for a minute: If you bill third-party payers for your clinical services, you are bound to wonder, "What if I don't have enough sessions to work with the client? It may take forever to build rapport!" Indeed, some of us are luckier than others when it comes to the timeframe in which we are given to work with each client. If you work with private-pay clients or have an agency contract with a public source of funding, you may be in a better position to work with a client long term than clinicians who simply bill insurance companies.

I suggest being as upfront as possible with clients when they want to pay with insurance. Find out ahead of time how many sessions are covered and let clients know that the EMDR treatment process may take longer than the number of sessions the managed care company is allowing. This situation can get sticky if you are not clear, especially if a more complicated client has heard that EMDR is a "quick cure."

My general practice is to explain the three stages of trauma treatment within which I work (see the consensus model in Chapter 3) and let clients know I can't make any promises about how long treatment will take. If a client is agreeable, I proceed with Stage 1 stabilization work and see how we're doing after the first two or three sessions in terms of rapport and the client's ability to learn the stabilization skills. As is explained in Chapter 5, the client's progress during the stabilization phase is generally a good litmus test of how he or she will handle Stage 2 work.

My overall experience has been that if you don't make lofty promises to clients and you assess progress on a session-by-session basis, you may be able to get quite a lot done in a limited number of sessions. You may find that you earn a great deal of respect and trust from clients by being direct. The decision of whether to work with clients on a self-pay plan to continue treatment after insurance runs out is up to you.

If possible, when clinicians within my company refer clients to me for EMDR, I have the original clinician introduce the client to me. Even if this introduction is just a brief 1-2 minutes in the hallway after our therapeutic hours are over, I find it to be helpful. Jeff, one of the clinicians in my office with whom I work closely, always tries to make the original introduction; as a result, his clients usually arrive for their EMDR evaluations ready to work.

Like with so many aspects of our practice, it is important to uphold the highest ethical standards when evaluating other therapists' clients for EMDR. Just because one of your colleagues insists the client needs EMDR, you are ultimately the one making the judgment call. This is a sensitive issue that requires the utmost humility and commitment to ethics on the EMDR practitioner's part. Just because you, as the practitioner, are excited about EMDR and the potential it holds to help people doesn't mean it is right for every client. Moreover, it is important not to fall into the trap of wanting to impress colleagues and referents (an error I admit to committing once or twice) in the attempt to be a good ambassador of EMDR and its therapeutic potential. The bottom line is that EMDR works for some clients and doesn't for others, and the same can be said for just about any currently available, validated treatment for PTSD and trauma-related issues.

Tailoring the Treatment to the Client

My belief is that one of the marks of a truly gifted EMDR practitioner is when he or she can recognize that EMDR may not be the treatment of choice for a client or when he or she can try something else when the treatment isn't helping a client reach his or her goals. That may sound like an odd statement in a book promoting itself as a guide for using EMDR with any clients. With all the talk in our helping professions about research, validation, best practices, and evidenced-based care, my experience has taught me that the best measure, the best validation of whether a treatment is working is if it is helping the client achieve the goals and objectives of his or her treatment plan.

Chapter 4: It's the Relationship that Heals

Most of us have been taught to involve clients in the treatment planning process—to find out what the client wants to get out of treatment, not what you believe he or she can achieve. This is the central axiom of honoring the relational imperative. Even if the therapist believes a client can reach for the stars and benefit from EMDR or another therapy, it is important not to push one's own agenda. Meet the client where he or she *is*. After the first goal or set of goals is achieved, it may be possible to go further. We have been taught to write treatment plans using specific terminology and measureable goals and to review these plans on a regular basis. Including the client in this process and getting his or her feedback is not only advantageous clinically (Duncan, Miller, Wampold, & Hubbard, 2009), but it is also the most respectful to the client.

This may all sound like common sense, yet sometimes we lose our common sense when we get wrapped up in the technical elements of our craft or push a client further than he or she is willing to go. I admit that I was guilty of committing both of these sins early in my career and advanced trauma training. It may sound paradoxical, but it was when I was able to contain my excitement about EMDR and see it as just one tool in my eclectic toolbox that my EMDR outcomes (as measured by meeting and sustaining objectives on client treatment plans) improved.

Psychotherapists can be a peculiar lot. Often, we find one treatment we really like and want to run with it. This may result in attempts to tailor the client to fit the treatment modality rather than the other way around and can be detrimental to honoring the relationship. Clinicians who subscribe to a particular school of therapeutic approach often scramble to justify their position with the latest research, and I have seen EMDR therapists do this. An oft-cited meta-analysis of EMDR literature is from Bisson and Andrew (2007), who found that *trauma-oriented* PTSD treatments were far superior to *coping-skill-only* PTSD treatments. Past-oriented or trauma-oriented treatments can include trauma-focused cognitive behavioral therapy, exposure therapy, hypnosis, or EMDR. Yes, this study bolsters the legitimacy of EMDR, but it primarily shows that EMDR is in the same league as some of the standard treatment modalities for trauma, not that it is better.

But let's step back for a minute and take a look at another one of those meta-analyses; you may find this one surprising. Another meta-analysis examined all studies on "bona fide" treatments for PTSD that compared two or more treatment interventions (e.g., desensitization, hypnotherapy, psychological debriefing, trauma treatment protocol, EMDR, stress inoculation, exposure, cognitive, present centered, prolonged exposure, Thought Field Therapy, imaginal exposure) conducted between 1989 and 2007 and found no statistical significance in effect size among the treatments (Benish, Imel, & Wampold, 2008). The authors ultimately concluded that although there is strong evidence that the treatments studied work for PTSD compared with no treatment, *no one therapy should be considered the only option for PTSD clients.* Thus, according to Benish and colleagues, "Having several psychotherapies to choose from may enable a better match of patients to type of psychotherapy that fits the patient's worldview and is more tolerable to that particular patient" (pp. 755-756).

Benish and colleagues (2008) convey a common-sense, client-centered approach to treatment. Although the meta-analysis is not without its critics, specifically over what constitutes a "bona fide treatment" (Ehlers, Bisson, Clark, et al., 2010), their conclusion resonates with clinicians who do not believe in a *one-size fits all* approach to therapy. Of course, that does not mean one should take an *anything goes* approach to trauma treatment, but it affirms that you, as a therapist working with a complex client, have choices for treating PTSD. Keeping your eye on this big picture can take some of the pressure off if you and one of your more complicated clients decide to try EMDR. If it doesn't work or goes awry for whatever reason, you have other options to help the client meet his or her goals within a trauma-sensitive model of treatment. (See the consensus model in Chapter 3.)

Chapter 4: It's the Relationship that Heals

If you have been trained and supervised as an eclectic therapist, you are at an advantage when it comes to doing EMDR with a complex client. As I shared in my Face 2 description of EMDR, I was lucky enough to work with a therapist who knew when it was time to give the official EMDR treatment a rest and just talk to me in a manner that, looking back, was informed by the sum total of her skills as a therapist. If you have the ability to do what my therapist did, let me assure you that you have what it takes to try EMDR with difficult, complex clients.

Chapter 5: Preparation, Preparation, Preparation

"How poor are they that have not patience! What wound did ever heal but by degrees?"
—William Shakespeare

When you use EMDR to do Stage 2 trauma processing work within the consensus model, it can be like taking a journey into a dark forest of memories and pain. Whereas it may be necessary to travel through this forest to get to the light at the other side, the journey can be hell. I see the preparation work we do with clients as part of EMDR or any trauma work to be absolutely vital, similar to preparing for a long and arduous hike through a dark forest. To make such a hike, you need to be healthy enough to make the journey. Carrying a backpack with plenty of tools in it to help you deal with the struggles that you encounter on the hike is also advantageous. Moreover, making such a trek with a trusted guide can ensure that the journey is less traumatic.

To carry this metaphor into EMDR, we, as therapists, are the guides. Imagine how you would feel taking a journey through a dark forest with someone you didn't trust. The backpack represents the client's skills for dealing with the stress of the journey. Some clients present for treatment with several skills already in their backpacks. However, for others, especially complex ones, the backpacks are close to empty. This doesn't rule out making the journey, but it does mean that the backpack needs to be filled with emotional regulation skills before we set off (Stage 1 of the consensus model). As therapist-guides, we are also in the position to assess whether the patient-traveler is in good enough health to make the trip.

With complex clients, the journey through the dark forest is typically longer and potentially more difficult than for clients whose trauma is simpler. The journey becomes further complicated when a complex client comes to treatment in poor overall health and has few coping skills or advantages. When such a client presents for treatment, it doesn't necessarily rule them out as being appropriate for EMDR. What it does mean is that the therapist needs to do more stabilization work before beginning the journey. I have alluded to this earlier in the text and can't stress it enough.

In Shapiro's traditional eight-phase protocol, an entire phase is devoted to client preparation (Phase 2). Indeed, Shapiro (2001) has written extensively about the importance of determining client appropriateness for EMDR (Phase 1: History Taking) and assessing the client's affect regulation skills (Phase 2: Preparation) before proceeding with the protocol. Shapiro also noted that preparation is not processing.

My observation is that many EMDR therapists have interpreted this to mean that you're not really doing the EMDR until you've gone back to the trauma with Phases 3 through 6 of the traditional Shapiro protocol. As a result, I have seen many well-intentioned clinicians rush into trauma work before a client is adequately prepared. I think Shapiro would agree that the more complicated a client's trauma and contextual history (something that is assessed in Phase 1: History Taking), the more preparatory work is needed before trauma processing. The issue of how much preparation is enough remains a source of debate. Certain clinicians assert that a client is only able to hold so much in terms of stabilization until he or she can get into his or her brain and begin the neurological restructuring that is involved in the processing of trauma. Other clinicians maintain that you can and should adequately stabilize a client before even thinking about taking the journey into the forest of the past.

Well, who's right? As with many issues in EMDR, it depends on whom you ask.

Chapter 5: Preparation, Preparation, Preparation

My general position, which serves as the foundation of this chapter, is that it's better to be safe than sorry in terms of adequate preparation. It's all about the safety. In this chapter, I explore some of the particulars of client history-taking, assessing for EMDR readiness, and skills for enhancing client stabilization. The more I have done EMDR, the more cautious I have become about preparing clients and focusing on Stage 1 stabilization work. As a result, I have found that EMDR can work well for even the most complicated clients whom I initially thought couldn't handle EMDR. This is where Face 3 EMDR practitioners are often at an advantage over those who practice Face 1 and Face 2 EMDR. Face 3 EMDR practitioners typically prepare their clients so well using their modalities and orientations of choice that the EMDR procedures typically work like a charm in processing trauma. In my experience, Face 3 EMDR practitioners often achieve better results than those who call themselves "EMDR therapists."

The Case of Judy

Judy, a lower-income Caucasian woman in her late-thirties, found herself in and out of community mental health facilities for the better part of her adult life. She suffered from both bipolar disorder and PTSD, resulting from a series of abuses at the hands of her alcoholic parents and sexual assaults in late adolescence. Although Judy was never diagnosed with a substance dependence disorder, she reported periods of substance abuse throughout her adult life to cope with stress, usually when she was not compliant with her medications for the bipolar disorder. She struggled significantly with medication compliance. Although her bipolar symptoms were regulated when she was medicated, she often complained about the side effects and cost of the medications.

137

Judy presented to a community treatment center that offered EMDR several years ago. Her therapist initially did not consider EMDR because Judy seemed so unstable. Judy was adamant that if she just got on the right medication, all of her problems would go away. During the first 2 months of treatment, Judy's therapist was careful to meet her where she was and not use overt confrontation, even about behaviors that were clearly detrimental to her mental health progress (e.g., choosing certain friends, attempting to reason with her equally troubled ex-husband). As a result, a solid alliance formed. Through some trial and error, Judy's psychiatrist was able to find a medication that worked well in keeping the bipolar symptoms reasonably stabilized, and the level of Judy's day-to-day lability significantly decreased.

During these first couple of months, Judy's therapist worked with her on coping skills, including guided imagery and deep breathing. Judy responded well to these two exercises, so her therapist suggested that they try adding some tactile bilateral stimulation. Judy's therapist explained the tapping as a process that may help to further enhance her relaxation. They worked on a light stream guided imagery technique, together with some tactile stimulation, and Judy reported that she felt more relaxed than ever before. During the next session, the therapist taught Judy a guided imagery safe place exercise using bilateral stimulation, and Judy reported that she liked that exercise as well. For the next 1 to 2 months, Judy and her therapist engaged in what would qualify as RDI, the process of coupling bilateral stimulation with exercises designed to enhance and build a client's positive material (Korn & Leeds, 2002). Because Judy did not have much good going on in her life, aside from receiving a government housing apartment and having solid relationships with her case manager and therapist, building resources became incredibly important.

The therapist, after seeing how well Judy responded to the RDI exercises, explained how the stimulation could be used in a different way to help process some of the traumatic memories. Judy was game. The first several sessions of trauma processing with EMDR were all over the place, and the therapist had to use a significant amount of interweave (see Chapter 6), or open-ended questions/statements typically used to assist complex clients work through emotional blocks. However, after these first several sessions, Judy was able to quickly process a series of traumatic memories that were both recent(e.g., an accident) and deep seated (e.g., past abuse). Judy and her therapist used EMDR off and on over a 9-month period (breaks in EMDR occurred because during some sessions, Judy stated a need to just talk), which led to significant improvements in Judy's overall self-image and decision-making. When I last had contact with Judy by phone, she remained on her bipolar medications and realized that she would probably need to do so for the rest of her life. However, her mood swings were no longer as violent and her lifestyle choices had improved because so much of the underlying traumatic material had been processed.

Judy's therapist believed that if she had rushed into EMDR, more harm would have resulted. It was important to introduce coping skills slowly and carefully, then add the bilateral stimulation, and then proceed with trauma processing. This is completely in line with the three-stage consensus model that was presented in Chapter 3. Prepare for the journey, and the journey will go a lot smoother.

History-Taking

In Shapiro's (2001) traditional protocol, Phase 1 is client history-taking. With any form of psychotherapy or clinical treatment, history-taking should be the first step. It is important to get a sense of what brings the client into treatment, and taking a thorough biopsychosocial history helps the therapist see the context around the presenting problem so that the best course of action can be recommended. If you are a graduate-level clinician, you most likely had a course in assessment as part of your curriculum, and your effectiveness with this skill is something you continually hone in your clinical practice. Everyone has his or her own assessment style, and I am not going to teach you how to reinvent the wheel. Rather, I'd like to give a few suggestions on how to use the initial history-taking session as a vehicle for beginning a solid therapeutic relationship and treatment experience for the client.

The initial history-taking[4] session is not the same for every client. Certain clients come in with a clear sense of what they want to get out of treatment. Some are seeking you specifically for EMDR because of what they have heard about you and your approach. Others may have been referred for reasons other than EMDR treatment, which means that the assessment should be more global to determine what the client wants to get out of treatment.

With clients referred for EMDR, you will probably be asking trauma-specific questions early on. Clients who are not really sure what they want from treatment typically need to be handled more gently, especially if they are at a lower stage of change (see Chapter 4). Within the first few minutes of meeting a client, through making small talk and asking the age-old question "So, what brings you here today?," you can get a sense of how direct you can be with the client as you take his or her history.

---

[4] I use the term *history-taking* here in place of *assessment*, since Phase 3 of the original Shapiro protocol is called assessment, which means locating the targets that need to be addressed with EMDR. There is often overlap between history-taking and assessment; thus assessment issues, in the Shapiro Phase 3 sense of the word, may be covered as you are taking the history.

Chapter 5: Preparation, Preparation, Preparation

I fully recognize that client history-taking, especially with a complex client, may take place over the course of several sessions, but that's okay. History-taking/assessment should be an ongoing process. Keeping some of these factors in mind, I have assembled a list of best practices for questioning during a history-taking session that I feel apply to work with any potentially complex client, whether or not you end up doing EMDR with him or her:

1. *Do not re-traumatize!* Many well-intentioned clinicians can re-traumatize a client when they ask questions in an interrogatory manner, minimize clients' experiences, or ask a client to talk about some aspect of his or her life or trauma before he or she is ready to talk about it.

2. *Do consider the role of shame in complex presentations.* Shame refers to the belief that who you are, at the core of your being, is bad or defective. Almost every person coming into treatment with an addiction issue struggles with shame on some level. Shame is also pervasive in many survivors of abuse or other trauma-based scenarios and in people who feel they are defective because they haven't been able to "get better" from the disorder that brought them into treatment. From the initial history-taking session, you have the power to reinforce this shame (through some of the re-traumatizing behaviors that I explained in #1) or begin dispelling it by edifying the client.

3. *Do be genuine and build rapport from the first greeting.* As I discussed in Chapter 4, edifying a client does not mean that you have to be fake and phony with goodness. Be yourself, but be attuned to how you present yourself, and always show the client dignity and respect.

4. *Do ask open-ended questions.* Just as you learned in Counseling 101, open-ended questions (e.g., typically those starting with *what or how*) tend to be less interrogatory. For example, a question like "What were things like for you growing up?" or "How did that experience effect you?" allows the client to steer

the interview in a direction that his or her current comfort level can tolerate. Avoid using leading or closed-ended questions like "So, was that experience traumatic for you?" or others that can be answered with a simple yes or no.

5. *Make use of the stop sign technique.* Any training course in EMDR covers the "stop sign" technique, or the process by which a client can signal you to stop the processing if he or she is not comfortable going any further with the past-oriented material. This technique is just as relevant in history-taking. At the beginning of sessions, I let clients know that if they are not comfortable answering any questions I'm asking they can let me know by telling me or flashing me a stop sign.

6. *Do be non-judgmental.* This should be a given for clinicians who are embarking on doing any type of trauma work. However, this is an area where we need to check ourselves: Might our brilliant interpretations and diagnostic proclamations, for instance, come across as judgmental to a client? Remember that you may be dealing with a person with a high degree of shame-based baggage; how he or she interprets things may be different from how you would.

7. *Do assure clients that they may not be alone in their experiences (if appropriate).* This is a strategy to use with caution, but it can be effective if used appropriately. Many clients present for treatment bogged down with shame, feeling they are uniquely bad or crazy for feeling a certain way or engaging in a certain behavior. Sometimes the simple assurance that they are not alone can make a world of difference. Only do this if you can be genuine about it, and be careful not to make it sound like you are minimizing their experience.

8. *Send the client away with a quick affect regulation technique or assignment (if appropriate).* If, during the first session, you have talked about a lot of trauma-related issues or if the client engaged in an unexpected catharsis, make sure he or she is feeling okay to leave. Consider teaching him or her a quick

breathing exercise or other body-based coping technique (e.g., pressure points, muscular clench and release, mindfulness) to effectively "shut down" the session, just like you would with complicated EMDR sessions.

9. *Treatment planning: Find out what the client really wants to get out of treatment.* This question may not get addressed until Session 2 or later because the client may need time to think about what he or she wants out of treatment. It is, however, important to find this out. If the client is just looking for coping skills to deal with stress, it is unethical to forge ahead with an intense trauma-resolution treatment plan. Sure, we can discuss the advantages and disadvantages of certain goals and strategies, but it is important to keep the sessions about the clients and his or her preferences. If you don't feel comfortable helping a client with his or her preferred set of treatment goals, consider referring out or seeking consultation.

10. *Treatment planning: Assess the client's level of willingness/stage of change.* See Chapter 4 for more on the stages of change. It is very important to ascertain where a client is when it comes to how he or she feels about change and how much work/commitment he or she is ready to put into the process. Keep in mind that if a client is at a lower stage of change (e.g., precontemplative), it doesn't rule out EMDR; however, it means you should not bombard him or her with lots of information about it right away. Start with the basics (e.g., rapport building; discussions about problems, solutions, and treatment options; motivational enhancement) and then work your way from there. As discussed in Chapter 4, stage-wise treatment is vital, especially with more complex clients.

Hopefully this list makes sense to you. In other words, the basics of good counseling apply as a foundation for good EMDR.

Assessing for EMDR Readiness

In my clinical view, *preparation* refers to Stage 1 stabilization activities in the consensus model (Chapter 3). Just to refresh your memory, the consensus model follows these stages:

1.) Stabilization (EMDR Phases 1 and 2)
2.) Working through the trauma (EMDR Phases 3–7; some of the Phase 7 work calls for the stabilization skills built in Phase 2)
3.) Reintegration/reconnection with society (EMDR Phase 8)

In assessing for EMDR readiness, the question is rarely whether a person can handle the stabilization phases (Phases 1 and 2: History-Taking and Preparation in the Shapiro protocol [2001]), but whether he or she is ready to move into working through the trauma. As discussed throughout this book, we must honor the fact that *stabilization* is trauma work and a very important part of trauma work at that. Many therapies for PTSD are purely stabilization oriented, such as the *Seeking Safety* program (Najavits, 2001). Thus, if you hope to do EMDR with a client, *you are doing an important part of EMDR by preparing.* Very often, how well the preparation activities play out is a good litmus test for assessing client willingness and motivation and predicting how well he or she will do with bilateral stimulation.

Remember the case of Judy presented earlier in this chapter. The therapist was not certain whether Judy was going to be a candidate for EMDR. However, when she saw how well Judy responded to the preparation exercises after bilateral stimulation was gradually introduced, she felt more comfortable about proceeding with trauma processing.

When working with most EMDR clients, especially complex ones, preparation entails more than doing a few relaxation exercises with bilateral stimulation. **Preparation is the sum total of clinical** activities in which we engage to ensure a client's safety before proceeding with trauma processing work. Having worked mostly with complicated clients in my time as an EMDR therapist, I have developed the following list of best practices for evaluating the quality of preparation and thus determining whether a client can move into the trauma processing stage:

1. *Have I assessed for secondary gains?*
Secondary gains are what a person is "getting" out of staying sick. These gains can be as tangible as procuring a government disability check due to a diagnosis or as subtle as maintaining an excuse for irresponsible behavior because of being "ill." Shapiro (2001) wrote about the importance of secondary gain assessment. Typically, I am direct with clients about what I mean by secondary gains, and if they are holding on to reasons for staying stuck in maladaptive behavior, I talk about it with them in the context of our therapeutic alliance. In some cases, I use a specialized sequence that I developed for targeting secondary gains, assuming that all of the other preparation steps listed below have seen completed (see inset on *Addressing Secondary Gains*).

2. *What is the client's motivation for wanting to do trauma processing work?*
I am reticent to do EMDR with a client, especially a complex one prone to destructive behaviors, when the reason given for seeking treatment is "to find out why I am the way I am." I am especially reluctant to use EMDR with a client if no effort has been made to embrace lifestyle change (e.g., if the client is in a precontemplative or contemplative stage of change) and he or she feels that a simple explanation for his or her problems lies in the past. Many therapists disagree with me on this one. However, in the spirit of safety, I will not do trauma processing work unless I am reasonably convinced that a client's motivations for doing so are based on getting well and not ascribing blame to others or finding "magic" answers. EMDR, as well as other trauma work, may reveal some clues from the past, but I make sure a client knows that it's what they do with those clues that matters.

3. *Does the client understand what may happen if change results and the effects of the trauma on his or her life start to shift?*
If EMDR works for the client, there is a very good chance he or she will change and adopt healthier lifestyle patterns. It is important that you discuss this with a client ahead of time to make sure he or she is aware of what's to come, especially if people in his or her life are used to the client being sick or unhealthy. If a client is in the middle of a legal or court case, it is especially important that he or she knows EMDR can impact how memories are stored, especially if he or she is being called to testify against a perpetrator (see inset on *EMDR and Legal Issues*). One time I did EMDR with a woman with a serious history of abuse who was in an emotionally controlling relationship at the time of her treatment. I asked, "If you make these changes, how might that affect your marriage?" Of course, we do not have these conversations with our clients to dissuade change but rather, to ensure that they know what they are potentially getting into with EMDR or any Stage 2 trauma processing intervention. This is why, in my clinical view, orientation to the EMDR process is especially critical (moreso before the trauma processing component) as part of preparation.

4. *Does the client have emotional support resources, including, but not limited to, an A.A. sponsor, home group and support network, a church group, access to healthy and easily accessible friends and family?*
The essential question is this: If the client has an emotionally draining EMDR session and has some disturbance after he or she goes home, is there someone healthy and supportive, besides you, whom he or she can call? I always encourage clients to let at least one person in their life know they are going through EMDR. The absence of a support system does not necessarily rule out doing EMDR with a client. It does, however, mean that you will need to spend more time bolstering preparation. If the client is genuinely without any positive social support, explore whether there are 24-hour on-call services in your community or ask yourself whether you would be willing to be contacted more regularly via your answering service during this complex client's trauma processing.

5. *Is the client able to reasonably calm and/or relax himself or herself when distressed?*

Of course, the client does not have to be able to perfectly calm himself or herself down when distressed; if he or she could, your services would not be necessary. However, as Shapiro (2001) wrote, the client needs some ability to regulate affect. Can he or she use one or more coping skills to self-soothe? Skills can include imagery exercises, music, somatic techniques, talking to someone, and others. Practicing these exercises and building up an arsenal of options for self-soothing is critical to EMDR preparation. At very least, a client should be able to return to a state of emotional equilibrium before leaving your office after a difficult session. Moreover, it becomes vital for clients to be able to do these exercises on their own if disturbance from processing emotional material emerges between sessions. I have clients test out, on their own time, the affect regulation exercises on which we have worked together before I am comfortable proceeding with trauma processing.

6. *Is there a sufficient amount of adaptive, healthy material in the client's life?*

As Fadalia (see case in Chapter 4) shared with me during her follow-up interview, "It is important that a person who does EMDR isn't coming emotionally unglued." This reflection speaks to the importance of stabilization and having an adequate amount of positive material in one's life so that the negative has something to which it can be linked. Positive material can include everything from acquisition of the basic needs (e.g., food, water, shelter), to work, hobbies, a supportive family, life goals, and healthy friends. The absence of such positive material does not rule out EMDR but does necessitate more advanced preparation in the realm of resource development. The concept of *frontloading* this positive material is discussed more fully in the next section.

7. *Am I comfortable working with a specific client and his or her general population group?*

This is where you must check yourself as part of the preparation process. Shapiro (2001) wisely recommended not doing EMDR with a client whom you wouldn't treat using other modalities. An essential question you may want to ask yourself is whether you have the clinical skills, especially in the relational realm, to bring clients back to equilibrium *without* EMDR if the EMDR session takes an unexpected turn. The more carefully you're prepared, the less complicated such a process becomes. I explain more fully in Chapter 6 how relying on yourself and your own style can be the most effective technique with which to handle troublesome EMDR processing sessions.

These questions can't be answered with a simple yes or no, and meeting X number of the items on the list does not mean you can automatically proceed with EMDR. It is the quality of your collective answers that should determine if you and your client proceed with trauma processing. Ultimately, proceeding with Stage 2 processing work with EMDR (or any other trauma therapy) is a judgment call that you and the client must make together.

Skills for Enhancing Client Stabilization

Frontloading

Frontloading is a concept that I learned in my first basic EMDR training, and it resonated strongly. As it was explained to me, the art of processing is like trying to link up two train tracks. The maladaptive or dysfunctional material is like a train track that is moving in a haphazard direction, not really going anywhere. Through processing, the goal is to link up that maladaptive train track with a track that is heading in a healthy direction. Makes sense, right?

My experience has been that clients who have many functional resources in their life and a variety of healthy experiences aside from their trauma (i.e., the healthy train track) do well with EMDR. Presumably, the maladaptive train track has something with which to link up. The problem is that many of our complex clients have a healthy train track that is in total disrepair—if they have a healthy train track at all. *Frontloading* refers to the process by which we assist a client in laying down a series of planks to build or strengthen the track that is heading in the healthy direction. For the complex client, this is a critical Stage 1 (stabilization) activity that must occur before Stage 2 (trauma processing).

Frontloading can occur in a variety of ways during the stabilization stage. Clinicians who practice Face 3 and Face 4 EMDR are at an advantage in this task because they have already used their existing therapeutic orientations and modalities to frontload. Adhering to the fundamentals of building a strong therapeutic alliance (as discussed in Chapter 4) in the first several sessions can also be part of frontloading. Using the questions from the previous section can help you determine how much frontloading you need to do in the stabilization process. Remember that stabilization is the foundation of treating complex clients and is not to be minimized.

Often, frontloading can be as straightforward as the Maslow hierarchy: Ensuring that a client's basic needs are met. Social work fundamentals can be used to link up a client with a qualified case manager and other resources. For instance, doing the trauma processing phases of EMDR with someone who is living alone in a crack house is not advisable. Although various clinicians have different opinions about whether you can do trauma processing work with someone who is still living in a traumatic environment (e.g., a physically abusive home, a correctional facility), I err on the side of caution and work only with stabilization activities until the client is willing or able to move into a safer situation. Of course, there can be exceptions; for instance, if a client is living in a traumatic environment and has fantastic affect regulations skills and a good spiritual outlook (e.g., a well-structured healthy train track), he or she may be able to move into trauma processing. EMDR (and any psychotherapy for that matter) needs to be conceptualized on a case-by-case basis.

Multisensory Stabilization

Many clinicians struggle because they get excited about the prospect of EMDR helping a troubled client who has not experienced success with traditional psychotherapy and believe that if they can just get in there and *process*, the root cause of the disturbance can be corrected. However, as stated previously, jumping right into processing can be dangerous: Adequate stabilization and frontloading need to be done first. What some clinicians don't realize is that using body-based EMDR strategies for stabilization and frontloading can lead to more successful trauma processing.

In EMDR trainings, clinicians typically learn some variations of the safe place or "calm safe place" (as many trainings are now using) guided imagery exercise and the light stream exercise. These are excellent activities, and I often use them, but there is a whole arsenal of stabilization exercises using all of the senses and slow, bilateral stimulation to enhance the positive experiences. It is important to learn a variety of stabilization skills so that you can work with the client on finding the set that are best for him or her. The skills presented in this section are just a few of the exercises you can use to assist a client with stabilization. There are many resources available to provide additional ideas (Box 10), and you may even draw from affect regulation skills you have used in your clinical practice. When using an affect regulation skill with bilateral stimulation for the purposes of frontloading, resource installation, or stabilization, I use (and recommend) the following general pattern, which has been informed by my reading, EMDR training, and clinical experience:

Resourcing
- Teach the exercise as you normally would.
- Use slow sets of bilateral stimulation to enhance relaxation and other positive responses. Parnell (2008) calls this process *tapping in* a resource.

Chapter 5: Preparation, Preparation, Preparation

After a period (at your discretion) of enhancing or further eliciting positive responses, have the client give the experience a "cue name" (e.g., with safe place-type exercises, this can be the name of the place; with sacred figures or supportive people, this can simply be the name of the person). Enhance that cue name with a *slow, short set of bilateral stimulation.*

> *Cuing (Optional, but recommended for enhanced preparation)*
> - Have the client bring up something that causes him or her mild disturbance (SUDs = 5 is a general guideline).
> - Have the client describe how he or she feels that experience in the body and get as specific as possible: location, color, shape, texture, sound, etc.
> - Ask the client to say the cue name of his or her positive experience silently, and invite the client to take himself or herself back to that positive experience.
> - You may need to help the client return to that positive place at first, but the ultimate goal is for the client to be able to go back to that positive experience when triggered or distressed without your direct assistance.
> - If you think it is appropriate and you feel confident that the client will follow your instructions and use slow tapping or eye movements to enhance a relaxation response he or she has been able to bring up, you can teach him or her how to create some slow sets of bilateral stimulation on his or her own to enhance the relaxation responses when needed. **Caution the client that tapping without bringing up something positive probably won't be helpful.**

The following are descriptions of some basic stabilization techniques. I have also presented cases to further elucidate how these techniques are used clinically.

Using Positive Cognitions for Resourcing

The purpose of effective stabilization is to fortify anything *good* that the client has going for him. Although the client may be coming in for EMDR riddled with negative cognitions due to trauma, most clients have it least one positive belief about self that can be enhanced and installed. If a client is having difficulty identifying positive beliefs about self, consider using the "Greatest Hits List of Positive Beliefs" tool. The simplest way to use this tool is to give it to the client and have her identify any positive beliefs that she has on that list. Then, you can go through each positive belief, pair it together with a time in the past or an instance of evidence in the present that supports that positive belief. While holding the association together, go ahead and do the short sets of bilateral stimulation to enhance, and see where it goes.

The "Greatest Hits" List of Positive Beliefs
(May be duplicated for use in clinical settings)

Responsibility
I did the best I could.
I do the best I can with what I have.
I did/do my best.
I am not at fault.
I can be trusted.

Value
I am good enough.
I am a good person.
I am whole.
I am blessed.
I am unique.

Safety
I can trust myself.
I can choose who to trust.
I am safe now.
I can create my sense of safety.
I can show my emotions.

I am worthy.
I am significant.
I am important.
I deserve to live.
I deserve only good things.
I am smart.

Power
I am in control.
I have power now.
I can help myself.
I have a way out.
I have options.
I can get what I want.
I can succeed.
I can stand up for myself.
I can let it out.

I can belong.
I am special.
I am a success.
I am beautiful.
My body is sacred.
I can make friends.
It's okay to make mistakes.
I can only please myself.
I cannot please everyone.

Others Not Listed:

Feeling and Body Sensation Skills

The simplest place to start with building a series of body-based stabilization skills is with breath work. Teaching a client how to breathe seems simple; however, breathing mindfully is so simple that people often overlook it. As world-renowned physician, Dr. Andrew Weil (2010) shared on his website, "Practicing regular, mindful breathing can be calming and energizing and can even help with stress-related health problems ranging from panic attacks to digestive disorders." Mindful breathing simply means to focus only on one's breath in a nonjudgmental fashion. It is believed that practicing mindful breathing for as few as 3 minutes a day can yield significant long-term benefits.

Living with traumatic experiences is like holding your breath in a figurative—and sometimes literal—sense. Although it may be easy to dismiss breathwork as too simplistic, it is a good place to start. Teaching a client a series of breathing exercises may offer him or her a new, radical approach to stabilization because he or she has never *thought* about breathing before. Moreover, you will find that once the client has a strong sense of how to regulate his or her breath, other sensory skills can be practiced more effectively. For instance, someone who can regulate his or her breath will likely derive more benefit from a guided imagery exercise than someone whose breathing is all over the place.

The three basic breath exercises with which I start are diaphragmatic breathing, complete breathing, and ujjayi (pronounced EW-djeye) breathing:

> **Diaphragmatic breathing (or belly breathing):** Have the client breathe in through the nose and out through the mouth, focusing only on the rise and fall of the belly (not the whole rib cage). Challenge the client to expand the belly as far as it will go as he or she inhales. Sometimes it helps for the client to put his or her hand on the belly to concentrate on this motion.

Complete breathing: Have the client begin with the belly breath. When the stomach expands as far as it will go, teach the client to inhale through the nose again and concentrate on the air coming into and fully expanding the rib cage. In yoga, this is called a three-part breath. You can use two variations on the release: either a slow, steady release, which helps promote tranquility and mindfulness; or a sudden, rapid release, which can help the client experience how good "letting go" can feel.

Ujjayi breathing ("ocean breathing" or "Darth Vader breathing"): This breath, which is effective as an affect regulator during moments of high stress or intensity, is a noisy in-through-the-nose, out-through-the-nose technique. The mouth should stay closed, although it should also feel as if one is sucking through a straw. This allows for a greater flow of oxygen into the lungs, which can stimulate a relaxation response. For clients who are not used to mindful breathing, it is especially important to start slow with this exercise, doing no more than five breaths at a time. Let the client know that the louder this breath sounds (even if he or she feels self-conscious at first), the better it is likely to work.

This list is by no means exhaustive. Box 10 lists several additional resources, including two free online sites where you can access more breath activities. Build your repertoire and find out what works for your practice. The nice thing about breathing is that it can be accessed by clients at any time. When you demonstrate mindful breathing exercises in your office it is important, as yoga instructors typically do, to have the client notice how his or her body feels after taking a set of specific breaths. If the client reports a relaxing or otherwise positive emotional state, you can reinforce that with a few sets of slow bilateral stimulation.

Many clinicians also use pressure points from the acupuncture/acupressure tradition and energy psychology tapping points to help enhance relaxation responses. The two that I am most likely to use are the "sea of tranquility point" (on the breastbone; see photo), and the "letting go points" (on the collarbones; see photo). The great thing great thing about the letting go points is that they are in a perfect position to be used as a "butterfly hug," a form of bilateral stimulation often used when EMDR is done with children. An excellent exercise I often incorporate is to have a client apply pressure to the letting go points, crossing the arms over the chest. I have them breathe and focus on the points and then begin a set of slow, alternate tapping, as is done with a butterfly hug.

Breath and body-based skills have been used for millennia by those who practice yoga. Yoga has different connotations for different people. For example, some devout Christians see it as Eastern, scary, and New Age, whereas others simply associate yoga with a class that's offered at the gym. *Yoga*, which literally means *union*, refers to a series of breath exercises and physical poses that are designed to build mental discipline and foster a greater sense of connectedness among body, mind, and spirit. Many see yoga as an ideal treatment (or adjunct to treatment) for mental health disorders, because those who suffer from them (including PTSD) experience disconnectedness. From my experience, yoga elegantly compliments any face of EMDR.

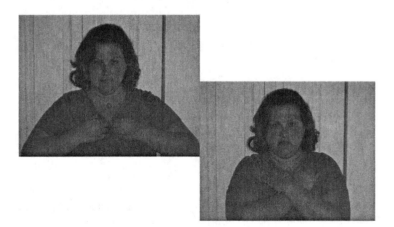

Box 10. Resources on Stabilization Skills.

A-B-C of Yoga Website: Accessed August 12, 2009, from
http://www.abc-of-yoga.com/pranayama/.

Curran, L. (2010). *Trauma competency: A clinician's guide.* Eau
Claire, WI: PESI.

Grenough, M. (2005). *Oasis in the overwhelm: 60-second
strategies for balance in a busy world.* New Haven,
CT: Beaver Hill Press.

Parnell, L. (2008). *Tapping in: A step-by-step guide to activating
your healing resources through bilateral stimulation.*
Boulder, CO: Sounds True Books.

Weintraub, A. (2004). *Yoga for depression: A compassionate guide
to relieve suffering through yoga.* New York:
Broadway Books.

Dr. Andrew Weil's website: Accessed January 11, 2010, from
*http://www.drweil.com/drw/u/ART00521/three-
breathing-exercises.html.*

Visual Skills

Guided imagery often comes to mind when we think of visually-based
coping skills. The purpose of guided imagery as a stabilization
exercise is to provide the client with a safe, healthy mental escape
that he or she can access when needed. At first, your voice is the
guide to take the client to this place. If you do not feel comfortable
developing your own guided imagery scenarios, there are many
good free scripts available online, including hundreds of variations
on the standard calm, happy, or safe place. (See Box 11 for some

resources.) To use guided imagery as a stabilization skill, pick your exercise of choice but do not talk the whole way through. After setting up the first part of the imagery, have the client focus in a nonjudgmental way on what he or she is experiencing, and add slow, short sets of bilateral stimulation. If the client does not like the bilateral stimulation or feels that it is taking him or her too far too fast, you do not have to use it at first.

My greatest caution about doing guided imagery as part of trauma stabilization is to screen for what image or place the client would view as calm, happy, or safe (or any other positive emotion). If the client says that he or she feels safe locked in the closet that is probably not the most adaptive place to use for an exercise. A problem I have encountered doing imagery with clients is that many complex clients have no conception of what the word *safety* even means. That's okay—the client does not have to have a safe place. An alternative construct, such as *calm* or *happy*, could work. With a few exceptions, it is also advisable to give the client a general orientation to imagery and to let him or her know that it is typically best not to have other people involved in their image, especially at first, because this can complicate the image.

If an early guided imagery exercise takes a bad turn for the client, fear not: You have options. One is to ask the client if he or she would feel more comfortable using another place instead and start over (with imagery or another stabilization exercise). Another option is to ask the client if he or she would like to talk about what came up. If you have established a solid therapeutic alliance, the talking approach will likely be effective, and if handled well, it can help assure the client that you will not push him or her into an area that he or she is not yet ready to visit.

Although I have used a variety of guided imagery exercises for trauma stabilization, I almost always start with a light stream exercise, because I feel it is the most benign while being the most effective. Emerging from the Buddhist tradition, variations of the light stream exercise have been used and recorded by Shapiro (1991,

1995) and many others. The essential principle of light stream imagery is to have the client imagine a bright, healing light of any color or with any characteristic. If the client is spiritual, you can have this light emerge from a spiritual source. As the guide, you describe the light entering through the client's body (typically through the top of the head, but this can vary) and then moving through the rest of the body. You can enhance the exercise with slow, bilateral stimulation at various points, and if you are familiar with hypnotic suggestion strategies, you can also insert some of those.

To really make the exercise effective, it helps to have a client start with a disturbance and have him or her describe the disturbance in his or her body (see my description at the beginning of the Multisensory Stabilization section). Then, as just described, introduce the concept of the bright and healing light and guide its passage through the client's body. After you have observed some type of affective shift, you can ask the client what happened to the original disturbance. If the client reports that the disturbance has been absorbed by the light, enhance the experience of the light in place of the disturbance with a set of bilateral stimulation. If the client is still experiencing some level of disturbance, invite him or her to turn up the intensity of the light or to think about the light being refreshed with every breath. Help the client to reduce the disturbance to being as small as possible through the use of slow, short sets of bilateral stimulation.

You can use the cuing principle with the light stream as well by inviting the client to give the light a special name or to focus on saying the color *white* (or the client's chosen color). I ask clients if they have an object that is the same color as the light that can be kept at their house, at the office, or in their car. If not, I suggest that they purchase a scented candle at the dollar store that is the color of their light.

Visual capital can be enhanced without the use of a guided imagery exercise. One option is to ask the client if he or she has any pictures that he or she finds especially calming or edifying. Sometimes, a client has a picture of himself or herself as a small child that represents a state of freedom that he or she would like to access. Often, recovering addicts will carry pictures of their family and children for motivation. Any picture that represents something positive to a client can be tapped in (using Parnell nomenclature) and used as a resource, and such pictures are easy to carry around.

The Case of Marta (Part I)

Marta did a traditional safe place exercise with her EMDR therapist and reported a moderate state of relaxation. She discussed seeing rainbows and flowers in the relaxation imagery that she found particularly soothing, and she said to her therapist, "I wish that I had a picture of those rainbows and flowers to hang in my room." Marta's therapist used rainbows and flowers for a Google Image search and then showed Marta three pages of search results before Marta pointed to a picture and exclaimed, "That's what I need to see to calm down!" Fortunately, Marta's therapist had a color printer and was able to print out a few copies of the image. When the therapist saw Marta's face glow at the sight of the picture, she invited Marta to notice her smile, and she reinforced it with a few short sets of slow, bilateral stimulation.

When Marta returned home, she hung copies of the picture of the rainbows and flowers in her bedroom (where she experienced night terrors), on her refrigerator, and on her dashboard. The picture became a calming cue for her in her daily life and served as the perfect image to bring up during closure when she did EMDR trauma processing work.

Box 11. Resources on Guided Imagery.

Lusk, J. T. (Ed.) (1992). *30 scripts for relaxation and healing
imagery.* Duluth, MN: Whole Person Associates.

Naparstek, B. R. (1994). *Staying well with guided imagery.* New
York: Warner Books/Grand Central Publishing.

Naparstek, B. R. (2004). *Invisible heroes: Survivors of trauma and
how they heal.* New York: Bantam Books.

Music and Sound

Guided imageries are wonderful, but not everyone can optimally
visualize. Music has been used as a coping skill since the dawn of
time, and many great historical figures have written about its healing
effects. In stabilization and preparation work, you can replace the
image with a piece of music that you and the client have determined
to be relaxing, healing, or empowering. Many of your clients will
have an mp3 player in their pocket or bag when they arrive for
sessions, so a resource is often right at your fingertips. Sometimes
in preparing for trauma work, I instruct a client to make a mix
CD or mp3 playlist that can be accessed at any time for affect
regulation. Clients may choose a variety of songs—everything
from Mozart to the Beatles to hypnotic trance music to New Kids
on the Block! The same principle already discussed applies here:
Find what works for the client.

Here is an exercise I developed called "Musical Safe Place" that
you are free to try with any of your clients whom you think would
benefit from it. Although I'm sure that others have used similar
exercises, I developed this version of it in my office after observing
many of my clients having problems with guided imagery.

- Have a client choose a song that he or she identifies as uplifting or meaningful to his or her recovery.
- Use your discretion to determine whether the song is a positive resource (e.g., avoid songs with traumatic references unless there is some healing message by the end of the song).
- Have the client listen to the song in your office, and add short sets of bilateral stimulation at a few points during the song.
- Have the client take notice of his or her feeling just after hearing the song and enforce it with short sets of stimulation.
- Make sure the client has access to the song after he or she leaves your office. Playing this song is the ultimate "cuing" experience when the client is distressed.

Although I created this activity for use with a song, it doesn't necessarily have to use a whole song. Sometimes a simple sound may be helpful. One client told me that the sound of children laughing is the most joyous sound in the world to her, so in my office, I found a sound sample online of children laughing. I had her listen to the sound as I added some short sets of bilateral tapping. We then practiced eliciting a disturbance and having her bring up the sound of children laughing, and she was able to calm herself down.

Taste and Smell

Just as you can create a "Musical Safe Place," you also can create safety with the senses of smell and taste. Find out which smells and tastes a client finds pleasurable and calming. If a person has compulsive eating habits, you may want to avoid using taste because it can reinforce the notion of eating as self-soothing. However, many people without eating problems report that chewing on a piece of gum or sucking on their favorite candy can be calming, so if you determine that this is not maladaptive, you can set up an exercise in which the client slowly and mindfully eats this substance, noticing the body-level responses as he or she does. Then, you can reinforce with slow, short sets of bilateral stimulation.

I find this works well with smell. I keep a variety of scented candles and other pleasantly scented items, such as lotions and body sprays, in my office. If a client samples some of these and identifies any as being particularly relaxing or soothing, you can have her light the candle or spread the lotion on her hands and smell, noting how her body feels when he or she engages with those scents. As before, you would enhance this experience by using slow sets of bilateral stimulation. You can practice the cuing component by bringing up a disturbance and then testing whether the client can use the scent to return to this relaxation state. The nice thing about olfactory capital is that the client can typically purchase a scented candle or lotion in the same fragrance inexpensively and keep it at strategic places around the house or carry it with her to access the calming cue at any time.

Applying Spiritual Principles

As part of history-taking, it is important to find out if the client has a spiritual belief system and if so, whether he or she is open to incorporating those principles into therapy. Many EMDR exercises can take on a spiritual dimension. For instance, with light stream exercises, I often describe the calm, healing light as coming from the God (or spiritual source) of the client's understanding. Judy, the case that I presented earlier in the chapter, identified as a devout Christian. Thus, when I did the light stream exercise with her, I had her imagine that Jesus was coming to touch her forehead, like a healing scene out of the Bible, and the healing light emerged from Jesus' hand into her body. Several of the resources listed in Boxes 10 and 11 contain other exercises, such as "sacred space" and "supportive figures," which can have spiritual components. For instance, many people believe that relatives who have died are in a better place looking down on them; you can use and enhance these spiritual connections as a positive, healing resource.

Blended

Three stabilization exercises that I often use tap into a blend of the senses: installing positive memories, installing hopeful future scenarios, and journaling. Installing positive memories, when carefully done, can be a tremendously healing resource, especially as a front-loading strategy. With this technique, you help the client take a positive memory or experience and use it as a safe place of sorts. The same principles already described for techniques using the other senses apply: Elicit the memory in detail, reinforce it with positive bilateral stimulation, and have the client give that experience a cue name. If appropriate, the cue name can be a positive cognition. Following is a case that helps illustrate this technique.

The Case of Allen

Allen presented for treatment in a hopeless state after years of trying to cope with complex PTSD resulting from abuse in his family. Over time, he had formed a problematically enmeshed "trauma bond" with the abusers in his family. One of Allen's goals for treatment was to separate himself from his family, but he battled with profound guilt at the thought of abandoning them because they were, after all, his family. During the history-taking process, Allen revealed that the happiest he had ever been was the year he lived in his own apartment in another town. He said that the apartment wasn't much, but it was his place, where he was free to come and go as he pleased.

The therapist asked Allen if he would be willing to use his memory of the apartment as a calm and safe place, and he was willing. As Allen described the apartment and focused on the body sensations and positive feelings that came up, the therapist enhanced these feelings with slow, short sets of bilateral stimulation. Bilateral stimulation was also added when Allen made insightful statements, such as, "That apartment was a dump, but it was mine." Ultimately, Allen had the positive cognition that he believed he had choices when he pictured himself in that apartment. The therapy helped reinforce this cognition Allen was able to give the apartment imagery a cue name and pair it with the positive belief, "I have choices."

Allen's case is a classic example of how to enhance some of the positive planks on the healthy train track through frontloading. I often suggest journaling to clients for similar purposes, and also to serve as an outlet for thoughts and feelings they might be suppressing. Allen made use of journaling in his preparation and throughout his EMDR treatment, and it gave his feelings a place to "go" between sessions.

Journaling worked for Allen, but it is not for everybody. However, some clients may have never considered the benefits of journaling until you bring it up, and the stabilization stage is the perfect time to do it. If the client can get into the habit of journaling, it can prove to be a fantastic supplement to EMDR treatment or any other trauma therapy. When I teach clients how to journal, I let them know that there is no wrong way to do it. I tell them to just take out a pen and paper and write whatever comes out. I also let them know that if they are afraid of someone finding their work, they rip it up after they've written it. The point is not to keep the work and bring it into sessions for analysis, but to get the troublesome stuff out, like taking emotional garbage out to the curb.

As a client once pointed out to me, a potentially potent connection between journaling and the bilateral stimulation of EMDR is that during journaling, whether by writing or by typing, the eyes inevitably move back and forth on the page. This client felt that journaling helped to enhance the work she did in between EMDR sessions, and the eye movement connection made total sense to her.

Just as a past scenario was used in Allen's case, a future template or scenario can also be used. You can have a client bring to mind the goal that he has for his future. In Allen's case, I could have elected to have him visualize what it will look like down the road to imagine himself in his own apartment or house. I might have him imagine, describing in as much detail as he can, what it will be like for him to live apart from his family. Then, that healthy, future projection can be "tapped in" or installed. This is another powerful way to incorporate frontloading.

The Case of Bill

Bill, a recovering alcoholic in his fifties, presented for treatment following a horrible motorcycle accident. The accident set off a flurry of PTSD symptoms, namely troublesome nightmares and night terrors that occurred at least five times a week.

Bill's therapist did Face 2 and Face 3 EMDR with him. It was clear from the history-taking session that Bill was a talkative man, and that thwarting this too soon to jump right into EMDR would have harmed the therapeutic relationship. In the early sessions of preparation, Bill's therapist suggested a few strategies he could try to help contain his troublesome emotions, and one of those was journaling. Although Bill had never really fancied himself a writer, he was willing to give it a try, and he found that he really enjoyed it. His journaling eventually moved into fiction writing, an avenue he was able to use to work out a lot of the demons connected to his accident. Here, Bill tells his story in his own words and describes how the fusion of journaling and EMDR helped him:

I've been involved with motorcycles for over 45 years. I have raced them, worked on them, and traveled a lot of miles on them. On one of my motorcycles I have logged over 125,000 miles in the almost 35 years of ownership. In 2003, I successfully passed a state authorized motorcycle safety course. But my troubles all started back in August of 2008, when my wife and I were on an outing that we usually make several times a year to a small resort town about 70 miles away. Needless to say, we were excited. We hadn't been able to make this ride in a while, due to work ... and we are both caregivers for our ailing parents.

The day before, I went over the motorcycle for any possible problems and everything checked out fine. I then spent the next several hours cleaning the motorcycle for our pilgrimage. We were well rested, and the sun was coming up fast and warming up nicely. Both eager, we were finally on the road. Arriving at our destination always brings back a lot of fond memories because we have been coming here for over 35 years together. We've made this trip well over a hundred times. As things went, we ate at our favorite restaurant and then visited a state park nearby. But we noticed a storm brewing and headed in our direction. We decided to make our way through the resort town one last time, which was on the way to the interstate, our quickest way home.

Then it happened: Halfway to the interstate, a full-sized bright red pickup truck pulled into our path. There were only two options and less than 10 seconds to make the correct decision: Hit the truck or lay the motorcycle down. I chose to lay the motorcycle down, avoiding the impact. I still feel that to this day if I would have hit the truck I would be dead. My wife would have landed on my back pushing my chest into the gas tank breaking my ribs, thus puncturing a lung.

Shortly after that fateful afternoon, I was diagnosed with PTSD. During the 15 months of at times grueling EMDR sessions, other things were tried as efforts to cope with the recurring nightmares of the red truck pulling into my path. At one point I went for more than 4 days without any sleep—I did not want to sleep to avoid the possibility of another nightmare. This resulted in me needing an emergency EMDR session, which helped.

Triggers that would cause these recurring nightmares were at first difficult to spot. Triggers were simple things like the letters from the girl's insurance company, dealing with five different adjusters over the issues of repairing the motorcycle, the return address label on their envelopes (after all of the frustration from adjusters). I even had recurring nightmares from watching motorcycle racing on TV when a motorcycle would be laid down and the motorcycle and rider would go tumbling. Also, there was a TV show that showed a motorcycle accident similar to mine that triggered a nightmare. The strangest one was during an NFL football game when an auto manufacturer showed one of their autos and two motorcycles and one of the motorcycles running into the auto. My wife and I looked at each other and knew what was going to happen. And it did—that night I had another nightmare. But thanks to some self-tapping that my counselor taught me, I was able to cope and make it to work the following morning.

Thanks to my counselor, as a way of getting the whole accident out of my system, I was asked to write down the whole experience. I started from our leaving home and all of the events throughout the day, accident, and our journey home. (I was able to ride the motorcycle home 64 miles approximately 5 hours after the accident.) This read like a short story but evolved into a complete book (9 chapters), and at present is not finished because the medical part of our accident has not been settled. I had so much fun with the writing of this "book" that I tried to write another—this one is fiction. I have just completed my first book of fiction and will be seeking a publisher. By the way, my second book of fiction has already been started and progressing well.

*I was very skeptical at first about the EMDR process, but I am a firm believer and advocate now. I have the utmost praise for my counselor and her expertise in her field and EMDR. **From such a negative action came such a positive reaction.** I am very grateful for her "pointing me to the pen."*

You Have Options

Hopefully, this chapter has inspired you to think outside the box when it comes to preparing a complex client for EMDR. Granted, for some of your simpler clients, doing a calm, safe place visualization may be enough, but with complex clients, this is rarely sufficient. I have explained the importance of preparation using some of Shapiro's traditional concepts, along with the principles of stabilization (from the consensus model), resource development and installation, and frontloading. Hopefully one of these explanations sticks with you and inspires you to take the preparation process seriously. The higher the level of disturbance in a client (not to mention the more complicated the contextual lifestyle factors) the more rigorous preparation will need to be. If you follow these guidelines, you will find that the trauma processing phases of the EMDR will go much more smoothly.

This chapter also explored some of the particulars of client history-taking, assessing for EMDR readiness, and skills for enhancing client stabilization. I hope that these discussions have helped you to realize that EMDR preparation is not one size fits all. Various avenues of exploration may be needed in preparation and in helping a client develop a series of body-based stabilization exercises; you can draw on exercises that are multi-sensory and multi-dimensional. In the next chapter, I continue describing ways to meet the client where he or she is principally and tailor the treatment to address a specific client's needs and level of disturbance.

Explaining EMDR to a Client

EMDR can sound bizarre, especially to a client whom has never had counseling before or has only experienced talk therapy. A critical part of EMDR preparation is orientation, and one of the biggest hang-ups therapists have is how to explain what EMDR is and how it is believed to work. Of course, there is no cut-and-dry answer on how to do this, because so many variables must be considered: the therapist's understanding of EMDR, which of the four faces of EMDR the therapist predominantly practices, the client's learning style and cognitive ability, the overall treatment goals, and the client's stage of change.

Whenever or however you were trained in EMDR, you were likely given some verbatim statement to read to the client about the approach; from my experience, this usually goes over the client's head. Often, you can give a client a pamphlet about EMDR or recommend a website (which does have some value in showcasing the legitimacy of the therapy), but this can come across as esoteric and theoretical. Here are some tips based on my clinical practice that seem to resonate with most clients. Of course, you may need to adjust your language depending on variables such as the client's cognitive/educational abilities and stage of change.

- Explain the story of how Shapiro created EMDR—most people can connect with a story.

- Get into some basics of the triune brain. Explain that sometimes the part of our brain that is rational (the pre-frontal cortex) goes offline when we are triggered by traumatic experiences and that there is a good reason for this: The emotionally driven part of our brain (the limbic brain) and/or the survival instincts (the reptilian brain) take over. Explain that the back-and-forth bilateral stimulation of EMDR helps the various parts of the brain talk to each other.

- If a client has had talk therapy in the past and it hasn't helped, some of these triune brain basics can be especially helpful, because you can explain that whereas talk therapy is designed to activate only the rational part of the brain, many traumatic memories are locked inside the other two parts of the brain that can't be accessed easily through just talking. Bilateral stimulation can help access those memories.

- Let a client know that the bilateral stimulation itself won't produce effects; rather, we need to bring up material (either positive or negative) together while doing bilateral stimulation that will point the brain in the direction it needs to go. I often compare bilateral stimulation with a gas pedal on a car. When we do the initial preparation activities, such as safe place or light stream, we use slow bilateral stimulation, which is like taking a nice slow drive in the car to soak in the scenery. However, when we get into the disturbing material, we use fast bilateral stimulation to drive away from the bad memories as quickly as possible.

Addressing Secondary Gains

If a client has significant secondary gains for staying stuck in maladaptive behaviors, I am hesitant to proceed with the Stage 2 trauma processing component of EMDR (phases 3–7 in the traditional Shapiro protocol [2001]). On occasion, I have used a variation of an EMDR targeting sequence: I target the secondary gain itself using medium-fast bilateral stimulation after the client has developed the affect regulation skills needed in preparation. Here is an example:

The therapist, using his or her own personal style, asks what the client's concerns and fears are about getting better.

> *Client: "If I get better, people will stop feeling sorry for me."*

The therapist asks if there is an image related to this fear or a worst part of this concern.

> *Client: "I would become just another ordinary person."*

The therapist then proceeds in a manner resembling a standard EMDR protocol:

> *Negative cognition: "I am ordinary."*
> *Preferred/Positive cognition: "I am a survivor."*
> *(The therapist can take a VoC reading if desired.)*
> *Emotions elicited by the worst part:*
> *Disgust, fear, worry*
> *(The therapist can take an SUDs reading if desired.)*
> *Ask about the place of body sensations*

Begin the processing and see what happens.

EMDR and Legal Issues

Shapiro (2001) has addressed the impact that transmuted memories from EMDR can have on a client's ability to offer testimony in legal cases. For instance, you can imagine that a client who has gone through EMDR and has done work on the effects of a sexual assault may have learned to talk about it calmly and rationally. Most would suggest that such calm, rational testimony is not what would be required to get the perpetrator brought to justice. This is one reason it is important to offer full disclosure about what EMDR can and can't do to a client and his or her legal team if the client is involved in a court case.

A client's involvement in criminal or other legal proceedings does not necessarily rule out EMDR. I suggest getting a release of information to the attorney or legal team, explaining the client's therapeutic concerns, and seeking the legal team's advice. On one occasion, a lawyer specifically asked that I do EMDR with a highly traumatized client because her disturbance was so great that she couldn't even bring herself to show up at the pre-trials. The thought of seeing the perpetrator in the same room was so disturbing that she refused to testify. Thus, the attorney and client both insisted on some EMDR before the trial, which ended up helping.

The long and short of it is that there are no absolutes when it comes to EMDR and legal issues. The best guidance I can give is to offer full disclosure, consult with all parties involved, and document everything. This is part of careful preparation.

Chapter 6: Processing Trauma with the Complex Client

"Eyes that do not cry, do not see."
—Swedish proverb

In your EMDR training, you were likely advised to prepare for Phase 4 of the Shapiro (2001) eight-phase protocol, Desensitization, in a manner similar to this:

- Identify the presenting issue or memory.

- Ask, "What picture represents the worst part of that incident?"

- Ask, "What words go best with that picture to describe how you feel about yourself now?" (e.g., "I'm worthless").

- Ask, "When you bring up that picture, what would you like to believe about yourself now?" (e.g., "I'm worthy").

- Ask, "When you think of that picture, how true does 'I am worthy' feel to you now?"
(1 = completely false to 7 = completely true).

- Ask, "When you bring up that picture and those words 'I'm worthless,' what emotions do you feel now?"

- Assess subjective disturbance: Ask, "On a scale of 0 (no disturbance) to 10 (the most disturbance imaginable), how disturbing does the incident feel to you now?"

- Ask, "Where do you feel it in your body?"

- Desensitize (using chosen form of bilateral stimulation): Saying to client, *GO WITH THAT!*

Look familiar? The goal is to desensitize the target down to a SUDs score of 0, get the VoC score up to a 7 (out of 7), install the positive cognition (Shapiro Phase 5), and do a body scan (Shapiro Phase 6) to see if the client is "all clear." Stimulation continues until this happens (with some exceptions, like if a person sees the SUDs of 0 as an impossible goal), and then a session is closed (Shapiro Phase 7). With complex clients, it may be nearly impossible to get through a single target in a session or two, so closure will need to be executed effectively to safely shut down incomplete sessions before installation or body scan.

In her modified protocol, Parnell (2007) streamlined the set-up to be a little less clunky, and a lot less numeric:

- Identify the target memory.
- Identify an associated image (or worst part of the incident).
- Identify emotions.
- Describe body sensation or discomfort.
- Identify negative cognition.
- When the client is visibly distressed, begin desensitization.

Clinically, Parnell, and many Face 2 and Face 3 EMDR therapists have found this approach to work just as well as the longer set-up because the essential ingredient of EMDR is being met: The traumatic neural network is being accessed and then stimulated.

In my experience, both the traditional and the modified approaches can work. You may even find yourself using a combination of the two in your practice, which I often do. Many clinicians find themselves getting weighed down by the numbers in the Shapiro protocol (2001), and the Parnell (2007) modification is an ideal solution. I do like to get a SUDs reading at the beginning of a session and periodically get other SUDs scores, although I often tell the client he or she doesn't have to give a number; he or she could just give me a general idea of how bad it hurts. The number scales were introduced during EMDR's infancy. New trainees often get tripped up with worries like, "Oh no, if I miss taking a VoC reading, will EMDR not work!?," and their confidence wavers, which can come across to the client. As Parnell observed, the numbers are not totally necessary for EMDR to be effective, so put your mind at ease.

There are many ways to set up a trauma processing session with EMDR. Face 1 EMDR therapists will likely find that statement blasphemous, yet it is compatible with the approaches of many Face 2 EMDR therapists and most Face 3 and 4 EMDR therapists. To refresh your memory, review Parnell's (2007) Four Essential Elements for EMDR Protocol:

1. Create safety.
2. Stimulate the traumatic neural network.
3. Add alternating bilateral stimulation.
4. End with safety.

As long as you follow the general guidelines discussed in this chapter, the details of how you prepare for trauma processing are completely up to you, based on your style and how you predict the client will best adapt to it. To refresh your memory, when Duncan and colleagues (2009) wrote about the four common elements of psychotherapy in *The Heart and Soul of Change: Delivering What Works in Psychotherapy*, they advised that techniques and methods should be used in a way that engages and inspires clients. Thus, if Shapiro's approach, with which I opened this chapter, goes over your client's head and confuses him or her, why would you use it? Find out what works for you and your clients.

A common question that new trainees ask me, especially with complex clients, is "Where do I begin?" "When there is so much trauma and so many areas that can be targeted, how do I know which one to get at first?" Both of these questions are explored in depth in the remainder of this chapter, informed by my experiences in the clinical trenches of agencies and private practice. The other common questions I get, and address in this chapter, are how to work with the client who is simply not processing, how to handle the client who severely abreacts and opens up the potential for destabilization in symptoms, and how to most effectively close down a session.

Processing: Where Do We Begin?

Clients will sometimes come for EMDR knowing exactly what the traumatic memory is that they need to work on, particularly with trauma that is single incident. For these clients, life has been pretty decent in general, but there is one thing that they can't seem to shake. For complex clients, life has typically been a warped web of various traumas, both small "t" and Large "T," and it can be a challenge to decide where to start with processing after stabilization has been achieved.

I recommend several approaches and have some tips to help with this decision-making. The first approach is to look at the treatment plan and ask what the client wants to get out of counseling. More specifically, what does the client hope to get out of EMDR? For example, if one of the client's stated goals was, "To decrease the frequency of nightmares from 5 nights a week to less than once a week," I may ask the client to further explore with me the content of the nightmares. From that exploration, we are typically able to pinpoint a memory or cluster of memories to which the nightmares relate.

Let's say that a client associates the nightmares with two memories: Being raped at age 18 and seeing her mother try to murder her father at age 3. Although traditional EMDR training advises you to go back to the earliest memory, that doesn't have to be the case to get at the root of the traumatic neural network (although the earliest is often the best). What I would do in this situation is ask the client to consider her rape at age 18 and then shift her attention to witnessing the attempted murder at age 3. Then, I would ask her which one seems to cause the strongest reaction in her body; if she can give me a definitive answer that is where I start the processing setup. If there is no definitive answer, I leave the choice up to her as to which memory we should begin with. Starting with a later (or even a recent memory) can still allow antecedent material to come up in the processing; it just may take a little longer to get there.

The second approach, and the one I most often use, is to do a negative cognitions list screening. In her text, Shapiro (2001) presented a list of sample negative and positive cognitions that traumatized clients often have. She suggested that the list can be given to a client if, when you are setting up the processing protocol, the client cannot pinpoint a negative cognition that goes with a certain event. I have modified the list for use in my own clinical practice (see The "Greatest Hits" List of Problematic Beliefs), and I use it slightly differently than Shapiro originally suggested.

In working with a complex client (and with clients who have single-incident trauma when I sense something else may be going on), I give them a copy of The "Greatest Hits" List of Problematic Beliefs, a list of negative beliefs that people with disturbance often experience. There are tons of these lists on the market, especially in CBT-type books and in Shapiro's original text (2001); use whichever one makes the most sense to you and your clients. I give clients the list and ask them to check off which of the negative beliefs they still struggle with, telling them that there is no specific number of items they should check off. A client may return the list with 2, 10, or 20 items marked. You may notice that a client's beliefs are concentrated in one of the categorical areas (Responsibility, Safety, Value, Power [see unnumbered box]), or they may span across categories. There is much semantic overlap between certain items on the list, but that's a good thing: Client A may connect with an idea worded in one way (e.g., "I'm worthless") that Client B may experience in a different way (e.g., "I'm no good").

The "Greatest Hits" List of Problematic Beliefs
(May be duplicated for use in clinical settings)

Responsibility
I should have known better.
I should have done something.
I did something wrong.
I am to blame.
I cannot be trusted.

Safety
I cannot trust myself.
I cannot trust anyone.
I am in danger.
I am not safe.
I cannot show my emotions.

Power
I am not in control.
I am powerless/helpless.
I am weak.
I am trapped.
I have no options.
I cannot get what I want.
I cannot succeed.
I cannot stand up for myself.
I cannot let it out.

Value
I am not good enough.
I am a bad person.
I am permanently damaged.
I am defective.
I am terrible.

I am worthless/inadequate.
I am insignificant.
I am not important.
I deserve to die.
I deserve only bad things.
I am stupid.

I do not belong.
I am different.
I am a failure.
I am ugly.
My body is ugly.
I am alone.
I have to be perfect.
I have to please everyone.

Others Not Listed:

RSPV-C

In her text, Shapiro (2001) stated that negative cognitions among traumatized individuals fall into one of three categories: Responsibility, safety, and choice. Dr. Earl Grey, a neuropsychotherapist based in Pittsburgh, Pennsylvania, is in the process of a years-long research project on the holistic experience of stress in all human beings, not just those who have experienced Large "T" traumas. He believes that in order for us to understand human reactions, we must first start by understanding "what's normal." As he explains it, everyone has little "t" distresses, but not everyone has Large "T" traumas. His research (Grey 2008, 2010; Stewart-Grey, 2008) has shown that people experience maladaptive conclusions or decisions about themselves in one of four thematic areas: responsibility, safety, value, and power. The thematic area of choice manifests as the adaptive resolution toward which people are driven. Grey described his developing construct as *RSPV-C*, which is the organizational basis I have used for my version of The "Greatest Hits" List of Problematic Beliefs.

I then return the list to the client and ask him or her if it is possible to rank his or her top three most disturbing cognitions. Typically, clients are able to do this. Whatever the client ranks the most disturbing cognition is typically where you should begin processing. Let's say that the client ranks his or her negative cognitions in this order:

1. I am worthless.
2. I cannot show my emotions.
3. My body is ugly.

Starting with "I am worthless," ask the "floatback" question (Shapiro, 2001), which is designed to get to the root of the traumatic neural network. My typical wording of the floatback question is, "Thinking back over the course of your whole life, when's the first time you remember getting the message 'I am worthless.'" Following this, set up the trauma processing using one of the approaches (or a combination of approaches) presented at the beginning of this chapter. If it is clear that the client's remembering the *first* incident of that message is not kicking up any disturbance or distress (which is rare but can happen), adjust your floatback question to, "When was the time in your life when that message, 'I am worthless,' felt the worst?"

There is one important situation in which you do not start with the number-one most disturbing cognition, and that is when the cognition "I cannot show my emotions" or some variant of this is endorsed by the client but is not ranked first. Even if this cognition is not in the top three, start there. Let's revisit the list I just presented:

1. I am worthless.
2. **I cannot show my emotions.**
3. My body is ugly.

Common sense dictates that starting with the second item on the list is wise. Think about it: EMDR is a highly emotional process. The neural networks that we are assisting the client to stimulate are in the limbic brain, the part of the brain that regulates emotion. If a client's core belief is that he or she cannot show emotion, why would he or she start showing it just because you're beginning the EMDR process? The following case study illuminates this point.

The Case of Britta

Britta, a Caucasian woman in her fifties, heard of my services working with chronic addiction relapsers, and she was willing to do just about anything to get to the root of her problems. Britta was in and out of active polysubstance remission for a period of 26 years, achieving almost 10 years of sobriety at one point. However, in the 2 years prior to coming to my counseling practice, Britta has been struggling to maintain more than a couple of weeks of sobriety at a time and was riddled with shame and self-loathing because she was not able to keep herself sober. In addition to meeting criteria for PTSD and polysubstance dependence, Britta was also being treated for bipolar disorder and felt better when she was medication compliant.

Britta and I engaged in 3 to 4 months of stabilization activities, which included helping her get active again with AA and "work the steps" with her sponsor. After hearing the benefits and risks of EMDR, Britta was more than willing to try it, well aware that messages she received in early childhood about herself kept her stuck in self-loathing and self-pity. Like with many a complex client, we could not pinpoint a specific memory as a starting point, since her whole childhood seemed tortured, so I gave her the negative cognitions list, and "I'm not good enough" was clearly her number-one choice. We set up a protocol tracing "I'm not good enough" back to an early childhood memory, but Britta began blocking (i.e., not being able to process) right away, saying, "I can't do this, I'm not feeling anything."

When we used some traditional cognitive interweave, or the open-ended questions that are taught by Shapiro (2001) to move along stuck processing, Britta revealed that she can't feel anything because she's not allowed to feel. A light bulb went on in my head, and I thought, "Adjust the setup! If Britta really believes she's not allowed to feel, we must start there." So, I readjusted the processing setup and had Britta remember the first time she ever got the message "I'm not allowed to feel my emotions." She also recalled a similar childhood memory, but in this one, her father specifically told her that she was not allowed to cry. We began the processing there, and although she blocked a little at first, the EMDR soon worked like a charm.

We spent about 7 active processing sessions on "I'm not allowed to feel my emotions," and when we later revisited "I'm not good enough," it took less than a session to process the remaining material. Clearly, a generalization effect had taken place. At the time of this writing, Britta had attained 18 months of sobriety, and she indicated that it's the first time in her recovery process that she does not feel burdened by self-loathing. As a result, she was able to complete all of the steps in her 12-step fellowship, this time in a more thorough manner.

Eyes That Do Not Cry, Do Not See

This Swedish proverb gives us good direction in preparing for trauma processing. If a client cannot access his or her emotions, especially if he or she has negative beliefs about emotions, it is unlikely that processing will get as deep as it needs to. Remember, if a client cites or endorses the belief that it's not okay to show his or her emotions, begin EMDR by targeting that cognition, even if it's not the primary issue he or she needs to address. If the client can work through that cognition and shift his or her beliefs about the ability to feel, the rest of the EMDR work will go more smoothly.

Another option to commence target sequencing informed by the treatment plan (one that my neurologically-informed colleagues have recently turned me on to) is starting with the future...yes, starting with the future. This is because the left frontal lobe is responsible for managing the time periods of past and future simultaneously. In other words, the past and the future are managed by the same part of the brain.

The easiest way to set this up is to start by having the client picture "what it will look like" when he reaches his wellness goal. Have the client get as descriptive as possible, then go ahead and commence the stimulation. Stay positive through as many sets as you can, although what usually happens is that the client will, through processing, come to the issue or roadblock that keeps them from getting to this future scenario. In essence, the client has just revealed his own "target" that you need to address. From there, you can set up a traditional protocol or your chosen modification (e.g., Parnell's modified protocol).

When Processing Gets Stuck: Tools for Unclogging the Drain

In the ideal EMDR session, once you've stimulated the traumatic neural network, the client brings up everything he or she needs to emotionally, cognitively, and somatically bridge the gap between the limbic and neocortical brain, allowing for adaptive resolution to result. As clinicians know, sessions rarely go perfectly, especially with complex clients. In such cases, the most common problem is blocking, the phenomenon of shutting down emotionally when bilateral processing brings something up for the client. Common sense suggests that this is likely to happen. Complex clients typically have problems with emotional regulation. They either repress or stuff the emotion, or they are not able to regulate the emotion properly (e.g., sad emotions can only come out as anger). In EMDR, by stimulating the traumatic neural network, all of these avoided feelings start coming up, and a person's defenses can kick into overdrive, especially if he or she doesn't believe it is safe to feel, as in Britta's case. Adjusting your setup to address the negative belief of "I cannot show my emotion," like I did with Britta, is the best way I have found to deal with blocking (i.e., not being able to process). If you can address that core belief, the rest of the EMDR process goes more smoothly.

Let's say that you've followed this advice and the client is still blocking. There are many other strategies you can try, including the use of interweaves, which come in many forms. Shapiro (2001, 2006) proposed the use of the *cognitive* interweave (a statement, question, or direction by the clinician) when a client is looping, when the session is running out of time, when there is a lack of generalization, or during extreme emotional distress. Similar to blocking, *looping* refers to when the client dwells on the same content and does not move through it. I typically see looping happen as a blocking response. Shapiro (2001) stated:

The term interweave refers to the fact that this strategy calls for the clinician to offer statements that therapeutically weave together the appropriate neuro networks and associations. The clinician initiates interweaves through questions or instructions that elicit thoughts, actions, or imagery (p. 249).

Shapiro further indicated that the purpose of an interweave is to "jump start blocked processing by introducing certain material rather than depending on the client to provide all of it" (p. 249). Shapiro clearly advised that interweaves should only be used when a client's spontaneous processing is stuck. In other words, an interweave is when we prod the client along. The therapist applies an interweave statement to the processing like a plunger to a clogged drain: Try one interweave, see if it works, and if the drain is still clogged, you can try another statement (e.g., giving the plunger another push). Clinicians with clinical training in areas other than EMDR can use statements similar to those used in general talk therapy sessions. (See following list for examples)

Chapter 6: Processing Trauma with the Complex Client

During ideal processing situations, interweaves are used sparingly. However, there seems to be a general consensus among many EMDR practitioners that the higher the level of disturbance, the more (or more intense) interweave will need to be incorporated. This is a judgment call—how much interweave to use and in what situations depends on whom you ask. Find the interweave strategies that work best for you and your clients. Here are some common blocking or looping scenarios I typically encounter and statements I frequently use to help unclog the drain:

- Client: *"I'm just not getting (feeling) anything right now."*

Possible statements or questions before next set of stimulation:

"That's okay—just notice what's happening in your body right now."

"What does that mean to you that you're not getting anything?"

"So if you can't feel, what are you thinking about right now?"

"What was the last thing that you noticed before the feeling stopped?"

- Client: *"I don't think that this EMDR is working."*

Possible statements or questions before next set of stimulation:

"What makes you think/say it's not working?"

"What does that mean to you when something isn't working?"

"Could it be that you're trying to make sense of it all instead of just letting the feelings come up on their own?"

- Client repeatedly makes the following statement: *"I just feel so guilty about the whole thing."* [looping]

Possible statements or questions before next set of stimulation:

"What does guilt mean to you?"

"What does being guilty say about you?"

"Where do you seem to experience/feel that guilt the strongest in your body?"

(If the guilt or looped feeling is present focused): *"Does the guilt you're feeling about this incident remind you of how you felt at an earlier time in your life?"*

- Client: *"I go to feel something and then I just shut down or get distracted."*

Possible statements or questions before next set of stimulation:

"It's okay—just notice what it feels like to be shut down (or distracted)."

"What was so troubling/disturbing about the last thing you felt before you shut down?"

"Thinking over the course of your whole life, when did you seem to develop this shutting down response?"

- Client: *"I'm just trying to make sense of it all."* [or similar incidences of staying in cognitive-only processing without accessing the feeling]

Possible statements or questions before next set of stimulation:

"What does that mean to you that you can't make sense of it all?"

"How does it feel that you can't make sense of it all?"

"What's happening in your body right now as you're going through all these thoughts?"

"How has it worked for you so far to try and think it through?"

• Client: *"I'm stuck on this obsession with going back and changing the past."*

Possible statements or questions before next set of stimulation:

"If you could change the past, what would you do?"

"What does it mean for you that you're obsessed with changing the past?"

"What happens in your body when you obsess over changing the past?"

This list of situations is by no means exhaustive, nor is my list of responses. I simply share them here to give you some ideas. The essential rationale of interweaves is that if a person is stuck in one area of the brain, you need to think of what to say to elicit a response in another part of the brain (Grey, 2010). In the next section, this logic is revisited in a discussion of handling abreactions and other messy situations.

Interweaves do not have to be verbal statements to be effective. The same logic of preparation being multisensory and multidimensional applies to interweaves as well. With clients who are emotionally blocked, using some of the statements I proposed here may help us get somewhere but not remove the clog from the drain entirely. A strategy Shapiro has suggested is that if processing is not progressing, change the direction of the eye movements or the form of the eye movements (e.g., going from straight line to diagonal). As an EMDR therapist who is open to different forms of stimulation, I often ask a client if he or she is willing to try another form of the stimulation. For instance, if eye movements aren't working, I'll suggest changing to audio tones or tapping. If tapping with the machine isn't working, I'll suggest eye movements or tones, or, if sufficient rapport has been established, I may ask the client if he or she would feel comfortable with me using my hands to tap directly on his or her legs or hands. For reasons that are unclear (although I think it has something to do with the energy of human connection), switching to actual touch can open up the floodgates of processing. That method has worked for me every time but requires caution with populations averse to touch. Only use it with client consent and assure the client that you can discontinue if it is making him or her uncomfortable.

The directness of human touch is powerful. Sometimes, incorporating a more direct form of exposure, such as a sound, smell, a piece of music, or visual aid (e.g., an actual picture) that reminds the client of the trauma, can move processing along. As mentioned, these strategies should be used with caution and only with clients who have developed good stabilization skills as part of preparation. One of my clients was blocked emotionally and had a hard time visualizing his trauma, but he remembered that a certain piece of music was playing on the radio when he was abused. After several sessions of trying traditional interweaves, I located the song he had referenced and used that (instead of the traditional image/worst part) in setting up our next session. It helped the client to get more in touch with the material emotionally, probably because music is not only stored in a state-specific form, but it is one of the first mechanisms that an infant brain uses to promote connectivity between the three regions of the triune brain (Levitin, 2006). Let's take a look at another case using musical interweave.

The Case of Peter

Peter, a white male, entered outpatient counseling at age 29. In the client history, Peter revealed a series of small "t" traumas throughout his life related to being bullied in school due to his visual learning disorders and to maneuvering the household dynamics in his family of origin. Both of his parents were severe alcoholics and addicts. Peter experienced a Large "T" trauma at age 12, when his alcoholic father, who imparted to the client his love of music, died in the client's presence. All of these experiences yielded problematic negative cognitions, including "It's not okay to show my emotions," and "I am stupid." Both of these cognitions appeared to be at the root of Peter's depressive symptoms. He first manifested these symptoms (e.g., low motivation, hopelessness, poor energy, fleeting suicidal ideations) at 13, and they intensified over the years as various life stressors were introduced.

Before coming for treatment, Peter had been involved with five other counselors who were primarily cognitive-behavioral in their orientation. Peter found these treatments only minimally helpful; thus, EMDR was attractive to him because it was "something different." Peter was considered a candidate for EMDR, although he was unable to develop a traditional, visually based safe place (which makes sense considering his history with visual learning problems). He responded well to a musical safe place activity and felt confident about using his two chosen songs to help him regulate stress and affect.

The therapist prepared for a traditional EMDR protocol by beginning with the cognition, "It's not okay to show my emotions," and the client began blocking immediately. All three major forms of stimulation were tried (eye movements, tactile, audio), and Peter was able to do some processing when the audio stimulation was applied. After every major interweave strategy and Shapiro-based (2001) suggestions for blocked processing was tried, the client experienced no major movement. Peter's SUDs of a touchstone event remained unchanged at 8, and his VoC of the preferred cognition ("It is okay to show my emotions") never rose above 1.

During Peter's twelfth EMDR session (with the SUDs at 8 and the VoC at 1), the therapist made a decision to have a few musical tracks on hand that she determined (based on her musical experience and what the client had shared about his musical preferences) could potentially unblock Peter if he got stuck in one of his "I can't feel" loops. In session twelve, Peter experienced a major block regarding his parents, and the counselor chose to play a song that was specifically meaningful to Peter's father. As Peter listened to the song, audio stimulation was applied. For the first time in his EMDR treatment, the client was able to cry and release feelings he'd been holding onto about his parents. At the next session, the SUDs of the touchstone had decreased to 5, and the VoC of the preferred cognition rose to 4.

Peter participated in three more traditional EMDR sessions after this use of a musical interweave, with no major shifts in SUDs or VoC level but numerous reported improvements in depressive symptoms. Peter, who had been on extended leave from work due to the depression, was able to return to work. He also graduated from college despite initial thoughts that he couldn't pass his senior capstone course. Due to financial concerns and the belief that EMDR had helped him get to a "better, more manageable" place overall, Peter elected to terminate treatment.

Chapter 6: Processing Trauma with the Complex Client

When Processing Goes Awry: Handling Abreactions and Other Messy Situations

This is an area in which an ounce of prevention is superior to a pound of cure. If you have taken your time and gone through proper preparation, even messy situations can be handled in an elegant way. In a proper course of preparation, the wise EMDR practitioner will orient the client to what's coming. I often use the dark forest metaphor, letting the client know that things may get intense. I let him know that it is to his advantage to keep going and let the stuffed emotional material come out when processing gets intense. I also use the rather crude parallel of vomiting: When you are physically sick and vomit, you typically feel better after you've let it all out. **I reiterate that it is the client's choice to stop processing at any time.** This is when it is critical to review the stop sign technique and assure the client that you won't think he or she is bad or weak if he or she decides to stop the processing: This is something I do as a best practice at the beginning of every processing session. Once again, preparation is key.

Abreaction

The technical definition of *abreaction*, as it appears in the American Psychological Association's *Dictionary of Psychology* (VandenBos, 2007) is, "The therapeutic process of bringing forgotten or inhibited material (i.e., experiences, memories) from the unconscious into consciousness, with concurrent emotional release and discharge of tension and anxiety" (p. 3). Take a while to absorb that technical definition and then think about what it means in layman's terms. An abreaction is when a client hits on something that he or she has long repressed, and it causes a heavy-duty emotional reaction: crying, screaming, foaming at the mouth, catatonia, or vomiting in extreme circumstances. If you consider the logic, it's actually a good thing that all of this repressed material is coming out, *as long as it can be linked to something positive.* (Recall the discussion on frontloading in Chapter 5 This is a case in which that ounce of prevention (preparation)can be better than a pound of cure for a bad abreaction. From my clinical observations and research on effective and struggling EMDR therapists, what you *do* to handle an abreaction is not as important as what you *don't do*. Therapists who are comfortable working with trauma in a global sense are able to sit with the client, be with him or her through the catharsis, demonstrating a positive and supporting presence. During some of my most intense EMDR sessions with clients, my focused presence, coupled with a few softly spoken positive affirmations, such as, "You're doing great, just keep letting it come out," does the trick.

A client abreaction is disturbing but does not mean that the session is going off track. In fact, it probably means you're getting somewhere. Of course, if you notice that the abreaction is causing marked physical distress for the client, it is important to take steps to help him or her end the abreaction. Your clinical discretion is important when it comes to how long you let a client stay in that state when no link up to positive material is apparent. Seeking consultation or peer support from other EMDR therapists who have worked with complex clients and their intense abreactions is an important way to develop your clinical judgment.

If it becomes clear that the client is continuing to abreact and isn't yet linking up with anything positive, that's okay. Try to allow at least 15 to 20 minutes at the session's end to close it down. When a client is having an intense emotional reaction, the limbic brain is in control. Ask an interweave question that will get the client back to the cognitive/neocortical (i.e., rational) brain. Statement-questions, such as, "I know that you are feeling very deeply right now, but what are you thinking about as you feel all of this?" work beautifully. Another strategy I use is to let the client know when we are running low on time. As I tell him or her in preparation (and reiterate at the beginning of each processing session), "When I tell you that we're low on time, it's not because I want to cut you off, but it's because I want to make sure that you are safe to leave the office that day." This is a strategy clients generally respect because it shows them that you are interested in their safety and well-being (Marich, 2010).

Chapter 6: Processing Trauma with the Complex Client

During preparation, I establish with the client that it is her choice to go back to one of her regulation strategies (e.g., safe place), talk for a while, or do a combination of the two when I give the "we're low on time" signal. Often, particularly if a solid, safe therapeutic alliance is in place, pulling back from the techniques of EMDR processing and just talking for a few minutes, connecting in human conversation, can be a wonderful way to end the session with safety. It can also help the client get out of the emotional brain and back into the rational brain, especially if you weave in questions such as, "So what did you *think* about what came up today?"

When the Client Wants to Stop

Shapiro (2001) was very clear that we as EMDR therapists should never force a client to continue with processing when he or she wants to stop. Assuming that you have established how to handle this in your preparation with the client by using something like the stop sign technique or asking the client to verbalize that he or she wants to stop, let's cover what to do when the client gives you that signal. When a client flashes you a stop sign, it is important to clarify verbally, "Does that mean that you want to stop this right now?" The clarification is important, because sometimes clients may flash a stop sign as part of the processing, such as telling an abuser to stop (Shapiro, 2001).

When a client has clearly asked me to stop because it has become too much for him or her, I honor that choice, and I ask the client what he or she would like to do: Go back to safe place or one of the stabilization techniques, or just talk for a while. This is similar to how I handle closure. Using one of the stabilization strategies is a good sign to the client that you recognize that he or she has had enough for that session and that you are fine with that. When the client chooses to talk for a few minutes to close, a good question with which to start (again, something I picked up from a colleague) is, "Can you tell me what was disturbing you the most about all of that before we stopped?"

Another strategy, in line with the rational brain logic, is to ask the client, "So what are you thinking about right now?" There's nothing wrong with "just talk" in complex EMDR. You may even find that after you've talked for a while, the client is willing to continue with the bilateral stimulation processing. If he or she does not want to continue with processing that session, it is important to sensitively ask in the following session how the client would like to proceed. From my experience, most clients are willing to continue with the EMDR, but some will need to talk instead. Honoring that client preference is paramount.

Closing It Down

There is no *right* or *wrong* way to close down an EMDR session, as long as it is done in a way that brings the client back to safety. The strategies that I described in the previous two sections can also work well for closure. Of course, closure can be a relatively simple process, especially if (in looking at it in Face 1 terms) you have processed the distress level of the target memory down to a 0, have installed the positive cognition, and ensured a clear body scan (Phases 4–6). If you are using a modified protocol, the key becomes focusing less on numeric scores and ensuring that the client is in a good place to stop processing and feel safe before leaving. Whether you are using the traditional approach or other variations, closure can be relatively simple if the session has gone well or more involved if a lot of heavy material was kicked up for the client. The following case illustrates this point.

The Case of Mae

Mae, an African-American woman in her forties, engaged in EMDR during treatment at a long-term residential addiction recovery program. A recovering crack cocaine addict and alcoholic with complex PTSD,

Mae was resistant to trying EMDR again after a bad experience with it a decade prior but eventually agreed after a long preparation. With 6.5 years of sobriety, Mae reflected on her experiences with EMDR when she had been sober for 2 or 3 years. One of the things she most remembered was how the EMDR clinician took great care to close down each session:

She'd never let me go out of that office messed up. And always told me that if something else kicked up again while you're at home, call the crisis counselor. It was like we went way up there or down deep in there, and before I left, I was OK. I was hurting but not hurting enough to go out and drink. That meant a lot to me because the stuff that we went through with the EMDR was the stuff that I used to drink and use over.

It is vital to ensure that the EMDR client feels secure enough to leave your office. If you have another client coming in right after that one, try to find your EMDR client an empty office or waiting room where he or she can hang out for a while if necessary. If you have office personnel at your front desk, make them aware of the situation. Some of my clients have chosen to sit in their car for awhile and listen to music or go next door to the pizza shop before they drive any distance. Collaborate on a plan that works for your client.

Another situation that requires careful preparation is when you know you will be getting into a major, heavy-duty trauma processing session with a complex client. If this is the case, schedule that client last on your schedule for the day. Then, if you need to run over, you have more flexibility to do so. Don't do this if you need to get out of the office promptly after your last client leaves or if you yourself feel you might have an abreaction if you don't get paid "overtime" for sessions that run long!

Many EMDR therapists make a regular habit of calling clients the evening after their first major EMDR processing session or after a particularly difficult session. This is a judgment call. I have called clients after rough sessions, especially with clients who have a history of self-destructive behavior. At very least, I provide the client with the number to my company's answering service, which allows him or her to reach an on-call counselor and me in case of an emergency. During my preparation work with clients, I also make sure they make a list of people in their support network whom they can call if they have a rough night after a session. The following case illustrates some of these issues.

The Case of Frances

Frances, a white woman, sought EMDR treatment in her mid-twenties following 2 years of successful recovery from an eating disorder. A very sensitive woman, Frances knew that EMDR would probably take her to a very deep place, so she and her therapist came up with a safety plan to follow after her EMDR sessions. Frances explains it in her own words:

My therapist, Donna, and I figured out that it would be best if I got together with one of my close friends on the nights when I did my EMDR sessions during the day. Although the point would be to do something fun, I was to warn my friend ahead of time that I might be kind of out of it and I might just need her to be there. I picked one of my friends who also had a rough childhood and really supported my decision to do this deep therapy. That helped. One day, my session was so emotional, Donna let me sit in the office of one of the other counselors until I felt calmed down enough to drive. Fortunately, that counselor had a couch, and I just laid there and rested my head until my tears cleared. That really helped. I only had to use Donna's answering service one time, but trust me, I really needed it after that session, and I'm glad that she didn't make me feel like a heel for using it.

———————————————

Part II : Special Populations

Chapter 7: Complex PTSD

"Traumatized people suffer damage to the basic structures of the self. They lose trust in themselves, in other people, in God ... The identity they have formed prior to the trauma is irrevocably destroyed."

—Judith Herman

Reflect on the passage that opens this chapter and think about how many of your clients fit this picture. Judith Herman, who introduced the term *complex PTSD* in the early 1990s, accurately identified that trauma is more than a diagnosis, more than a pathology: It is an experience that, especially if endured over time, can leave a lasting impression on one's selfhood.

In the DSM-IV-TR (American Psychiatric Association, 2000), complex PTSD is also referred to as Disorders of Extreme Stress Not Otherwise Specified (DESNOS). Although it has received a great deal of attention since the publication of Judith Herman's book *Trauma and Recovery* in 1992, complex PTSD was not an official diagnosis in the DSM-IV in 1994. Herman accurately identified that the standard PTSD definition was not sufficient to address the long-term effects of trauma in an individual who had experienced prolonged exposure to a trauma or traumas. DESNOS is currently under review for the forthcoming DSM-5, as are some modifications to the existing PTSD diagnosis (American Psychiatric Association, 2010). Although not an official DSM-IV or DSM-IV-TR diagnosis, complex traumatic stress disorders are real to many clinicians. The label of *complex PTSD* suggests that the healing of original, traumatic wounds can be further complicated due to a variety of conditions. Courtis and Ford (2009, p. 1) described these conditions as traumatic stressors that:

(1) are repetitive or prolonged;
(2) involve direct harm and/or neglect or abandonment by caregivers or ostensibly responsible adults;
(3) occur at developmentally vulnerable times in the victim's life, such as early childhood;
(4) have great potential to compromise severely a child's development.

Simply put, it is widely accepted that trauma can seriously affect someone's life. But let's look at some of the more complicated scenarios. Have you ever met a person who grew up in a culture of trauma? Have you ever worked with someone who has so many wounds to the psyche that you are stumped when it comes to commencing treatment? Have you ever met a client for the first time who, when you ask if he or she has experienced trauma says, "Where do I even start?" If so, you have probably encountered complex trauma.

You may be asking yourself, "Where do I start?" in treating a complex PTSD client with EMDR. The good news is that if you read through the first six chapters of this book and obtained a solid grasp on the principles of trauma, therapeutic alliance, preparation, and addressing potential complications in sessions, you have the foundation you need. The simple awareness that doing EMDR or any trauma work with a complex PTSD case will take longer than for a single-incident PTSD case is often the reality check that you need to be successful. Having this realization can help you remember to lay a solid foundation in the basics of relationship-building and preparation/stabilization. It also can allow you to keep your expectations realistic and not push a client into trauma processing work before he or she is ready. Keeping this in mind can help keep you grounded and remind you not to expect miracles in the first trauma processing session: With complex PTSD clients, it will usually take several sessions to get somewhere. It is good practice to help your clients avoid unrealistic expectations by making them aware of this reality in your EMDR orientation.

EMDR has not been as widely studied with complex PTSD as it has with single-incident or adult-onset cases of PTSD (Korn, 2009). Some conclusions that have emerged from large-scale, randomized controlled studies on EMDR that are especially significant to clinicians are as follows:

- Eight weeks of EMDR therapy was not enough to resolve the long-term effects of traumatic sequelae in a population of adults with child-onset trauma, compared with a group of similar adults with adult-onset trauma (van der Kolk, et al., 2007).

- Despite improvements in an overall population of adult survivors of childhood sexual abuse after six EMDR sessions, this length of treatment was not sufficient to adequately address all of the survivors' issues (Edmond, Rubin, & Wambach, 1999).

- Earlier studies showed that EMDR yielded mixed results with combat-related PTSD. It is now believed that this was due to an insufficient number of EMDR sessions; positive outcomes with this population in a later study were attributed largely to extending length of treatment to 12 sessions (Carlson, Chemtob, Rusnak, Hedlund, & Muroka, 1998).

Several qualitative studies by Kim and Choi (2004), Brown and Shapiro (2006), and Marich (2009) demonstrate some level of EMDR impact with complex PTSD. In the Brown and Shapiro study, EMDR was successfully implemented in the treatment of a patient with borderline personality disorder, often conceptualized as a form of complex PTSD (Santoro & Cohen, 1997). With this case, 20 sessions were needed over a 6-month period, and a series of affect regulation skills were incorporated for preparation. In the Kim and Choi study, the existing therapeutic alliance was one of the major reasons EMDR was successful; the client had an existing therapeutic relationship of more than a year with the clinician. Interestingly, the existence of that relationship and the strategies used by the client and therapist prior to EMDR served as the preparation (Korn, 2009).

The Case of Nancy (Marich, 2009a)

Nancy entered a county community drug and alcohol treatment facility several years ago. A white woman in her forties, she had been treated for dependence to multiple substances (alcohol, marijuana, sedatives) approximately 12 to 13 times over a 12-year period in both inpatient and outpatient facilities. She presented to the county agency following her third conviction for driving under the influence. In the initial interview, Nancy described herself as a chronic relapser who was not able to be sober for more than 4 months at any given time. She was diagnosed with PTSD at one of her prior treatment facilities, a diagnosis that was confirmed by her treating counselor at the community agency. In Nancy's opinion, avoiding the issues underlaying her PTSD kept her from staying clean, but she found the prospect of working on those issues daunting.

On further assessment, it was clear that Nancy's case of PTSD was not so cut and dry; it was clearly complicated. Nancy grew up in a broken, alcoholic home, and her first experience of sexual coercion happened at age 10. Over a prolonged period, children in the neighborhood made Nancy do things sexually that she wasn't comfortable doing. When she was 12, she was raped by a family member, and no one in the family believed Nancy's side of the story. Nancy's addiction began during her adolescence, and she dropped out of high school to marry a man who was also addicted to multiple substances. Throughout the marriage, Nancy's husband coerced her sexually, often subjecting her to sexual activity that placed her life in danger. When Nancy divorced her husband after 20 years of marriage, her addiction was fully progressed, and she continued to subject herself to sexual activity that was degrading.

Using Courtis and Ford's definition of complex PTSD (2009) as a guide, we can see that Nancy's sexual trauma was repetitive and prolonged and that it began during the developmentally vulnerable milestones of childhood and adolescence. Moreover, there was no protection from family members, and the abuser in her most impacting experience of sexual assault was a relative.

We will hear more about Nancy in the following chapter on addictions. However, I have presented the vignette of her background here to give you an idea of what complex PTSD looks like. If Nancy had been raped once after growing up in a supportive environment and had reached her developmental milestones without having commenced polysubstance use, her case could be defined as single-incident PTSD. However, because of the context of repetitive trauma and lack of a healing environment that surrounded Nancy throughout her life, her case clearly fits more into the realm of complex PTSD.

Better Understanding Complex PTSD

A Chinese proverb says something to the effect of, "Once you've been bitten by a snake, you're afraid even of a piece of coiled rope."

One day, I shared this quote in a workshop, and a participant wisely responded, "Well, what if you're still living with the snake?" This potent comment speaks volumes about how many people with complex PTSD live: If they are living in environments (and with people) that are traumatizing, rather than dealing with "ropes," they are continually dealing with "snakes." People with standard PTSD may fit the original proverb well; however, those with complex PTSD fit the variation that my participant proposed.

To help you better understand the intricacies of complex PTSD, let's go back to the original wound parallel I proposed in Chapter 3. Remember Rhonda, the soccer player who got injured while playing? Rhonda collided with Erin, another soccer player who was in good health and was given a chance to heal. Rhonda, in contrast, had a series of health problems (particularly low vitamin C levels and white blood cell counts), and she returned to playing soccer before the wounds she suffered during the original collision had a chance to heal.

In this scenario, Rhonda continues to play soccer all season. Sure, she puts adhesive bandages and gauze on her original lacerations to keep them from opening up during the game, but soccer is rigorous. She falls down a lot and gets kicked here and there; many of those injuries agitate her original wound and make her more vulnerable when she returns to games. One day, Rhonda is feeling particularly weak. She notices that some blood is seeping through the gauze on her legs but, at her coach's insistence, decides to shake it off. She goes into the game, running at full force to tough it through the pain. Then her ankles buckle, and before she knows it, she's down on the ground in shock. Soon, Rhonda's coaches and teammates are all surrounding her; they seem like a blurry vision as she looks up. Rhonda's coach asks her to move her leg, and she screams tortuously when she tries.

"It's broken," the coach declares. Rhonda is taken to the hospital, her leg is set, and the doctor orders her to stay off her feet for a minimum of 6 weeks. Rhonda's parents are cooperative at first, but by the fourth week, they accuse her of milking her injury, and Rhonda is expected to do her share of housework while still navigating on her crutches. When the doctor puts on a walking cast, Rhonda is still advised to take it easy, but she resumes her normal activities at school and work. The doctor is concerned because after several weeks, Rhonda is walking with a limp because the injury didn't heal properly. She insists that she is okay. Before long, spring rolls around and it is track and field season. Rhonda cannot even imagine that she would not run track that season, even though her leg continues to hurt.

Hopefully, you get the picture and see where I am going with this. Common sense would suggest that if Rhonda would just allow her leg some time to heal, especially considering her other health complications, she might fully recover in the long run. The same common sense would suggest that people who experience an emotional injury should have all of the help and support they need to be able to heal. Yet we know that this often doesn't happen for many who bravely enter our offices. Festered wounds are bad enough when they are singular in nature and are experienced by a person who is in relatively good health. But when the wounds are multiple and healing is not only forbidden but discouraged (remember Rhonda's coach and parents), the result is traumatic stress that is clearly complex in nature.

Rhonda continues to work and play on her damaged leg for several years, but by time she is 30, her doctors are recommending a total knee replacement. Rhonda is willing to have the surgery, but her doctors are recommending a complete lifestyle change regarding how she cares for her health. The proper course of rest is advised, followed by physical therapy. Obviously, if Rhonda has the surgery and follows through with the recommendations, she maximizes her chances of long-term healing. Yet if Rhonda has the surgery and resumes her learned lifestyle of working through the pain without letting her leg heal, she is setting herself up for further complications.

Doing advanced treatments like EMDR on traumatized individuals can be helpful, just as surgery on a chronic, prolonged injury can be helpful. However, if the lifestyle changes that will support the healing are not addressed and implemented by the trauma survivor, the chances of the EMDR taking lasting effect are minimized. EMDR can be successfully applied with complex PTSD, but we need to conceptualize it similarly to the treatment of physical injuries. Standard injuries on overall healthy people can be easily addressed with EMDR, requiring a modicum of preparation. However, with complicated emotional injuries that parallel Rhonda's physical injuries, more advanced preparation is needed, the treatment may be more intense and take longer, and the reintegration process following the treatment is likely to be more involved.

Tips from the Trenches on Working with Complex PTSD

From my own clinical work, I have learned that there is no big secret to successfully doing EMDR with complex PTSD clients. The success of EMDR treatment with this population lies in the understanding that their condition is more complicated than a standard case of PTSD, and thus more preparation and stabilization are needed. Ensuring that a solid therapeutic alliance is in place is part of this preparation. EMDR with complex PTSD can go to a very dark place, and I don't believe that any client (especially one with fragile trust issues), would be willing to go to that dark place without trusting her therapist. Building this relationship can take time and patience. To repeat the quotation by William Shakespeare that opens Chapter 5, "How poor are they that have not patience! What wound did ever heal but by degrees?" With this in mind, I have created a list of best practices that I incorporate into my daily clinical work with complex PTSD clients:

- Find out how many sessions you have to work with the client. If the client has complex PTSD and only a limited number of sessions are possible, you will do more good giving the client a solid set of stabilization skills than rushing through stabilization and jumping into processing that will likely remain unfinished.

- Get a solid understanding of how the complex trauma has affected the client's life, even if it is clear that he or she is not ready to talk about or go into all of the details of the trauma. In obtaining this understanding and getting a sense of what the client wants from treatment, you will be able to formulate a treatment plan. Depending on what face of EMDR you predominantly practice, you can then determine how you will incorporate EMDR and/or related techniques into the treatment.

- Putting the therapeutic alliance in the driver's seat of treatment is absolutely imperative with this population. I explained the rationale for this guidance in Chapter 4.

- Careful preparation and stabilization skills are vital with this population. I instructed you to err on the side of caution in Chapter 5. To reiterate here, *the higher the level of distress, the greater the level of preparation and stabilization needed.* Monitoring the successful progress of preparation will help you determine the right time to segue into trauma processing.

- Many clients with complex PTSD are being treated with psychotropic medications, and many are prone to dissociative episodes. Both of these issues are discussed in greater detail in Chapter 10, but I mention them here as a simple heads up in doing stabilization work with complex PTSD clients.

- Make sure the decision to commence trauma processing is a collaborative one between you and your client. Taking the client by surprise or leading him or her into trauma preparation before he or she is ready can be particularly damaging with this population, for whom trust and safety have likely been violated in the past.

I believe that the relational elements are most important with this population. Nancy, whose case we examined earlier in the chapter, shed some light on the role of the therapeutic relationship in her treatment:

I had many therapists in the past, never felt connected to any of them. With the therapist who took me through EMDR, I somehow felt such a connection that it was almost unreal ... I felt kind of like a heart-to-heart connection. I look at it as if it was God doing for me what I couldn't do for myself. He put the right people in my life at just the right time, and I knew it. I just knew it. I somehow sensed it in my spirit. I just felt a connection. I never felt it before, and I just knew it was like God was telling me, "This is the one that I sent to help you." I felt a sense of, "I can relate to her." I can relate because the last few counselors that I had had, I couldn't relate to them at all. I just could not, and I really felt the sense of "I can relate to this person, and she can relate to me"... and I don't know any other way to describe it.

It would be a mistake to let the excitement of what EMDR can offer overshadow the therapeutic relationship.

Assisting Complex PTSD Clients with Reintegration

Many books on PTSD and trauma-related disorders focus largely on Stage 1 (stabilization) and Stage 2 (trauma processing), taking the third stage, reintegration, for granted. These chapters on special populations emphasize the importance of reintegration issues with which we can assist. In the traditional Shapiro model (2001), the purpose of Phase 8, re-evaluation, is to determine the success of the EMDR over time. In my own practice, Phase 8 is very important in helping clients integrate the results of the breakthroughs they experience with EMDR treatment into their everyday lives. With complex PTSD clients, it is important to start every session with a general check-in. It is helpful to ask how things have gone since the previous session, especially if it included significant trauma processing work. Although this is good practice with all EMDR clients, it is vital with complex PTSD clients, whose struggles with activities of daily living and functioning are likely more pronounced than those of simple PTSD clients. If powerful material is coming up in sessions but a client can't cope with it or integrate it, then the therapy can end up being counterproductive in the long run. A good strategy is to ask the client what his or her questions may be about material elicited by the EMDR and then integrate the questions into a conversation that meets the client where he or she is.

For example, let's say you've worked through a long course of EMDR with a complex PTSD client. It is important, if feasible, to arrange for follow-up sessions after you have formally wrapped up the EMDR processing. Even if it is a simple check-in 3 to 6 months after treatment, I have found follow up to be critical in ensuring that clients are maintaining the gains that emerged during EMDR. If the client is struggling, you can conduct a needs assessment at the follow-up to see if more work or some other type of follow-up care is necessary. Sometimes that care is additional EMDR sessions, a different form of therapy, or a more logistical service, such as case management. Case managers or other local community resources (e.g., vocational rehabilitation, public housing authorities, educational assistance) may offer services to assist the client in reaching his or her goals for integrating or reintegrating into society. If the client has been doing well, you can use your follow-up session to discuss the progress he or she has been able to make.

It is important not to leave our most complicated clients hanging, especially after an intense treatment like EMDR. Consider the parallel that I made to surgery in Chapter 3. Even if a surgery goes successfully, the vast majority of medical providers recommend some type of follow-up care. The same logic prevails with complex PTSD. See Box 12 for further resources.

Box 12. Resources on EMDR with Complex PTSD.

Forgash, C., & Copeley, M. (2008). *Healing the heart of trauma and dissociation with EMDR and ego state therapy.* New York: Springer Publishing.

Greenwald, R. (2007). *EMDR within a phase model of trauma-informed treatment.* New York: The Haworth Press.

Korn, D. (2009). EMDR and the treatment of complex PTSD: A review. *Journal of EMDR Practice and Research*, 3(4), 264–278.

Parnell, L. (2007). *A therapist's guide to EMDR: Tools and techniques for successful treatment.* New York: W. W. Norton & Company.

Chapter 8: Addictions

*"Just 'cause you got the monkey off your back doesn't mean
the circus has left town."*

—George Carlin

When I first took a job in the addictions field, I was disheartened
by how many of my colleagues operated with a rigid, status quo
attitude. You may have heard comments in your work setting, such
as, "They just act that way because they're still in denial," or "They
just need to sit down and shut up." I was taught to do treatment
plans that were rigidly cognitive-behavioral or 12-step in nature. I'm
not saying that these approaches are detrimental; however, for some
clients with major trauma issues, they are not sufficient.

One such experience stands out as being formative in my decision to become an EMDR therapist and bring the approach to
struggling alcoholics and addicts. I was working in a reputable inpatient treatment facility. This was my first "real" job after graduate school and my own EMDR experience. I worked under a traditionally rigid clinical director, and he would not entertain any
discussions with me about the role that trauma played in the lives
of our clients. I tried to plead my case with him based on my own
experience, saying something to the effect of, "Do you think I
just took opiates and became hooked at such a young age because
things were great?" He insisted, "No, that happened because you
were an addict." Part of me saw his point: Yes, my body had a pre-

disposition for addiction. However, I was not convinced that the answer was so straightforward.

Following my conversation with him, I was drawn to seek out addiction professionals who were not rigid but instead embraced an "all of the above" approach to the treatment of addiction. To me, "all of the above" does not mean throwing every intervention available at the client to see what will stick, but rather, meeting clients where they are and providing them with the best intervention or combination of interventions possible. After leaving that hospital, I transitioned into providing outpatient treatment to clients with a dual diagnoses. I currently practice in a facility that is mental health oriented, although I still work with dually diagnosed clients, and I appreciate my colleagues who reject rigidity and are willing to be flexible in meeting client needs.

Case evidence and usual care research (i.e., research that is conducted in clinical settings as opposed to artificially created research studies) continues to support the use of EMDR as a plausible intervention for addiction (Abel & O'Brien, 2010; Brown & Gilman, 2007; Cox & Howard, 2007; Hase, Schallmayer & Sack, 2008; Henry, 1995; Marich, 2009a; Shapiro, Vogelman-Sine, & Sine, 1994; Zweben & Yeary, 2006), especially when implemented appropriately alongside other supportive care (Marich, 2009a; 2010; Shapiro & Forrest, 1997). In one of the first books she published on EMDR, Shapiro expressed that EMDR is best implemented

---

...As part of a system designed to make the client feel safe and supported. It works best when it is used in conjunction with counseling groups that provide a nurturing atmosphere, such as group therapy, Alcoholics Anonymous (A.A.), and Narcotics Anonymous (N.A.) (Shapiro & Forrest, 1997; p. 178).

My general position on how to use EMDR with addicted clients does not differ significantly from what Shapiro wrote in this early book. Even though the push by many is to view EMDR as an approach to psychotherapy, my practice and research continues to inform me that EMDR can be effectively used in concert with other approaches to augment addiction treatment (Marich, 2010). EMDR can help the addict resolve the negative cognitions that fueled the addiction in the first place (Shapiro & Forrest, 1997), and it can assist in breaking down both cognitive and experiential roadblocks that exist to meaningful addiction recovery.

Clarifying the Terminology: Addiction, Relapse, and Recovery

Addiction Defined

Addiction can be a tricky phenomenon to study, simply because there is disagreement in the literature on what constitutes addiction, relapse, and recovery. For some, addiction is a disease, whereas others see it as a state of mind or a moral problem. In terms of relapse, some people view it as the return to any addictive substances or behaviors, whereas others see it as a return to pretreatment levels of use. In my opinion, recovery is the construct that is the most widely open to interpretation. For the purposes of better understanding how to use EMDR with complex clients, it is important to discuss some of the disparities in definition and propose the best possible working definition of each construct.

Addiction, which comes from the Latin root meaning "to be assigned to or favoring something," is not a diagnosis in the DSM-IV-TR (American Psychiatric Association, 2000). The DSM favors Substance Dependence, and only some of the behavioral addictions (e.g., pathological gambling disorder) are addressed. *Addiction* is a broad-sweeping cultural term that can be used to describe both chemical and behavioral manifestations. Indeed, medical and psychotherapeutic professionals often use the term *addiction* to refer to the phenomenon of continuing to do something over and over, even when it causes repeated pain and consequences (GWC, 1993).

There are many definitions of *addiction*, each being informed by the specific model that is being used to conceptualize it. For instance, the disease model of addiction has been predominant in the medical and psychotherapeutic professions since the 1950s. This model purports that addiction is a primary disease with a predictable course and symptoms, and that it is chronic, progressive, and fatal if left untreated. As with many diseases, the causes of addiction can be multifarious and influenced by genetic predisposition.

Alternate models exist to describe addiction. Prior to the disease model, the moral model was used throughout most of the world to explain addiction. This model suggested that addicts are weak willed and that their consumption was tantamount to sinful behavior; meaningful religious conversion was the only hope for a cure. Around the world, there are cadres of faith-based programs that still rely on this model. Other models include the habit and pleasure models (behavioral paradigms), the allostatic model (addiction results as a response to accumulated stressors), and the cultural model. Regardless of which model you accept as a professional, it is important to consider that rigid acceptance of any of these models is not optimally trauma sensitive. Any of these models can be used to conceptualize and treat addiction, but if the critical role that trauma can play in the development and treatment of the addiction is dismissed, further harm can result for the trauma survivor in treatment. The attitudes that I encountered in the treatment center mentioned earlier in the chapter would be a clear example of the disease model predominating without taking the role of trauma into account.Noted sex addiction expert Patrick Carnes (1992) proposed an excellent general definition of addiction that arguably encompasses most of the models that we just discussed: "*Addiction* refers to the entire pattern of maladaptive behaviors, cognitions, belief systems, consequences and affects on others, not just the *behavior* as in compulsivity." Indeed, addiction is more than just a behavior gone out of control; there are many other factors fueling it (e.g., cognitions, effects of trauma) and many more factors affected by it (e.g., global functioning of the individual, impact on family and society). EMDR can play a powerful role in addressing these various factors.

In further exploring the meaning of addiction, it is wise for us to consider the words of those who have battled addiction. Ten women who experienced EMDR as part of their addiction treatment described who they had become in active addiction as cheater, liar (two participants), monster (two participants), and thief (two participants) and described themselves and their behavior in active addiction as angry, crazy, deceitful, dishonest, easily offended, entitled, exploitive, fearful, hopeless, insane, rationalizing, manipulative, miserable, promiscuous, rageful, sad, selfish, secretive, and unpredictable (Marich, 2009b). In the following pages, you can read Jennifer's story and a passage from Nancy, the woman whose case we first visited in Chapter 7, to further understand the experiences of addiction, relapse, and recovery.

"And There Within Ourselves, We Found Our Wings to Fly"
by Jennifer B.

I have been sober for a little over 10 years now. When I was 26, I got a fourth DUI and was ordered to A.A. I did 45 days in the work release program in the local county jail. They let me keep my job, so I slept in jail and went to work during the day. My whole life, I had control of everything except my drinking. I was a good student, graduating with a 3.4 GPA. Always worked a job, always paid my bills, did volunteer service, was involved in the local theater and was fairly responsible, except for my drinking. It was the one thing I had no control over. When I was 7 years old, my 8-year-old brother and I were molested by my blood aunt's boyfriend. I told my mom and she took him to court. My brother and I are biracial, and 2 "black" kids accusing a well known "white" man of this horrific thing was unheard of. So he hired a slick lawyer to scare us on the stand in court. Needless to say, he got away with it, and this began my drinking. He had given us our first taste of alcohol while he was sexually assaulting us, and I remember liking the feeling I got from the booze. I knew what was being done to me was wrong, but the booze took all my inhibitions away. My family already didn't accept us because we were "half breeds," and this whole thing just added to their disapproval.

At this tender age I found alcohol took all that guilt away. For years, I blamed myself for the destruction of our family. Half the family still talked to this man, and half wanted nothing to do with him. My aunt is still with him to this day. So I drank to numb those feelings of rejection. I grew up without a father also. He was an alcoholic. He passed in 1998. After being in recovery for 5 years, I hit a wall of severe depression. I became suicidal and just wanted to die and didn't know why. I was a manager at a flower shop, I was sober, I had friends and every reason to love life, but I was miserable. Someone in the program suggested I get counseling. I was apprehensive because I had been to so many therapists in the past (trying to figure out what was wrong with me), but never sober. So I made an appointment and started therapy. My counselor suggested that I try EMDR. He had seen very positive results from it.

I figured I had nothing to lose. So we did 2 months' worth of EMDR. Although the process was so painful, each time I started to feel a little better. We talked about the molestation, my family's rejection, my self-hatred, my physical abuse... After the 2 months were up, I did a few more therapy sessions, then that was it. I started a whole new journey to recovery. I started writing again and found a whole new lease on life. My depression lifted, and my suicidal thoughts went away. Occasionally I still get depressed even today, but I was given tools to take care of it. I write, I talk, I have even gone back for more therapy when needed. Just one of the greatest things that happened to me as a result of EMDR is the forgiveness I have received. In March of this year, I wanted to go see my grandma in New Mexico. She lives there in the same town as the man that molested me. When she moved there 11 years ago, I swore her off forever. I wasn't sober yet. So through getting sober, working steps and EMDR, I forgave her for her decision to live by him. I realized she was doing the best she could. I come to find out my aunt has blamed herself all these years for staying with him.

Of course he admitted to doing it years later. I had a wonderful time visiting with my aunt and grandma. My A.A. sponsor suggested that I only visit with them and not try to mend things with him. I told my aunt I forgave her and I forgave him for the past. I told her I work in a drug and alcohol treatment center and I have learned to love the unlovable and forgive the unforgivable, so why wouldn't I forgive him too. We all cried and healed together from this catastrophic event so many years ago. When I returned home, I still felt like things were unfinished, so I wrote him a letter and told him my life story and how I forgave him for what he did 29 years ago. To let go of the anger I held onto for that many years was like someone just handed me a million dollars. I feel so free and so clean! I would recommend EMDR to anyone that needs to recovery from a painful past!

Some Words from Nancy

Addiction devastated my life to the point where I really no longer had the will to live. I didn't want to live. Every day I hoped and prayed that today would be the day that I could drink myself to death. That pretty much sums it up as what went from maybe being fun at the beginning, escaping reality, turned on me like an enemy would and just totally devastated my life to the point where I just didn't care or have the will to live. You know I just—I could escape for a while but when I came to everything was just all the more worse. I mean it just didn't work for me anymore. It didn't—it didn't take away the pain. It didn't fulfill me, it just devastated my life; it just made me want to die. I would just keep thinking that I would rather be dead than have to live like this every single day of my life and feed this addiction.

My whole life went from being a caring, giving, loving person ... I turned into a cold, selfish, uncaring, unloving—unlovable person. Very hateful, very mean, very just negative attitude, I hated life, I hated myself ... I hated what I had become during my addiction, and ... the only way I could describe it is I just didn't want to live with myself anymore and I felt like the biggest failure. I had tried so many times to get out of it, to get sober and I never could and I, I just felt hopeless. I felt totally hopeless, devastated like the only way that it was ever going to end was death.

Relapse and Recovery

Nancy's story speaks to the vicious cycle that has often been used to describe addiction, relapse, and recovery. Now that we've illuminated the concept of addiction, let's explore relapse and recovery.

Delmonico and Griffin (2007) contended that, in explaining addictive behavior, different models tend to develop over time and independently of each other, even though they are all trying to investigate the causes of addiction and the implications for more effective treatment. Although various models abound to explain relapse, the common theme emerging from the literature is that poor self-efficacy and high volumes of negative emotion, coupled with poor coping skills, put an individual at greater risk for relapsing on alcohol or other drugs following a period of sobriety (Allsop, Saunders, & Phillips, 2000; Connors & Maisto, 2006; Donovan, 1996; El-Sheikh & Bashir, 2003; Moos & Moos, 2006; Tapert, Ozyurt, Myers, et al., 2004; Walitzer & Dearing, 2006; Walton, Blow, Bingham, et al., 2003). Relapse is a significant issue, and the literature seems to show some common themes regarding relapse risk; however, no definitive model has emerged to explain the relapse process (Allsop, Saunders, & Phillips, 2000). One possible explanation is that, as was mentioned previously, treatment professionals don't always agree on what constitutes a relapse (Donovan, 1996; Marlatt & George, 1984; Walitzer & Dearing, 2006); it is variously defined as any substance use, a return to pre-treatment levels of substance use, and the consumption of a certain number of drinks or the presence of a specific blood alcohol level (Walitzer & Dearing, 2006).

Miller and Guidry (2001), who developed the Addiction and Trauma Recovery Integration Model (ATRIUM), contended that traditional models of addiction fail to appropriately consider the significant role that unresolved trauma plays in an addicted individual's attempt to recover. They further stated that these traditional approaches tend to marginalize addicted traumatized women more than their male counterparts. Though Miller and Guidry did not discredit the merit of traditional models such as the 12 Step/Minnesota model of treatment or CBT, they suggested that these approaches do not sufficiently address the role of trauma in setting individuals up to fail in recovery. In their own work, Miller and Guidry expressed specific concern about female addicts. Though Miller and Guidry, like other authors, have cited factors such as poor self-efficacy and a high volume of negative emotion coupled with poor coping skills as risk factors for relapse, they have advocated a more holistic approach to promote long-term recovery and prevent potentially debilitating relapses. In other words, they have stated that treatment needs to extend beyond the cognitive interventions that have traditionally been used in relapse prevention counseling or the 12 Step–oriented methods associated with the Minnesota model.

The fact that most traditional treatment models ignore the impact of trauma is also identified by Zweben and Yeary (2006) in their EMDR-specific article on treating trauma as part of addiction treatment. They contended that EMDR answers the call for a more holistic approach to the treatment of trauma and addiction because it combines cognitive, body-oriented, emotional, and experiential matter into a single treatment protocol. Alan Moskovitz (2001), an internationally recognized figure in the treatment of borderline personality disorder, has called EMDR, "an artful blend of several therapeutic techniques, including exposure therapy, cognitive therapy, and even an abbreviated form of the free association of psychoanalytic psychotherapy" (p. 184).

EMDR clearly has a place in addiction treatment, but before considering how to integrate EMDR into *recovery*, we must first examine what recovery means. For some who follow a traditional 12 Step approach, *recovery* is synonymous with working the steps in a fellowship such as A.A. or N.A. However, it is imperative to consider that there are many paths to achieving a recovery-oriented lifestyle. In the most general, inclusive terms, *recovery* refers to the process by which an individual is actively taking measures to keep his or her addiction in remission (White & Kurtz, 2006). Recovery is more than abstinence from chemicals or problematic behavior; rather, it is a process in which an individual takes active measures to repair the life damage caused by addiction (Evans & Sullivan, 1995). Lifestyle change is a critical common denominator in most approaches to recovery (Fletcher, 2001).

A useful construct for using EMDR with a recovering addict is that of *recovery capital*. This refers to the "quality and quantity of internal and external resources that one can bring to bear on the initiation and maintenance of recovery" (Granfield & Cloud, 1999; White & Kurtz, 2006, p. 9). This concept can also be conceptualized as the tangible and intangible resources that an individual possesses to make recovery successful. Recovery capital can include a support group, 12-step meetings, a sponsor, a church group, a job, hobbies, supportive family, motivation, and a place to live—essentially, whatever the person has going for him or her. In assessing whether an addict is a candidate for incorporating EMDR into recovery, it is important to evaluate the depth of his or her recovery capital before proceeding with EMDR. This is an approach that is concomitant to preparation and stabilization stage work; i.e., using whatever you can to get the client ready for EMDR. Helping a client build recovery capital can be an important component of frontloading before proceeding with trauma-processing work using EMDR.

Tips from the Trenches on Using EMDR with Addiction

Hopefully, this book has inspired you to start thinking about the application of EMDR on a case-by-case basis with your clientele. There are no black and white guidelines, especially with complex populations. One of the common questions I often get is, "How much sober time should a person have before we do EMDR?" The simple answer is that there is no simple answer. The answer must be informed by the quality of a client's Stage 1 (stabilization) resources. Among professionals, I have seen two extremes when it comes to using EMDR with addicts. Many mental health therapists who are not comfortable treating addiction insist that they will not do EMDR with a recovering addict until he or she has 1 to 2 years of sobriety. On the other end of the spectrum, I have seen therapists do trauma-processing EMDR while a client is still actively using.

I do not believe that either extreme is optimal. Many of my clients cannot remain sober for a year or two without having addressed their trauma. In contrast, if you open up the Pandora's box of traumatic memories while substance use is still one of the predominant coping skills for regulating affect, you may be doing more harm than good for the client. Several of my colleagues, many whom I respect a great deal, have taken the position that for a person to really get sober, then the underlying trauma must be addressed, and they use this rationale to justify doing EMDR while a person is still using. I have never been comfortable with that. In my early days of doing EMDR, I attempted some trauma processing work with a few clients who were actively smoking marijuana or binge drinking on weekends, and I found it to be fruitless. They kept hitting too many walls during processing or could not handle what came up. When I shifted my energies to working with them on coping skills, some of which included the bilateral stimulation, resourcing skills that we see in EMDR, the clients did better.

So when the question comes up, "Can I do EMDR with someone who is still actively using?" I often say *yes*, as long as it's preparation-oriented EMDR (i.e., Shapiro Phases 1 and 2). Part of stabilization/preparation with a traumatized addict is to help him or her achieve a modicum of functional sobriety while building an arsenal of positive coping skills that he or she can use in place of the addictive substance or activity. Some of the classic resourcing skills that we see in EMDR (e.g., safe place, light stream, installation of positive memories or cognitions with bilateral stimulation) work brilliantly during stabilization. Several EMDR clinicians have written up specialized protocols that use bilateral stimulation to target the craving or urge instead of the traumatic memory (see Box 13). These specialized protocols appear to be very effective for clients who are not yet ready to do trauma processing. As I have emphasized throughout this book, even if you believe such a client might be a good candidate for trauma processing work in the future, don't *rush* it.

Chapter 8: Addictions

I typically begin trauma processing work with addicts when they have been sober 3 to 7 months. Again, this is an approximate range—I have begun processing as early as 1 month into recovery and as long as 1 to 2 years after recovery has commenced. I take these factors into consideration when engaging in clinical decision-making with this population:

- EMDR can work very well for the *sober but stuck* client. These are people who have achieved initial sobriety but then at a certain point experience a stalemate in their emotional growth in recovery. Typically, this happens when the so-called *pink cloud* of initial sobriety lifts and life starts to get harder to manage. When you, as the clinician, see this starting to happen, it's often a good time to commence trauma-processing (assuming that stabilization skills are in place).

- If a client is working a 12 Step recovery program, trauma-processing EMDR is best applied after an individual has completed the foundational steps 1 through 3. Many recovering addicts have difficulty with steps 4 and 5, the "moral inventory" steps. In these steps, a person is asked to look back at his/her past, and these steps can become a frightening prospect for traumatized people. I often use EMDR after a client has done steps 1 through 3 and is struggling with the notion of doing steps 4 and 5.

- Like with many therapeutic approaches, the client's willingness to participate is a critical element. In terms of doing EMDR with addicts, willingness to look at past issues is key. If a person isn't ready, keep working with him or her on stabilization skills.

- Examining a client's rationale for wanting to look at past issues is very critical. In Chapter 5, the importance of assessing for secondary gains was discussed. With addicts, failure to assess for secondary gains can be especially costly. If you hear an addict saying that he or she wants to go back to the past to find out the "reasons why" he or she drinks, that's typically a red flag for misguided motivation. Giving an addict "reasons why" in the absence of motivation for recovery and wellness may end up providing more excuses to drink, use, or engage in other dangerous activity. Using general, conversational rapport, you can help an addicted client understand that simply uncovering reasons why he or she has used substances is not going to make him or her better. This issue is addressed more thoroughly in the section on reintegration that concludes this chapter.

- Safety is key. Everything covered in Chapter 5 on preparation applies to and is vital for this population.

- Know yourself. To repeat Shapiro's (2001) wise suggestion, do not treat a client with EMDR whom you wouldn't normally treat with any other therapy. If you are comfortable working with addicts in general, you will probably do well using EMDR with this population in the relatively early stages of sobriety because you have other skills and experiences on which to rely if the EMDR backfires.

Assisting Recovering Addicts with Reintegration

One of the dangers of doing EMDR with an addicted client who has a long history of trauma is that the EMDR can be such an amazing experience that the client may believe he or she is "cured." Although restoration to wholeness is certainly a gain that can result from EMDR, it can make a person complacent and thus prone to slipping back into old lifestyle patterns. A longstanding debate among professionals is whether addiction requires a lifelong recovery or a one-time restoration. Although this book is not the forum for entertaining such a debate, I do make the following conjecture: Lifestyle change is the common denominator. Most current programs available for treating addiction are aimed at lifestyle change. True gains don't just happen in treatment; they must be applied to meaningful lifestyle change outside the therapy office. This is a primary goal of the reevaluation phase in the Shapiro (2001) protocol.

I have seen it happen on several occasions: A person has a great experience with EMDR (or another therapeutic approach), thinks he or she's *all better*, and stops doing what worked initially. Usually, this means that the client gradually slips back into old lifestyle patterns. This is why EMDR and some good old-fashioned relapse prevention planning are not mutually exclusive. In fact, I maintain that this combination is a best practice. This idea may be best illustrated through the following case.

The Case of Davy

> Davy was referred to an EMDR therapist following numerous failed chemical dependency treatment episodes over a 10-year-period. Davy clearly had complex PTSD caused by ritualistic torture that he experienced as a young child. He entered EMDR therapy with a heightened sense of awareness about his addiction and how his stuck cognitions in the area of trust inhibited him from getting close to the people in 12 Step recovery meetings whom he knew could help him. Together with help from the 12 Step support system, which he eventually allowed himself to trust, Davy had a powerfully cathartic experience with EMDR. In many ways, following some initial blocking, Davy's experience was textbook, with the SUDs levels on his targets coming down to 0 and the VoC levels on positive cognitions coming up to 7. Davy was optimistic about his healing and his future. His therapist suggested a series of follow-up sessions to ensure that these gains

would be maintained. Davy agreed but did not come back for any of the follow-up sessions.

The therapist later learned that Davy had taken the experience of "it's over" (e.g., his abuse) to such a heightened level that he got complacent in following the 12 Step recovery program that had helped him get sober in the first place. First, he began drinking a beer here and there, and before long, Davy slipped back into old, manipulative behaviors and eventually, full-blown addiction. Although the therapist believed that she had done all she could to make follow-up appointments available to Davy, she acknowledged that more careful orientation to what EMDR can and can't do toward the end of treatment and obtaining a release of information to contact the client's 12 Step sponsor might have helped.

Using EMDR to Target Recovery Roadblocks and Slippery Situations

A traditional, Face 1 EMDR belief that can get in the way of the therapy's effectiveness is targeting the worst or first target cognition can produce a "generalization effect," in which this progress causes all other problematic cognitions to clear. Rigidly assuming that a generalization effect will always take place (or assuming that it has already happened) is problematic.

In Davy's case, he maintained that all of the initial problematic cognitions he identified were gone after processing the two worst ones. This notion made sense to Davy's therapist, who was aware of the plausibility of a generalization effect. However, in Davy's daily life after EMDR treatment, he encountered roadblocks in maintaining his recovery lifestyle. EMDR can be applied to these specific roadblocks throughout treatment, and I often use modified EMDR protocols to target issues that come up in the reintegration stage. These sessions usually go quickly, especially if major trauma processing work was done beforehand.

Another resource I have developed is a list of common addiction-specific negative cognitions (see "The Greatest Hits List of Addiction-Specific Beliefs"). This list closely parallels the list of general negative cognitions that appeared in Chapter 6. You can use the addiction-specific list in a similar way. When a client is near to or in the reintegration stage (consensus model), have him check off which beliefs may still apply, then prepare the client for an EMDR session to clear out that potentially roadblocking belief (e.g., "My addiction is my identity"; "Sex/Alcohol is my most important need"). This approach can work with deeply ingrained addiction-specific beliefs and with relatively minor problems that could develop into major sticking points.

The "Greatest Hits" List of Addiction-Specific Beliefs
(May be duplicated for use in clinical settings)

I cannot cope without alcohol.

I cannot cope without drugs.

I cannot cope without cigarettes.

I cannot cope without acting out violently.

I cannot cope without victimizing others.

I cannot cope with emotions without eating.

I cannot live without sex.

Sex is my most important need.

Escaping reality is my most important need.

I cannot survive without a partner/relationship.

I am not capable of dealing with my feelings.

I am not capable of dealing with my life.

I cannot accept/deal with reality.

I am incapable of being social without drugs.

I must victimize others to cope with my past.

I must drink alcohol to be in control.

I must smoke cigarettes to be in control.

I must act out violently to be in control.

I must victimize others to be in control.

I am incapable of being social without alcohol.

I must be in a relationship to be in control.

I must act out violently to cope with my past.

I am incapable of being social without cigarettes.

I am nothing without my addiction.

I have no identity without my addiction.

I have no identity if I can't act out.

My addiction is my security.

I must use alcohol to cope with my past.

I must use drugs to cope with my past.

I must have sex to cope with my past.

I must eat to cope with my past.

I must have sex to be in control.

I must gamble to be in control.

I must smoke to cope with my past.

I must eat to be in control.

I must use drugs to be in control.

Other Beliefs Not Listed:

Let's say that a client is coming in for monthly check-ups following the establishment of initial sobriety and completion of major trauma-processing work. One day, she comes in for her session and tells you she's been struggling with letting go of something that her boyfriend said. The client comments, "I just can't let go of these little resentments." This is a perfect opportunity to set up a short sequence to target that belief. If you are more Face 1 or Face 2 in your orientation, you can set up a formal protocol to clear out this belief. If you are more open to modified protocols (e.g., Face 3 and Face 4), you can set this up very simply by asking the client to consider the negative belief, "I just can't let go of these little resentments" and notice where she feels the experience of holding on to the resentments in her body. Then, ask if an image or emotion is coming up and commence bilateral stimulation to see where the client goes with it. For clients who have already worked through Stage 1 (stabilization) and Stage 2 (trauma processing), these roadblock processing sessions go relatively quickly.

Because EMDR is a therapy that was designed to be a "three-pronged protocol" (i.e., past, present, and future; Shapiro, 2001), EMDR future templates (which are essentially imaginary scenarios) can have powerful applications for recovering addicts who often find themselves in slippery situations. Some of these situations, such as going to a holiday party, returning to school after 5 years away due to addiction, or having to set a boundary with an unhealthy partner can be addressed with EMDR future templates. If antecedent memories connected to the future templates have not been cleared out in the trauma-processing stage, they are likely to come up in this future template work, and that's okay. It shouldn't be an issue if the client has stabilization skills and has become used to doing EMDR.

How rigidly you want to set up future templates depends largely on which face of EMDR you predominantly practice. Here is a traditional example of how to set up a future template for a precarious situation in sobriety. Modify it as needed, depending on your personal style:

Situation: Going to a family Christmas party where there may be a lot of drinking.

Image/Worst part: Seeing my mother start to act silly ... goes along with the scent of the whiskey.

Negative cognition: "I can't stand it."

Positive cognition to work toward: "I can handle it." [Get a VoC level if desired.]

Emotions: Sadness, frustration.

SUDs: 6.

Body sensations: Throat, shooting down to stomach.

Therapist's response: "Go with that."

Box 13. Resources on Specialized Addiction Protocols.

Hase, M. (2010). CraveEx: An EMDR approach to treat substance abuse and addiction. In M. Luber (Ed.), *EMDR scripted protocols: Special populations* (pp. 467–488). New York: Springer Publishing Company.

Popky, A. J. (2005). DeTUR, an urge reduction protocol for addictions and dysfunctional behaviors. In R. Shapiro (Ed.), *EMDR solutions: Pathways to healing* (pp. 167–188). New York: W. W. Norton & Company.

Popky, A. J. (2010). The desensitization of triggers and urge reprocessing (DeTUR) protocol. In M. Luber (Ed.), *EMDR scripted protocols: Special populations* (pp. 489–516). New York: Springer Publishing Company.

Chapter 9: Violent and Acting Out Behaviors

"We fear violence less than our own feelings. Personal, private, solitary pain is more terrifying than what anyone else can inflict."

—Jim Morrison

The phrase *anger management* is one of the many buzz phrases circulating the halls of mental health in recent decades. Clients have been referred to us en masse from the courts due to problems with anger management. Clients come to couples counseling accusing their partner of having anger management issues. The phrase *anger management* even resulted in a hilarious movie of the same title staring Jack Nicholson and Adam Sandler.

However, violence and acting out behaviors are no laughing matter. According to the Bureau of Justice Statistics (2010), a violent crime can include murder, rape, sexual assault, robbery, and simple assault. To further illustrate the impact of violence on our collective society, consider the following statistics from the National Crime Victimization Survey in 2008 (Bureau of Justice Statistics, 2010):

- About 4.9 million nonfatal violent victimizations of people 12 years or older occurred that year.

- Violent crime victimizations were experienced by 19.3 per 1,000 people 12 or older.

- Simple assault is the most frequently occurring violent crime. In 2008, 3.3 million simple assault victimizations affected 13.9 per 1,000 people 12 or older.

- In 2008, of the female population in the United States older than 18, 0.6 per 1,000 were victims of a rape or sexual assault, and 0.3 per 1,000 of the total population (males and females) were victims of a rape or sexual assault.

- Only half of all nonfatal violent crimes were reported to the police in 2008.

Although the National Center for Health Statistics has continued to report a decline in the national murder rate since the mid-1980s, the latest numbers reveal that approximately 6.2 deaths per 100,000 in the United States are the result of homicide (Bureau of Justice Statistics, 2010).

As clinicians who use EMDR or other approaches to treat trauma, there is a great likelihood that we will see the victims of such crimes at one time or another in our practices. But are we equipped to deal with those who perpetrate crimes and other victimizing behaviors? Viktor Frankl surmised that it is one thing to help those who suffer, but if you really want to change the world, help those who are causing the suffering (Vesely, 2009). It is well-accepted logic that people who find their way to treatment for inflicting suffering on others typically have experienced a wellspring of suffering themselves. EMDR offers us a clinical avenue to address the underlying suffering and unresolved trauma in those who act out.

Chapter 9: Violent and Acting Out Behaviors

Better Understanding Violence and Acting Out

Like many concepts in this book, *violence* and *acting out* require some explanation in order to be better understood. *Violence* comes from the Middle English word meaning *short force*. As stated in Chapter 3, traumatic wounds, often a product of violence, take a short time to create but a long time to heal. Violence is often cyclical in nature: We must consider whether a person who inflicts violence does so in response to violence, or short force, that was inflicted on him or her. For some victims of violence, unhealed wounds become easier to deal with if they can ignore the pain or assert power by inflicting wounds on others. This idea relates to a standard definition of *acting out*:

The uncontrolled and inappropriate behavioral expression of denied emotions that serves to relieve tension associated with these emotions or to communicate them in a disguised, or indirect, way to others. Such behaviors may include (but are not limited to) arguing, fighting, stealing, threatening, or throwing tantrums (VandenBos, 2007; p. 12).

Many segments of the addiction treatment field have adopted the phrase *acting out* to describe the behavioral component of addictive disorders. For instance, a sex addict who engages in a compulsive sexual behavior instead of dealing with his or her core issues is said to be acting out.

As EMDR practitioners, it is important to tune into the link between acting out behaviors (which can be violent) and re-pressed emotions. EMDR can help the person find an avenue for identifying and expressing these pent-up emotions that have typically been let out inappropriately. Just as with addictive disorders, it is unrealistic to assume that as soon as a client receives EMDR, he or she will be able to feel and instantly stop acting out. However, a combination of interventions is typically the solution for helping those who act out attain meaningful lifestyle change.

Perhaps the best research on the role of EMDR in the treatment of violent and acting out behaviors comes from the team of Ronald Ricci and Cheryl Clayton. In their initial study (Ricci, Clayton, & Shapiro, 2006), 10 incarcerated male child molesters (who had been molested themselves as children) were treated with a course of EMDR therapy as an adjunct to standard CBT and relapse prevention therapy. The control group represented individuals who were receiving the standard therapies without EMDR. The authors found that significant differences existed among the EMDR group's decrease in sexual arousal (as measured by standardized scales), increase in motivation for treatment, and increase in empathy for the victim.

Ricci, Clayton, and Shapiro's (2006) study offered insight into the origins of sexual deviance and implications for treating it by resolving core traumatic memories. In a qualitative follow up to the original article, Ricci and Clayton (2008) conducted in-depth interviews with the 10 original participants. A noteworthy insight gained from the interviews was that study participants had difficulty with standard CBT and relapse prevention treatment for one of three reasons: (a) They were unable to discuss the specifics of their sexually deviant behavior without becoming "stalled in treatment" (p. 43), (b) Treatment gains were cognitive rather than emotional; thus, "there was no internalization of victim harm or reoffense risk awareness" (p. 43), or (c) "Emotional triggers were repeatedly activating lapse behaviors and hence increasing reoffense risk" (p. 43). Several themes emerged in analysis of the interviews: participants were better able to recognize distorted beliefs and cognitive distortions, they felt more accountability, they participated more in group therapy, they experienced increased empathy, they gained raised consciousness as a self-management tool, they had more self-esteem, and they were better able to recognize and manage emotions.

Although Ricci and Clayton's investigation (2008) primarily examined sexual offenders, these themes have implications for the treatment of acting out behaviors in general. The main implication is that gains made in treatment that are cognitive, lacking any emotional connection, are not as effective as gains that involve an emotional involvement or investment. In other words, if the client can verbalize that his or her acting out was wrong and identify the cognitive distortion behind the action but can't show some emotion in connection with that cognitive distortion, progress will likely be stymied.

This idea fits with the VandenBos definition of acting out offered earlier in the chapter. If acting out behaviors are the misplaced expressions of stifled emotions, shouldn't treatment be aimed at helping clients who act out connect with their emotional potential? This may be easier said than done, especially if a client has little emotional vocabulary. EMDR can help, as the following case illustrates.

The Case of Sasha (Marich, 2009b)

> Sasha, an African American woman, entered treatment in her mid-forties for cocaine addiction, although she identified acting out and violent behaviors as primary concerns that needed to be addressed. During many previous attempts at addiction recovery, her anger got in the way. Sasha was sexually molested as a small child and had a longstanding history of discord with her mother. The core negative cognition that defined her identity was "I am bad/shameful." After successfully completing a multifaceted treatment program that included EMDR and being sober for 3.5 years, Sasha was interviewed about her experiences (Marich, 2009b). She reflected on the role that anger played for her:

I was a cesspool of badness ... of dysfunction. I was very promiscuous...I was a liar, a thief, and a cheat. And I was very aggressive, real angry, and I had been molested at the age of 5, and me coming here [to treatment] had really helped me identify all those behaviors I had going on and connect the dots on why I did what I did. And in my addiction, I was just angry and I was covering up a lot of feelings, trying to suppress them. So when I came in here, the only feeling I could really identify with was anger. Anger and rage. And by me staying in that addiction as long as I did, I wasn't me, I wasn't my authentic self anymore. I just did what I had to do to survive and did what I did and had to do to get the drugs and alcohol.

I was a chronic relapser. And I think that was because, now that I have some awareness of a lot of that, I think it was because I didn't get to none of my core issues. I really didn't. And it was just surfacy stuff: the things you know to say that you say when you do the treatment thing, the treatment jargon. But for me today, it's just totally different, because I've gotten to my core issues. EMDR helped me get in touch with the things, with the resentments I had towards my mom and me wanting to know why my mom didn't love me or care anything about me. During the EMDR, I saw that it's none of my business of why she didn't love me or any of that. I did a lot of crying, I did a lot of that work.

Tips from the Trenches on Using EMDR with Violent and Acting Out Behaviors

Sasha's story provides us with a world of insight. For many people who act out, the only emotion they are capable of expressing is anger, so a big part of our work is to help them identify and learn to feel other feelings in a healthy way. The tip that I highlighted in Chapter 6—starting the trauma processing work by clearing out the negative belief "it's not okay to show my emotions"—is especially relevant with this population. If a person is incapable of showing any emotion besides anger, it is important to figure out where he or she got the message that it's not alright to show other feelings. My experience overwhelmingly suggests that if this core negative belief is blocking a person, and it usually is with this population, then the trauma processing EMDR is not going to go very far until the core belief is adaptively resolved.

In terms of other guidelines, many of the same suggestions I provided for working with addicted populations apply here as well:

- As with many therapeutic approaches, willingness is a critical element. With people who act out, willingness to look at past issues is key. If a person still isn't ready, keep working with him or her on stabilization skills.

- Examining a client's rationale for wanting to look at past issues is critical. The importance of assessing for secondary gains was discussed in Chapter 5. As with addicts, failure to assess for secondary gains can be especially costly with people who act out, especially those who act out violently. Once again, if you hear clients saying they want to go back to find out the "reasons why" they do the things they do, that's typically a red flag for misguided motivation. **Giving a person reasons for behavior in the absence of motivation for recovery and wellness can provide excuses to drink, use, or engage in other dangerous activity.**

- Safety is key. Everything covered in Chapter 5 on preparation applies to and is vital for this population.

- Know yourself. If a client who falls into this category of violence or acting out is pushing your buttons, seek consultation or supervision about the best course of action. It is generally not wise to take a person deeply into EMDR trauma processing work if your countertransference alarms are ringing at full volume.

Assisting Those Who Act Out with Reintegration

When working with clients who act out (as with many other special populations), the reintegration stage ensures that clients apply the gains made in EMDR treatment to their daily lives. With this population, the most obvious way to monitor reintegration is to directly track the acting out behaviors. Have they decreased? If so, work with the client to figure out whether new, healthier strategies have been learned to replace them. For instance, if a client formerly had a pattern of beating up his wife whenever he was under stress, discuss how he is currently handling his stress. For example, he may now be able to accept his feelings and take a walk to deal with those feelings as a positive replacement. Make sure clients can recognize that they are taking positive action and that taking positive action is an active choice. This strategy helps alleviate shame and magnify healthy, personal empowerment.

The themes that emerged from the Ricci and Clayton (2008) study offer some direction about what we should be listening for and working on with clients in reintegration: recognition of contributors to distorted beliefs and cognitive distortions, accountability, increased participation in group therapy [or group support/support system utilization], increased empathy, raised consciousness as a self-management tool, self-esteem, and emotion recognition and management. I often encourage clients to ask themselves, "What's this really about?" When the client identifies anger or another charged, "negative" emotion, he or she is able to work on raising his or her consciousness as a self-management tool. When a cognitive distortion is recognized, assess whether it could be addressed further in therapy. Sometimes, just becoming aware of the cognitive distortion following a rigorous course of trauma-focused EMDR work can get the client back on track.

Chapter 9: Violent and Acting Out Behaviors

Increased empathy in a person who has acted out is a major sign that their reintegration is progressing in a healthy direction. I encourage clients who feel emotionally stuck, especially in anger, to ask themselves, "How would I feel if I were in this person's shoes?" When a client gets in the habit of asking himself or herself this question, he or she will likely begin to connect more of the proverbial dots between how his or her acting out behaviors have been a recapitulation of the trauma that he or she once experienced. The reintegration stage is prime time for helping a client make such full-circle connections, which can potentially aid in relapse prevention.

As with addicted populations, EMDR future templates can be incorporated into reintegration work with clients who act out, especially as they become more aware of their triggers. Once again, how rigidly you set up future templates depends largely on which Face of EMDR you predominantly practice. Here is an example of how you may set up a future template for this population that you can modify as needed depending on your personal style:

Situation: Having to deal with people who disrespect me.

Image/Worst part: Seeing them laugh (even when it's not at me)

Negative cognition: "I am not in control."

Preferred/Positive cognition to work toward: "I am in control."
[Get a VoC level if desired.]

Emotions: anger, hurt

SUDs: 8

Body sensations: heart, hands

Go with that...

Box 14. Resources on Violent and Acting Out Behaviors.

Ricci, R. J., & Clayton, C. A. (2008). Trauma resolution treatment as an adjunct to standard treatment for child molesters. *Journal of EMDR Practice and Research*, 2(1), 41–50.

Ricci, R., & Clayton, C. A. (2009). EMDR with sex offenders in treatment. In R. Shapiro (Ed.), *EMDR Solutions II: For depression, eating disorders, performance, and more* (pp. 459–471). New York: Norton Professional Books.

Chapter 10: Other Axis I Disorders

"Disease is one of our languages. Doctors understand what disease has to say about itself. It's up to the person with the disease to understand what the disease has to say to her."

—Susanna Kaysen (*Girl, Interrupted*)

One of the most frequent questions colleagues ask me about EMDR is, "Can EMDR work for _____?" Truly, I have heard just about every Axis I (and Axis II) condition inserted into that blank. The simple answer is that even though most research on EMDR supports its use with PTSD, EMDR can be used with a variety of Axis I and Axis II conditions. This broad application makes sense if you agree with Shapiro's tenet that pathology is rooted in Large "T" and small "t" trauma. This tenet is rooted in the assumptions made in Chapter 3 that trauma consists of more than just major events that can yield a diagnosis of PTSD and that many of the cases we treat, from simple depression to kleptomania, can be rooted in some form of unresolved trauma. By following the logic that I presented in Part I of the book, especially the guidance offered on therapeutic alliance and client preparation, you will develop the basic skills you need to use EMDR with any Axis I presentation, with or without PTSD. The only caveat is that some Axis I conditions may require more attention and preparation than others because of certain special situations that may arise.

Better Understanding Axis I Disorders

If you've worked in the mental health field for any period of time, you have most likely acquired working familiarity with the common diagnoses: depression and other mood disorders, anxiety disorders, and adjustments disorders. If you are still not sure how trauma plays into the clinical picture of these presentations, I encourage you to re-read the primer on trauma in Chapter 3 and consider how trauma may have impacted some of your clients who present with these common disorders.

Often, it's the disorders that are more difficult to conceptualize that cause the most problems. For some of us, it's because we don't see certain disorders, such as trichotillomania (compulsive hair pulling) and male orgasmic disorder, for example, as frequently as we would see depression. Other clinicians are so accustomed to seeing the more common disorders that unusual clinical issues requiring attention can be missed. The key is to seek supervision or consultation if you are encountering a clinical presentation that is baffling to your frame of reference.

The mental health diagnostic system has been criticized for "putting people into boxes" based on their illness. The sad reality is that, in many mental health settings across the nation, this happens in practice (even more than in theory) when practitioners believe that a handful of diagnoses can explain every ill. During my first internship, every person who came into the hospital was slapped with a diagnosis of Bipolar Disorder. The only variations related to some of the qualifiers (e.g., Bipolar I vs. Bipolar II; with or without psychotic features). In numerous facilities, if a young child presents with any type of attention or behavioral problem, he or she is quickly labeled as having ADHD or Oppositional Defiant Disorder. Whenever a person hears voices, it is often immediately assumed that he or she has a psychotic disorder. However, as established in Chapter 3, in some cases, hallucinatory symptoms are better explained by trauma.

The key to offering quality treatment for a single or combination of Axis I disorders is to get to know the client, his or her psychosocial context, and the role that trauma (whether large or small) played in the development of the presenting problem. If you have to provide a diagnosis for billing purposes, you should, but don't let that diagnosis be so set in stone that it muddies your clinical vision (Yalom, 2001). If we allow the diagnosis to trip us up, we abandon many of the basics that make us good clinicians, such as providing trauma-informed treatment, building a therapeutic alliance, and preparing the client well for therapy. As suggested in Part I of this book, the more severe the presentation, the more advanced the preparation and stabilization is required to be before any trauma processing work with EMDR can commence.

Recall the case of Judy in Chapter 5. Even with severe bipolar disorder in addition to PTSD, she was able to benefit from EMDR because careful attention was paid to stabilization. The following cases help illustrate how EMDR can be used with clients presenting with trauma-related Axis I disorders.

The Case of Marta (Part II)

Marta, an African American woman whose case was introduced in Chapter 5, had spent most of her adult life in the community mental health system seeking relief. Although exact diagnoses could not be agreed upon (Marta had been diagnosed with everything from undifferentiated schizophrenia to bipolar disorder with psychotic features, to PTSD), Marta had been stable for several years on a combination of psychotropic medications. Moreover, she identified that her visual psychosis symptoms (which she called "the ghost") tended to arise when she was most stressed. Using a series of stress management exercises, both general and with bilateral stimulation (see Chapter 5), Marta reported that the frequency of her "ghost" decreased to almost nothing. As she continued to work on trauma processing with EMDR, she continued to report that her "ghost" no longer had a reason to appear and torture her.

The Case of Jim

Like Marta, Jim (introduced in Chapter 3) spent most of his adult life in and out of community mental health and addiction treatment facilities for comorbid cocaine addiction and psychotic symptoms. He had been virtually unresponsive to most antipsychotic medications. Jim was able to establish almost a year of sobriety through active involvement in N.A. but still struggled with dehabilitating mental health symptoms. His primary therapist, a trauma-sensitive clinician trained in EMDR, wisely began to explore the origin of Jim's mixed hallucinations. Over the years, Jim told providers that the voices were telling him to hurt himself, but it was not until he talked to the new therapist that he made the connection that the voices and images were really his abusive parents. Although Jim never elected to do full-scale trauma processing with EMDR, several resource development exercises using bilateral stimulation proved to be extremely helpful in keeping the intensity of the voice and images at a manageably low level.

During the session that ended up being a turning point in his treatment, Jim identified the imagined experience of "being up on the clouds" as a safe place for him, where the voices were relatively quiet. Jim's therapist set this up as a standard safe place-style guided imagery, and when she realized that Jim "being up in the clouds" was removed from the voices down on the ground, she invited him to "go higher" in the imagery, enhancing with bilateral stimulation. The higher that Jim moved, the quieter the voices became, and he continued to use this strategy whenever the voices became problematic.

At last report, Jim had over four years of sobriety, his mental health symptoms were described as manageable, and overall global functioning was high.

Tips from the Trenches on Working with Axis I Disorders

Jim and Marta's cases both demonstrate that with some careful preparation, EMDR and related techniques can produce great results, even for some of our most difficult clients, clients who at one time were thought to be inappropriate for EMDR. As you can see, the *preparation, preparation, preparation* logic that has run through this book is emphasized here as well. The following are some practical suggestions, both general and specific, for using EMDR with Axis I presentations:

- General recommendation: Can the client maintain dual awareness between past and present? In other words, if you do a safe place exercise with the client or set up a target on a past memory, will the client know that he or she is still in your office and not *really* going there? Dual awareness is essential for the most effective, safest EMDR.

- General recommendation: Use the RDI exercises as a litmus test to see how a client will handle the use of bilateral stimulation. I have consistently found that if a client gets freaked out by bilateral stimulation during a simple safe place or light stream, EMDR will probably not be the treatment of choice for him or her. The exception would be if you stabilized the client using other psychotherapeutic approaches. If he or she seems to gain more stability, you can try the EMDR again (see The Case of Ciara).

- General recommendation: The period when a client and the psychiatrist are experimenting to try to find the right combination of meds is not the best time to do any kind of trauma processing work. However, some stabilization/preparation-oriented exercises with or without bilateral stimulation could be appropriate during this time. For more on the interaction between psychotropic medications and EMDR treatment, see "Medications and EMDR."

- General recommendation: Use Maslow 101 logic. If the client's basic needs are not being met (e.g., food, water, shelter, safety), it is not a good time to do trauma processing work. Consider working with a case manger or other community resources to ensure the client's basic needs are being met; this is part of the preparation and stabilization process.

- General recommendation: Go slowly. As stated previously, the higher the level of disturbance, the more you will need to intervene. This means more preparation and more careful attention paid when the trauma processing actually begins. It is especially important that you do not bombard clients with high levels of disturbance with too much at once. Stick to the consensus model logic (stabilization, then trauma processing, then reintegration).

- Specific recommendation for clients with eating disorders: Much of the guidance provided for working with addictions applies to eating disorders as well. Simply eradicating the core trauma will not resolve the eating disorder. Rather, a sensible behavioral plan combined with stabilization work is needed as a base. Consider getting a nutritionist involved as a collaborator in care. Then, trauma processing can be titrated into the treatment to enhance the treatment gains and help with relapse prevention.

- Specific recommendation for clients with other behavioral concerns: Once again, just dealing with the root trauma will not eliminate the problem behavior or series of behaviors. Collaborative strategies, at which Face 2 and Face 3 EMDR practitioners excel, are key. For instance, behavioral modification plans and EMDR do not have to be mutually exclusive; they can work very well in concert.

The Case of Ciara: Combining Hypnotherapy with EMDR

Ciara, a young woman from a working-class family, entered treatment in her mid-twenties to deal with chronic low-grade depression (dysthymia) that traced back to years of childhood bullying endured because of Ciara's awkward appearance, shyness, and weight. Ciara's goals for treatment were to alleviate depressive symptoms that lowered her quality of life (e.g., low energy, chronic sadness, hopelessness) and to lose approximately 50 pounds. Although Ciara seemed to make some gains by building rapport with her counselor, it was clear that CBT would not be optimal for her, as she was always "fighting" the irrational beliefs that her counselor tried to confront. Ciara was open to EMDR, but that did not go well at the onset, mainly because she did not have a healthy amount of positive material to which the negative material could link up. (See "Frontloading" in Chapter 5.)

Ciara's therapist then made the decision to try a few sessions of hypnotherapy, specifically the Rational Living Hypnotherapy protocol developed by Aldo Pucci (www.nacbt.org). Using this strategy, Ciara's therapist was able to suggest several positive, edifying beliefs while Ciara was in a state of hypnosis. Ciara was able to work on clearing out most of her negative cognitive material. While Ciara was in a state of hypnosis, the therapist also made some suggestions about healthy lifestyle strategies that she could adopt for weight loss. Following 3 sessions of hypnotherapy (which included making a self-hypnosis tape for Ciara to use at home), Ciara was willing to try the EMDR again. This time, the negative charge behind her memory and cognition targets cleared out effectively in 3 to 4 sessions. Her case was a clear example of needing to utilize another approach to therapy to frontload positive material. Once that occurred, the EMDR helped Ciara come full circle in reaching her goals by connecting the emotional work with the cognitive work. At termination, Ciara was free of depressive symptoms and had shed 30 of the 50 pounds she set out to lose.

Medications and EMDR

Do psychotropic medications get in the way of EMDR working properly? I have heard this question many times from consultees, and when I was a consultee myself, it was one of the first questions I asked. Although no formal research exists on the topic, I can share my thoughts on this issue, thoughts that have been shaped by my clinical experiences and basic neurology. EMDR can work well for people who are on psychotropic medications, as long as they do not fall into the category of central nervous system depressants. Obviously, illegal drugs such as marijuana would fall into this category, as would the legal (but often abused) alcohol and opiate pain medications. In the psychotropic realm, benzodiazepines (e.g., Klonopin, Xanax, Valium, Librium) can be dangerous, potentially addictive medications. It becomes difficult to do successful trauma processing EMDR with someone who is on benzodiazepines, especially if he or she took the medication before the session. Although beta blockers (e.g., Inderal), drugs that are designed to reduce the effects of adrenaline and other stress hormones, are not a central nervous system depressant, they can cause similar problems. The general idea is that because EMDR accesses the emotional charge that benzodiazepines and beta blockers are trying to quell, the two will counteract each other. As one of my colleagues once said, "Trying to get someone on benzos to process is like trying to get wet wood to ignite."

There are some solutions. Several of my colleagues and I have been able to do reasonably successful EMDR with people who are still on a benzodiazepine or a beta blocker if they do not take a dose before a session. Because many of these meds are given "as needed," clients can make the decision about when to take them. You may decide to get the psychiatrist involved.

Another solution I have explored with some clients is to ask whether their long-term use of benzodiazepines has helped with their anxiety but hurt their emotional expression. Such medications were never intended to be used long term, but many clients have fallen into this trap. Ultimately, the choice is the client's, but a little education about the meds they take can go a long way, especially if therapeutic rapport is solid.

Dissociative Disorders

Dissociation is an area of such great concern to many clinicians that it deserves more than a bullet point in this chapter. Dissociation and trauma-related disorders often go hand in hand because dissociation is an extreme defense on which the mind may rely to deal with intense disturbance. The most extreme forms of dissociation, such as dissociative identity disorder (DID; formerly known as multiple personality disorder), dissociative amnesia, and dissociative fugue can be particularly baffling. However, these disorders are treatable using some of the principles covered in this book and a sense of adventure (not to mention open mindedness) on the clinician's part.

Dissociation is a part of the human experience. We've all done it, whether we realized it or not. In her outstanding book, *The Dissociative Mind*, Elizabeth Howell (2008) demystifies the phenomenon:

> The rising tide of trauma and dissociation studies has created a sea change in the way we think about psychopathology. Chronic trauma ... that occurs early in life has profound effects on personality development and can lead to the development of dissociative identity disorder (DID), other dissociative disorders, personality disorders, psychotic thinking, and a host of symptoms such as anxiety, depression, eating disorders, and substance abuse. In my view, DID is simply an extreme version of the dissociative structure of the psyche that characterizes us all. Dissociation, in a general sense, refers to the rigid separation of parts of experience, including somatic experience, consciousness, affects, perception, identity, and memory.

One of clinicians' worst fears may be that if clients who are prone to dissociation drift off during the EMDR process, they won't be able to bring them back.

The antidote to this fear: Careful preparation that includes multi-sensory grounding strategies. Visual-only strategies are rarely the best for grounding, or bringing the client back to a mindful state of awareness and reality. If you think about it critically, when we ask a client to do a safe place exercise, we are asking him or her to dissociate! Clearly, dissociation can be an inherently positive self-soothing mechanism. Case in point---how many of you have ever daydream or "drifted off" to cope with a particularly boring continuing education presentation or tedious meeting? Like many other self-soothing mechanisms, when it is utilized to an excessive degree and impairs functioning, it can be problematic.

Hence, the stabilization phase for a client who is prone to dehabilitating dissociation takes on even more importance. Learning more about whether a client is prone to zoning out is an important part of this preparation, and tools like the Dissociative Experiences Scale (DES) can be incorporated as a screening device. Such tools (see www.neurotransmitter.net/dissociationscales.html) allow the clinician to get a sense of which emotional areas are most likely to trigger a dissociative response. This data can make it easier to ensure that EMDR work, both preparatory and early trauma processing, begins in a less vulnerable area and thus eases clients into the process.

Stabilization is also a critical period for determining which coping strategies or bilateral techniques will work best to keep the client in a place of dual awareness. For some clients, grounding exercises in which they envision their feet rooted into the earth like trees are very effective. Add the multisensory component by inviting the client to press his or her feet into the ground and feel that sensation. Consider having the client give a cue word to this experience, and enhance it with some short sets of bilateral stimulation. You may find that other experiences, such as smelling a specific scent, feeling a certain tactile sensation (e.g., like wool, cotton, rubber), listening to a certain piece of music, or tasting a certain candy may make the client feel present, alert, and aware. Use the stabilization period to experiment and find out what works. Then, if dissociation happens during EMDR trauma processing and it becomes imperative to bring a client back to the here and now, you will have a strategy or group of strategies in place. Another matter related to dissociation during EMDR is determining which form of bilateral stimulation works best. Some maintain that having a client close his or her eyes promotes dissociation, so tactile or audio stimulation with closed eyes should be avoided and the original eye movements should be used. Other clinicians maintain that the audio stimulation seems to work best at keeping the client present (and I have experienced this to be true for the most part). The bottom line, which has been my anthem throughout this book, is that there's no singular, correct answer for every client. Use the preparation period to find out which modality of stimulation is going to work the best for the client and minimize the chances of dissociation.

If you have completed all of the necessary preparations, begin EMDR processing, and the client begins to dissociate, don't panic. In fact, it has been my experience that many clients do a lot of processing and working through traumatic material while in a state of mild dissociation. This makes perfect sense if you consider that dissociation is a commonly incorporated defense for many clients growing up with trauma.

Interweave strategies (see Chapter 6) become important in trauma processing with a dissociative client, especially those questions or strategies that invite the client to identify what is going on in his or her body if he or she gets stuck with processing. If it becomes clear that it is time to end a session, the client wants to stop, or the dissociation is causing the client more distress than is therapeutic, use the strategies you established during preparation and help the client get regrounded in the here and now.

As a clinician, you will become increasingly more comfortable handling dissociation the less you fear it. Education about dissociation, like trauma, is becoming increasingly more important for clinicians as clients affected by it become more common. Educating yourself can go a long way. Seek peer consultation or supervision with clinicians who are routinely comfortable handling dissociation. See Box 15 for additional resources, some of which are specific to EMDR and dissociation.

Assisting with Reintegration

Reintegration with Axis I disorders takes on various forms, depending on the severity and pervasiveness of the original presenting problem. A client being treated for a depressive disorder may require a simple follow-up 3 months after treatment to ensure that gains are being maintained. Other clients who have chronic mental illness may need to be involved with professional services on a more long-term basis to manage psychotropic medications and receive case management services. Find out the client's needs and long-term goals and formulate a workable plan from there.

Some clients may be appropriate for what I like to call "spot check" EMDR—when clients have concluded the majority of treatment and are no longer coming for regular counseling services but may need occasional help. For example, an event might come up that causes distress, even though the client is still doing well overall. Doing a session or two of EMDR in these circumstances may be appropriate.

Clients may also benefit from a couple sessions of EMDR when, together with their psychiatrist, they have decided to go off of their medications. This varies from client to client: Some are on psychotropics for a short time, and others are on them long term (or even permanently). Coming off of an antidepressant can be an emotional adjustment, especially if the emotional work that one did in therapy (with or without EMDR) was completed while the client was on the medication. Sometimes, untapped emotional material reveals itself in these situations, and EMDR can assist in clearing some of this out. This spot-check process can be smooth and effective if the client did EMDR as part of Stage 2 trauma processing work. Following is an example of a scenario that may apply to your practice:

> **Situation:** Going off an antidepressant medication
>
> **Image/Worst part:** Fear of what might happen without the medication

Negative cognition: "I am weak"

Preferred/Positive cognition to work toward: "I am capable"
(Get a VoC level if desired)

Emotions: Fear, worry

SUDs: 4

Body sensations: Heart, forehead

"Go with that."

Box 15. Resources on Special Axis I Scenarios and Dissociation.

Braddock, D. H. (2001). *The dissociative identity disorder sourcebook*. New York: McGraw Hill.

Forgash, C., & Copeley, M. (2008). *Healing the heart of trauma and dissociation with EMDR and ego state therapy*. New York: Springer Publishing.

Howell, E. (2008). *The dissociative mind*. New York: Routledge.

Manfield, P. (2003). *EMDR casebook: Expanded second edition*. New York: W. W. Norton & Company.

Shapiro, R. (2005). *EMDR solutions: Pathways to healing*. New York: W. W. Norton & Company.

Shapiro, R. (2009) *EMDR solutions II: For depression, eating disorders, performance, & more*. New York: W. W. Norton & Company.

Chapter 11: Grief, Loss, and Spiritual Concerns

> *"That whole Kubler-Ross thing? The separate stages of Denial, Anger, Bargaining, Dorothy and Toto, or whatever? TOTAL CRAP. What you get when someone dies is all those feelings ALL AT ONCE, warping and spinning around like grief's bad trip."*
>
> —Lily Burana (I Love a *Man* in Uniform)

When we think of grief, we typically think of death. But the reality is that grief, the broad range of feelings and behaviors that follow a loss (Worden, 2002), can result subsequent to any significant loss. Loss of a job, loss of a pet, loss of a relationship—any of these can lead to grief reactions. There has been no shortage of scholars who have weighed in on death and dying, grief and loss. Many have tried to describe these experiences in stages and models, attempting to distinguish between what constitutes *normal* grief and *pathological* grief. As author Lily Burana expressed in the quote that opens this chapter, grief is an experience that cannot be neatly categorized. What is clear is that the *warping* and *spinning* to which she refers can leave an indelible imprint on a person if left unexpressed or unresolved. This chapter explores grief, loss, and the spiritual concerns that often accompany them and presents tips on how to use EMDR in helping a person with resolution.

Better Understanding Grief, Loss, and Spiritual Concerns

There are numerous published works that elucidate the phenomena of grief, loss, and spirituality. This section examines how these constructs can be understood using what we know about trauma. Like trauma, a *loss* is a wound, a puncture, a removal that often takes a person by surprise. *Grief* is the process that ensues after a person has been wounded with a loss. Grief is the healing of the loss wound. Consider what Chapter 3 said about trauma: Some people heal more quickly and more healthfully than others, depending on the context of the original wounding and the conditions that exist for healing following the wounding. In Chapter 3, we looked at two soccer players who got injured in the same game. Rhonda was not given the proper time and conditions with which to heal and kept exposing herself to reinjury. It can be similar with loss and grief: They must flow naturally for the loss to heal. Too many times, people, especially young children, are taught to just deal with a loss, or "suck it up." This often happens after a death, and it is even more commonly stated in response to losses that seem insignificant to others but feel like the end of the world to the affected person (similar to small "t" trauma). For instance, think about a child who loses his favorite teddy bear. Sure, this would not be a major trauma that warrants a PTSD diagnosis, but consider what such loss *means* to that child. When people get the message that they must suck it up, they are never given the space, time, and emotional outlets they need to heal, and grief is repressed and stifled. So where does it all go?

A concept from the grief literature that closely parallels what we know about trauma is that of *masked grief*. First proposed by Helene Deutsch, one of Freud's colleagues, masked grief refers to the experience of maladaptive or problematic psychological symptoms that can be traced back to unresolved grief. Unexplained physical symptoms can also be attributed to a masked grief reaction (Worden, 2002). Asking the right questions in a sensitive manner is one of the first steps in determining if a person's disturbances or symptoms might have a connection to unresolved grief. If a connection exists, using trauma-sensitive approaches to treatment, which can include EMDR, could be beneficial in the facilitation of healing.

Sometimes unresolved or masked grief is accompanied by spiritual confusion. You may have heard clients say something like, "I'm so mad a God for taking him," or, "If there really was a God, how could he let my child die?" Often, these comments come from people who had some level of spiritual connection and sometimes even a deep sense of spirituality. Problems with spiritual connection sometimes accompany grief reactions. Other times, experiences earlier in life make it difficult for a person who wants to connect with something greater than himself or herself to tap into anything spiritual. The following case studies illustrate some of these issues.

The Case of Danyell

Danyell, a Caucasian, middle class woman in her late thirties who had struggled with the residual effects of complex PTSD since she was a child, openly talked about her dysfunctional upbringing. She had no doubt that this upbringing, which included multiple episodes of sexual abuse, scarred her for life. Despite her professional success, Danyell had been in and out of counseling since her late teens and had been unable to establish herself as a thriving woman with good interpersonal boundaries. Danyell's mother had a severe heroin addiction and other psychological issues. She often put Danyell into precarious situations with men that led to Danyell having sexual activity forced on her.

Danyell's father was a member of an extreme Evangelical religious sect. He made her go to private Christian school, and when she heard messages demonizing sex, she automatically believed that she was a demon because of the sexual activity that had been forced on her. Danyell was spiritually abused by her father and his group of ministers, who threatened the wrath of God on her if she didn't "act the right way." Throughout her upbringing, Danyell felt that God was only a punishing God who was out to get her for being a "bad girl."

In her most recent episode of therapy with an EMDR clinician, Danyell agreed that she needed to let go of baggage from the past but also knew that she had nowhere to "let it go to." Danyell struggled with the concept of God, yet felt that she had a sense of spirituality, a vital need to connect with the greater universe. Through the use of EMDR preparation activities that began with a light stream exercise, Danyell was able to develop a concept of a higher power that worked for her throughout her EMDR treatment.

As Danyell progressed into the trauma processing phase of EMDR treatment, she identified many of the negative cognitions that blocked her progress toward being spiritual; namely, "I am a bad girl in God's eyes" and "I deserve only bad things." One of the preferred cognitions that she decided to work toward was, "I am full of light." To do this, Danyell had to process several traumatic memories connected to experiences at her school, including an episode of sexual assault by another student that happened on school grounds.

The Case of Becky (Marich, 2009b)

The experience of loss and grief can be a turning point in a person's perception of how God works. Consider Becky, whose mother died of cancer following a long bout with the illness when Becky was 6 years old. From as early as Becky could remember, her mother was always going to the hospital and coming back. Many times, Becky would accompany her mother and father on such trips to the hospital. One day, Becky's mother didn't come back from the hospital, and Becky's father shared the news of her mother's death in a very awkward manner. Shortly thereafter, Becky's father remarried in an attempt to give Becky and her sister a mother figure. All the while, Becky was left confused, feeling somehow that the death was her fault, and unsure about what God had to do with all of this.

Becky's grief remained unprocessed for years. As a young person Becky began experimenting with drugs and alcohol, and by her early twenties, she was a full-blown heroin addict. Fortunately, Becky was able to enter long-term treatment in her mid-twenties following some legal consequences. At the facility, Becky was able to do EMDR as part of a comprehensive treatment plan for her addiction recovery. Three years after she established initial sobriety, Becky reflected on her experiences with EMDR and the role it played in helping her process her unresolved grief:

Before treatment I was resistant to talk about my mother's death; I was in denial about my mother's death for many years, despite being haunted by it. Through EMDR, I realized that her death was not the end of the world, and that I did not have to drink or use because of it. I also saw that my mother is now in a better place and did not choose to abandon me.

Clearly, a plethora of issues can surround an experience of loss under ordinary circumstances, but imagine trying to consolidate the experience Becky had at such a vulnerable age. The impact of the loss and unresolved grief on a client's developmental process is one of many issues that must be considered when conceptualizing such a case for EMDR treatment.

Tips from the Trenches on Using EMDR with Grief, Loss, and Spiritual Concerns

Like with many of the special populations that have been discussed in this book, the more that you know about the issue constituting the "special population" distinction, the more comfortable you ought to be with the EMDR. As a clinician, working with grief and spirituality were two issues that I readily addressed before my training in EMDR, so I found the incorporation of EMDR to be very elegant. It is likely that before delving into these areas too deeply with EMDR, especially with the intensity that EMDR can produce, you may want to do a serious check on yourself and make sure that you have done your own work on these issues. Moreover, it is critical to respect the construct of *meaning*. In other words, a client's conception of God or a Higher Power may be totally different than yours, and if you are willing to respect what God or Higher Power means to a client without reframing it through your own judgment, you will be optimizing the effectiveness of your work.

Here are some other critical strategies to consider:

- Keep in mind everything you have learned about developmental milestones when assessing the impact of unresolved grief, loss, and spiritual concerns. In the addiction field, it has often been said that a person's maturity halts or slows at the age at which he or she regularly began using drugs. I have observed a similar parallel with unresolved grief cases. Consider Becky's case. Her loss happened at age 6, and in many ways, Becky stayed stuck at that place emotionally until the grief was processed (e.g., took everything that happened to her personally, became very demanding when she didn't get her way).

- In working with complicated grieving, it is important to assess whether the client feels responsible for a death or disaster. If so, this self-blame is generally the best target with which to begin processing (see The Case of Christopher).

- It is very important to consider what message the client took from the loss experience or the dysfunctional spiritual experience. For instance, in Danyell's case, it was, "I'm a bad in God's eyes." A variety of negative belief messages can result from loss, including, "God must be punishing me for taking her away," "It's my fault that he died," or, "I should have done something to keep him from dying." If you can find out in assessment what the negative message is, you can build your EMDR setup quite effectively around that maladaptive cognition.

- I have found that working with grief, loss, and spiritual issues (either related or unrelated to grief) is similar to the conceptualization of trauma given at the beginning of this chapter. How you use EMDR preparation and setup with more standard traumas applies elegantly in these scenarios. Just as trauma varies in its degree and impact, depending on its nature and the person experiencing it, so too can loss and the grief that follows it. The material covered in the foundations section of this book applies here as well.

- In some cases of working with spiritual issues, it is not as obvious that a loss has occurred, such as in Danyell's case. Yet when issues that seem to be related to grief emerge, it is helpful to explore with the client whether a loss has occurred. For instance, Danyell was grieving over her lost childhood and the loss of the God that she once thought existed.

The Case of Christopher

"I Should Have Done Something"

Christopher was referred to counseling services, specifically for EMDR, due to suspected PTSD. He worked as an EMT/firefighter for almost 30 years and reported that approximately 5 years before presenting for treatment, he began going numb on the job and just stopped caring. Moreover, images of physical trauma patients whom he had treated in the field were seared in his memory, causing him to live in a near chronic state of anxiety while working.

When he came to treatment, Christopher had been placed him on a 3-month leave of absence from work due to the chronic anxiety. Using the Problem Severity Rating Scale (which operates on a scale of 0–10 like a SUDs reading), Christopher rated his struggles with grief and loss at a 10. After further assessment, Christopher met criteria for a formal PTSD diagnosis and was willing to proceed with EMDR.

Because Christopher was unable to pinpoint a single incident, memory, or issue, his therapist gave him a variation on the "Greatest Hits List of Problematic Beliefs" (see Chapter 6), and Christopher checked off several items. When the therapist asked him to go back and rank the top three, Christopher revealed that his overwhelming negative belief was, "I should have done something." On further assessment, it was clear that this belief related to many people he had helped over the years, but he recalled that it became more prominent about 6 years prior. At that time, Christopher's mother dropped to the floor and became unconscious at a family party, and Christopher was unable to resuscitate her using CPR. To make matters worse, all of his family members were looking on. It was later determined that his mother, who was in poor health, had a heart attack. Doctors stated that it was been miracle that she survived as long as she had, considering the extent of blockage found in her arteries.

Another complication of Christopher's grieving was the unhealthy relationship he had with his mother over the years. A demanding woman, she always accused Christopher of being lazy and not doing enough, and his belief that he didn't do enough to save her life further solidified the years of small "t" traumas from his mother's criticism.

Christopher responded well to EMDR with tactile stimulation. To clear out his blaming belief about his mother's death, he first had to process the earlier material. Once he did this, he was able to cry about her death and emerge from the processing believing he had done all he could. This shift in responsibility generalized to his work in the field. Within weeks after completing this major section of EMDR, Christopher was able to return to work.

At a follow-up session 18 months later, Christopher was asked to fill out the Problem Severity Rating Scale once again. Although he had a new set of life struggles surrounding his own physical health and his marriage, causing some items on the scale to be rated high, his rating on the grief and loss scale was a 0.

Assisting with Reintegration

Like with many of the special conditions discussed in this book, the purpose of reintegration for the clients with issues of grief, loss, and spiritual concerns is to help them transition into living their lives without the burden. For clients struggling with unresolved grief and spiritual issues, that burden often comes in the form of guilt, but they may also feel sadness, loneliness, terror, anger, or other emotions. An emotional burden is like a heavy backpack filled with rocks and other items, all of which weigh a person down, but when someone has been living with such a burden for months, years, or even decades, as painful and as bothersome as it may be, he or she may find some way, even if it's maladaptive, to carry that weight a long time (with credit to John Lennon and Paul McCartney for the song lyric).

When a client has managed to get rid of the burden through EMDR or some other process, it's fabulous. In fact, it's probably one of the most freeing feelings anyone could ever experience. You've probably been in sessions where a client has made a comment like, "I feel like a big weight has lifted." Too often, we and our clients stop there and don't consider that, after carrying a weight for such a long time, it may feel incredibly weird or even uncomfortable to maneuver through life without it. If, for instance, the client has released the burden of guilt over his father's death, he can begin to live his life with the new knowledge that he is a good person. But imagine how hard that would be if the people in his life had grown so used to his negative self-image that they took advantage of his low self-esteem. His new outlook on life could change the whole family dynamic. How does the client adapt to these new adjustments in living?

These adjustments and adaptations are not necessarily bad, but they may feel strange and new. The care and concern of a therapist who helped a client release the burden can be an invaluable asset to help him or her reintegrate into ordinary life. Simply being there to help the client answer, "What now?" or "How do I handle this person?"

is an important part of the overall therapy. Often, a key element of reintegration is helping a client who has released the grief burden cope when others in his or her life continue to carry that burden, or worse, try to put it back on the client. See Box 16 for resources on grief and loss and Box 17 for readings on one aspect of spiritual issues, spiritual abuse.

The Case of Yuka

Consider Yuka, a teenager of Japanese descent who lost her father in a tragic accident only a short time ago. Almost every day since their father's death, Yuka's brother has blamed her, saying that because she was such a bad girl, her father was stressed and thus vulnerable while he was driving on the road where the accident took place. Yuka was confused about the Buddhist spirituality of her rearing, which left her with a sense of uncertainty about the meaning of her father's death and where he was now. Because her spirituality left her with little comfort, Yuka believed her brother's accusations and began internalizing the guilt about her father's death. Although there was nothing in Yuka's history to suggest that she had done anything bad or scandalous by most people's standards, she believed that she had to live her life perfectly from this point on, which caused high levels of stress as she strived to do well in school and in all her extracurricular activities.

Through her engagement in EMDR, Yuka was able to release a great deal of the guilt, shame, anger, and fear that she experienced as the result of her father's death. Through processing, she was able to surmise that because her brother had been doing things that were

bringing shame to the family in the months before
their father's accident (e.g., legal problems, calling their
parents names on a daily basis), he could be projecting
his own guilt on to Yuka. This was a major perspective
shift that allowed the majority of Yuka's distress to clear.
However, the issue remained that Yuka still lived with
her brother and had to endure his heartless comments.

Yuka could not bring herself to stand up to her brother,
who was now the head of the household. However, she
found that the intensity of his comments seemed to
diminish and bother her less as time went on. Through
reintegration work (or Phase 8, re-evaluation), Yuka
was able to revisit some of the positive resources she
developed during preparation/stabilization to keep the
negativity away when it challenged her. For instance, she
was able to picture a healing purple light shielding her
and keepingout negative sounds or insults when she
needed it. Moreover, she felt that the EMDR process
helped her tune into one of the spiritual figures of
her childhood, whose presence she was able to sense
whenever she felt lonely or scared.

Box 16. Resources on EMDR with Grief and Loss Issues.

Botkin, A. (2005). *Induced after-death communication: A new
therapy for healing grief and trauma.* Charlottesville,
VA: Hampton Roads Publishing Company.

Shapiro, F. (1999). *Working with Grief* [DVD Demonstration].
Zeig & Tucker Publications. Available at:
http://www.emdrhap.org/store/.

Box 17. Resources on Spiritual Abuse Issues.

Farrell, D., Dworkin, M., Keenan, P., & Spierings, J. (2010). Using EMDR with survivors of sexual abuse perpetrated by Roman Catholic priests. *Journal of EMDR Practice and Research*, 4(3), 124–133.

Johnson, D., & Vanvonderen, J. (2005). *The subtle power of spiritual abuse: Recognizing and escaping spiritual manipulation and false spiritual authority within the church*. Grand Rapids, MI: Bethany House Publishing.

Chapter 12: Other Blocks to Wellness

"In a disordered mind, as in a disordered body, soundness of health is impossible."

—Cicero

A theme I have strived to convey in this book is that if a client is emotionally stymied, EMDR may be an appropriate intervention to help release the block, thus allowing information processing to flow. The ultimate hope is that this flow will allow for optimal connectivity among the regions of the triune brain. As I have mentioned previously, my colleagues often ask me whether EMDR can help with condition X or problem Y. No doubt, these questions have emerged from their own frustrations with attempting to treat condition X or problem Y; especially when traditional, talk interventions have been inadequate.

This chapter describes the use of EMDR with other conditions that sometimes contribute to a client being blocked in his or her progress toward wellness. These conditions include chronic pain, somatization, phobias, lifestyle choices, and performance enhancement issues. These issues are not included as an afterthought. However, they are not easily categorized into some of the other chapters of this book, and their treatment, especially with complex clients, continues to baffle many clinicians.

Understanding Problems Through a Trauma-Sensitive Lens

The issues addressed in this chapter can be conceptualized using the description of *trauma as wound* presented in Chapter 3. Chronic pain and somatization would be most likely to be traced back to large "T" traumas. Phobias are the ultimate grey area that may be related to small "t" or large "T" traumas, and most issues of lifestyle dilemma and performance enhancement I have treated result from small "t" trauma (with some exceptions, of course). Most of the published research in treating these conditions appears in the form of case studies, and there are some excellent articles on phobias (DeJongh & ten Broeke, 1998; DeJongh, van den Oord, & ten Broeke, 2002; Schurmans, 2007). For more resources, see Box 18. As I noted earlier, a full EMDR bibliography is available to the general public through the online Francine Shapiro Library at http://emdr.nku.edu/emdr.php. If you find yourself stumped with conceptualizing a specialty presentation and would like to read what others have done, the library is an excellent resource.

Box 18. Resources on Other Issues and EMDR.

Broad, R. D., & Wheeler, K. (2006). An adult with childhood medical trauma treated with psychoanalytic psychotherapy and EMDR: A case study. *Perspectives in Psychiatric Care, 42*(2), 95–108.

deGraffenried, D. (2007). EMDR and temporary assistance to needy families (TANF) recipients: A case study of trauma treatment in the home. *EMDRIA Newsletter, 12*(1), 6–9.

DeJongh, A., & ten Broeke, E. (1998). Treatment of choking phobia by targeting traumatic memories with EMDR: A case study. *Clinical Psychology and Psychotherapy, 5*, 264–269.

DeJongh, A., van den Oord, H. J. M., & ten Broeke, E. (2002). Efficacy of eye movement desensitization and reprocessing in the treatment of specific phobias: Four single case studies on dental phobia. *Journal of Clinical Psychology*, 58, 1489–1503.

Foster, S., & Lendl, J. (1996). Eye movement desensitization and reprocessing: Four case studies of a new tool for executive coaching and restoring employee performance after setbacks. *Consulting Psychology Journal: Practice & Research*, 48(3), 155–161.

Grant, M. (2009). *Change your brain, change your pain*. Wyong, NSW, Australia: Mark Grant.

Grant, M. *Overcoming pain*. Accessed June 12, 2010 at http://overcomingpain.com.

Grant, M., & Threlfo, C. (2002). EMDR in the treatment of chronic pain. *Journal of Clinical Psychology*, 58(12), 1505–1520.

Keenan, P. S., & Farrell, D. P. (2000). Treating morbid jealousy with eye movement desensitization and reprocessing utilizing a cognitive-interweave—a case report. *Counselling Psychology Quarterly*, 13(2), 175–189.

Manfield, P. (2003). *EMDR casebook: Expanded second edition*. New York: W. W. Norton & Company.

McGoldrick, T., Begum, M., & Brown, K. W. (2008). EMDR and olfactory reference syndrome: A case series. *Journal of EMDR Practice and Research*, 2(1), 63–68.

Miller, A. (2005). *The body never lies: The lingering effects of hurtful parenting*. New York: W. W. Norton & Company.

Rothschild, B. (2000). *The body remembers: The psychophysiology of trauma treatment.* New York: W. W. Norton & Company.

Schurmans, K. (2007). EMDR treatment of choking phobia. *Journal of EMDR Practice & Research, 1*(2), 118–121.

Shapiro, R. (2005). *EMDR solutions: Pathways to healing.* New York: W. W. Norton & Company.

Shapiro, R. (2009) *EMDR solutions II: For depression, eating disorders, performance, & more.* New York: W. W. Norton & Company.

This section does not explain each issue in great detail; however, each area is covered in the following Tips from the Trenches section. My challenge for you is to consider these separate problems and think of how you would conceptualize each using EMDR. When you explore the origin of any of these conditions, you can typically trace its maladaptiveness back to one of the negative cognitions listed as examples in Chapter 6. Using the floatback question, you can get a sense of when the first memory associated with that negative cognition occurred.

For phobias and performance enhancement issues, it is wise to get a sense of when the worst and/or most recent memories associated with that negative message happened. On questioning, if you get a sense that those are more relevant to the maladaptive behavior than the first memory, it is wise to include this hot-button area in your processing. In the traditional phobia protocol that I was taught, I was advised to process the first, the worst, the most recent, any ancillary events related to the phobia, any present stimuli, or any other physical sensations/signs of fear (Shapiro, 2006). I have found using all six to be superfluous. With phobias, performance enhancement, and the other conditions named in this chapter, as long as you can identify and accordingly target the first, the worst, the most recent, and set up a future template (massively critical in performance enhancement as well), you will be on your way to helping the client through the block. Often, a traditional setup is all you need with clearing out the antecedent memories connected to the phobia or performance block. Remember the basic structure that Parnell (2007) recommended for EMDR sessions, and you have a good blueprint for maneuvering any scenario that may come your way in EMDR:

1.)   Create safety.
2.)   Stimulate the traumatic neural network.
3.)   Add alternating bilateral stimulation.
4.)   End with safety.

As I have cautioned throughout the book, make sure to prepare the client carefully, because even with the complicated scenarios discussed in this chapter, EMDR can go well as long as adequate preparation has occurred. The following cases illustrate how EMDR can work with identity and lifestyle issues (The Case of Connor) and social phobia (The Case of Abbi).

The Case of Connor

Connor was an 18-year-old white man who grew up in a middle-class section of an affluent community. He presented for treatment because he was struggling with several identity and lifestyle issues; namely, how to attain a fulfilling romantic relationship. Connor recognized that that he struggled with having a "big ego" yet also admitted to disliking many things about himself, such as his "gut"

(NOTE: Connor was slightly overweight at the time of presentation). Connor recently graduated from high school and had been successful in many of his school activities, yet he always believed he was capable of performing better. He found himself in a deep depression after a girl in whom he was interested gave him mixed messages and, ultimately, rejected him. Connor had wanted to examine his issues for some time but grew especially concerned when, following the girl's rejection, he punched a wall and almost broke his hand.

Connor identified that the main negative message he heard when the girl rejected him was, "I'm a no-good piece of shit." Interestingly, some of the reasons the girl had rejected Connor existed long before she met him, including the fact that her conservative family pressured her not to date. Connor was unable to see that evidence.

Using a series of floatback questions, he traced the negative message, "I'm a no-good piece of shit" back to two instances that occurred roughly around the same time. The first was when he was in elementary school and didn't have many friends, and the second was when his parents made fun of him for being unpopular. When Connor was asked which issue had the most negative charge, it was clearly the incident with his parents, so active processing commenced with that target. Through processing, Connor was able to identify that this internalized negative message was a primary reason for his failure in prior romantic relationships. Furthermore, he was able to take responsibility for treating other girlfriends badly to meet his own ego needs.

The Case of Abbi

Abbi, a young, multiracial mother in her twenties, presented for treatment due to social phobia. After going through the standard EMDR preparation, Abbi was willing to begin processing the earliest memories she recalled of being afraid of people. Following a floatback question, she was able to remember times during her preschool years when she hid under tables whenever guests came into the room, and she noted that big parties or events filled her with terror.

When Abbi processed these early memories, she was able to tune into a memory from later in her school days (approximately fifth grade) when she performed in a school play in front of many people. She reported that she forgot how confident she had been. The therapist installed the positive feelings and beliefs that she remembered from that time.

Over the next several sessions, although Abbi reported feeling "better," she was still troubled by going out in public, which was connected to the negative cognition, "I am not in control." On further exploration, Abbi revealed that this same cognition described how she felt with several addicted members of her family with whom she was currently acting as an enabler. When those recent memories and distresses were finally cleared out, Abbi was able to integrate the social phobia processing that emerged from her past and ultimately take strides to interact more with the public. A simple task such as going to the grocery store used to terrify Abbi, and although at the termination of treatment it still wasn't her favorite activity, she found it more bearable.

Tips from the Trenches on Using EMDR with Other Issues

The following sections offer syntheses of how I have successfully used EMDR with various presentations. My hope is that you, as the reader, will make connections between the logic I'm offering in this list and the general principles that I've covered throughout the book:

- People with somatization conditions or other bodily manifestations of trauma (e.g., unexplained migraines or gastrointestinal difficulties) require a healthy amount of preparation to orient them to the process of listening to their bodies. Honoring body cues and "going with them" are a big part of EMDR. The bodily aspect of EMDR is extremely important in helping people with these problems process the antecedent traumas that may be causing the physical pain. However, if a person is shut off and disconnected from listening to what his or her body is trying to say, he or she is unlikely to suddenly start doing it once you start EMDR. Simple body cuing exercises (e.g., asking "When you see your mother-in-law's face, what happens in your body?") are help ful, as is assisting the client to identify a body sensation to accompany his or her existent or emerging emotional vocabulary (e.g., sadness equals empty pit in stomach; anger equals fireball in heart). After the client is comfortable with cuing, consider using preparation exercises such as light stream or breathing techniques to teach the client to self-soothe in a healthy way.

  Body cuing may be a very difficult task for the highly traumatized. As I advised in Chapter 5, start slowly. You may need to do rudimentary sensory activities with the client in the initial sessions, such as having the client hold an object or smell a scent and inviting him or her to try describing it. Mindfulness strategies are also incredibly helpful.

- Chronic pain work with EMDR can be multidimensional. If the pain has a clear connection to a trauma, significant relief may result if the case is properly conceptualized. More often than not, most of the pain work that I do with EMDR is when the client is experiencing organic pain that is connected to a trauma (e.g., a man's leg and back cause him significant and daily pain after he has fallen from a 30-foot billboard at work). As I explain to clients, EMDR cannot eliminate any pain that is organic, but it may be able to take some of the edge off psychological pain. Presenting treatment in a realistic fashion typically works well. Sometimes doing basic work on trauma can have an effect on pain; other times, directly targeting the experience of the pain as you would a traumatic memory is more effective (e.g., the SUDs level is the pain level, the body sensation is the experience of the pain, the image or worst part is how the client sees the injury in his or her body). For more on EMDR with chronic pain, I highly recommend work by Mark Grant (see Box 18).

- Don't let phobia work trip you up. Remember, a phobia is an anxiety disorder just like PTSD and can be conceptualized in a way that is similar to how you would handle a standard PTSD case. As explained in the previous section, a few extra dimensions of processing may be necessary.

- For phobias, performance enhancement issues, and other hang ups, it is important to keep Shapiro's (2001) "three prongs" in mind: Clear out: *past* disturbance, then work on improving *present* and *future* functioning. Once you clear out the original Large-"T" or small-"t" traumas (which could be anything from a near-fatal spider bite to tripping and falling on the ice during the last moments of your free skating program at the 2001 Eastern Great Lakes Regional finals), it is important to follow through with installation of the positive/preferred cognition to create a sense of empowerment in the present. Then, make liberal use of future templates.

EMDR with the Developmentally Disabled

Research on using EMDR with developmentally disabled clients is forthcoming from a team in New England that is currently working on a project that looks to be very exciting. Of course, people with developmental disabilities are not immune to the realities of trauma, and over the years, many have asserted that EMDR can work with this population as long as appropriate adjustments are made in language and style to accommodate the individual. In fact, the EMDRIA definition (2009) allows for modifications to the language of the protocol in phases 3 through 6 to accommodate those with developmental difficulties.

This is not one of my areas of expertise, which is why I do not personally do EMDR with this population. However, if you are comfortable working with developmental disabilities and are used to modifying your language and approach, I encourage you to apply EMDR as you see appropriate. Remember all of the fundamentals of the therapeutic relationship covered in Chapter 4; always keep the therapeutic relationship in the front seat. If you can do that with this or any other specialty population, your journey on the road to wellness using EMDR as your guide ought to be fruitful.

Chapter 12: Other Blocks to Wellness

Assisting with Reintegration

The future template is one of the most ingenious features of EMDR, for it is designed to help a client apply all that he or she has learned from processing and installation to life in the outside world. Future templates can be used with any special population to assist with reintegration. I have chosen to give them some special attention here because their use seems to be critically important when dealing with phobias and performance enhancement issues. It is important for the client to envision himself or herself in an empowered state and to use the healing bilateral stimulation process to help enhance that feeling.

With future templates, residual traumatic material that was not directly elucidated during the primary processing may emerge. In the work that I've done with future templates, having these last few shreds of material come up when a positive self-image has already been achieved leads to even more effective, integrative processing.

In the traditional, eight-phase Shapiro model (2001), future templates best fit into the reevaluation phase (Phase 8). Using the logic of the consensus model that I have favored throughout the book, future templates can be incorporated into Stage 2 trauma processing work and then implemented as a bridge into Stage 3 reintegration work. The consensus model stages are not set in stone; they are meant to be a general guide. We are helping many of our clients to reintegrate into their lives as we are doing the preparation and trauma work. Just like resource development and installation work can help with the process, so too can future templates.

Let's take a look at how Connor's therapist worked a future template into his treatment. Connor was able to process the past material connected to his negative message, "I'm a worthless piece of shit," to a more positive self-image defined by, "I am good enough." Connor was concerned about seeing the girl who rejected him, and the following setup was used:

> **Situation**: Seeing the girl who rejected me at a graduation party

Image/Worst part: Her pretty face with a rejecting scowl on it

Positive message: "I am good enough."

"Go with that."

In Connor's case, more material came up that needed to be processed when he worked on this future template, but it ultimately led him back to a stronger sense of "I am good enough." Chapter 8 included examples of how you can set up a future template on addictions, Chapter 9 included examples on violent and acting out behaviors, and Chapter 10 included examples on other Axis I disorders. My overwhelming belief is that with future templates (just like with trauma processing), there is no right or wrong way to set it up as long as you're adhering to the four basic elements of an EMDR protocol that Parnell (2007) presented.

A Final Note

This book does not contain all of the answers—far from it. I have strived to present streamlined, simplified solutions for working with some of the client presentations that are prone to baffle us the most. If you feel that you need to read further on a certain area to enhance your competency before attempting EMDR with an especially tricky presentation, you should. Always keep educating yourself: That is the key to doing well with EMDR and with the populations discussed in the book. However, keep in mind that education does not always come in the form of books, articles, or continuing education workshops. As Barry Duncan, Mark Hubble, and Scott Miller (1997) boldly asserted in their book *Psychotherapy with "Impossible" Cases: The Efficient Treatment of Therapy Veterans*, our clients are our best teachers. **Listen to their feedback about whether a certain approach you are trying with EMDR is working, and be willing to adapt.** Flexibility and adaptability are, without a doubt, two of the most important traits you can have when working with any clients.

References

Abel, N.J., & O'Brien, J.M. (2010). EMDR treatment of comorbid PTSD and alcohol dependence: A case example. *Journal of EMDR Practice and Research*, 4(2), 50-59.

Adler, A. (1931). What life could mean to you. In Stein, H.T. (Ed.), *The collected works of Alfred Adler*. Vol. 6. Bellingham, WA: The Alfred Adler Institute of Northwestern Washington.

Alexie, S. (1992). *The business of fancydancing: Stories and poems.* New York: Hanging Loose Press.

Alexie, S. (2009). *War dances.* New York: Grove Press.

Allsop, S., Saunders, B., & Phillips, M. (2000). The process of relapse in severely dependent male problem drinkers. *Addiction*, 95(1), 95–106.

American Psychiatric Association. (2000). D*iagnostic and statistical manual of mental disorders.* 4th ed., text revision. Washington, D. C.: American Psychiatric Association.

American Psychiatric Association. (2004). *Practice guidelines for the treatment of patients with acute stress disorder and posttraumatic stress disorder.* Arlington, VA: American Psychiatric Association.

American Psychiatric Association. (2010). *DSM-5 development.* Retrieved April 8, 2010, from http://www.dsm5.org/ ProposedRevisions/Pages/proposedrevision.aspx?rid=165.

American Psychological Association Presidential Task Force on Evidence-Based Practice. (2006). Evidence-based practice in psychology. *American Psychologist*, 61, 271–285.

Benish, S., Imel, Z., & Wampold, B. (2008). The relative efficacy of bona fide psychotherapies for treating post-traumatic stress disorder: A meta-analysis of direct comparisons. *Clinical Psychology Review*, 28(5), 746–758.

Bisson, J., & Andrew, M. (2007). Psychological treatment of post-traumatic stress disorder (PTSD). *Cochrane Database of Systematic Reviews 2007*, 3, 1–82. doi: 10.1002/ 14651858.

Borstein, S. (2009). *The effectiveness of brief adjunctive EMDR: A pilot study.* Poster presented at the annual meeting of the EMDR International Association, Atlanta, GA.

Botkin, A. (2005). *Induced after-death communication: A new therapy for healing grief and trauma.* Charlottesville, VA: Hampton Roads Publishing Company.

Braddock, D. H. (2001). *The dissociative identity disorder sourcebook.* New York: McGraw Hill.

Briere, J., & Scott, C. S. (2006). *Principles of trauma therapy: A guide to symptoms, evaluation, and treatment.* Thousand Oaks, CA: Sage Publications.

Broad, R. D., & Wheeler, K. (2006). An adult with childhood medical trauma treated with psychoanalytic psychotherapy and EMDR: A case study. *Perspectives in Psychiatric Care,* 42(2), 95–108.

Brown, S., & Gilman, S. (2007). *Utilizing an integrated trauma treatment program (ITTP) in the Thurston County Drug Court program: Enhancing outcomes by integrating an evidence-based, phase trauma treatment program for posttraumatic stress disorder, trauma, and substance abuse.* La Mesa, CA: Lifeforce Trauma Solutions.

Brown, S., & Shapiro, F. (2006). EMDR in the treatment of borderline personality disorder. *Clinical Case Studies,* 5(5), 403–420.

Burana, L. (2009). *I love a man in uniform: A memoir of love, war, and other battles.* New York: Weinstein Books.

Bureau of Justice Statistics. (2010). Bureau of Justice Statistics. *In Office of Justice Programs*. Retrieved June 6, 2010, from http://bjs.ojp.usdoj.gov/index.cfm.

Carlson, J. G., Chemtob, C. M., Rusnak, K., Hedlund, N. L., & Muraoka, M. Y. (1998). Eye movement desensitization and reprocessing (EMDR) treatment for combat-related posttraumatic stress disorder. *Journal of Traumatic Stress*, 11(1), 3–24.

Carnes, P. (1992). *Don't call it love: Recovery from sexual addiction*. New York: Bantam.

Chambless, D. L., Baker, M. J., Baucom, D. H., Beutler, L. E., Calhoun, K. S., Crits-Christoph, P., et al. (1998). Update of empirically validated therapies, II. *The Clinical Psychologist*, 51, 3–16.

Connors, G., & Maisto, S. (2006). Relapse in the addictive behaviors. *Clinical Psychology Review*, 26, 107–108.

Courtis, C. A., & Ford, J. D. (2009). *Treating complex traumatic stress disorders: An evidence-based guide*. New York: The Guilford Press.

Cox, R. P., & Howard, M. D. (2007). Utilization of EMDR in the treatment of sexual addiction: A case study. *Sexual Addiction & Compulsivity*, 14, 1–20.

Curran, L. (2010). *Trauma competency: A clinician's guide*. Eau Claire, WI: PESI.

deGraffenried, D. (2007). EMDR and temporary assistance to needy families (TANF) recipients: A case study of trauma treatment in the home. *EMDRIA Newsletter*, 12(1), 6–9.

DeJongh, A., & ten Broeke, E. (1998). Treatment of choking phobia by targeting traumatic memories with EMDR: A case study. *Clinical Psychology and Psychotherapy*, 5, 264–269.

DeJongh, A., van den Oord, H.J.M., & ten Broeke, E. (2002). Efficacy of eye movement desensitization and reprocessing in the treatment of specific phobias: Four single case studies on dental phobia. *Journal of Clinical Psychology*, 58, 1489–1503.

Delmonico, D., & Griffin, E. (2007). Problematic online sexual behavior. In M. Jarvis, L. Baxter, & J. Tanner (Eds.), *Ruth Fox course for physicians* (pp. 189–221). Miami, FL: The American Society of Addiction Medicine.

Department of Veterans Affairs & Department of Defense (2004). *VA/DoD clinical practice guidelines for the management of post-traumatic stress*. Washington, D.C.: Department of Veteran Affairs & Department of Defense.

Devilly, G. J. (2005). Power therapies and possible threats to the science of psychology and psychiatry. *Australian and New Zealand Journal of Psychiatry*, 39, 437–445.

DiGiorgio, K. E., Arnkoff, D. B., Glass, C. R., Lyhus, K. E., & Walter, R. C. (2004). EMDR and theoretical orientation: A qualitative study of how therapists integrate eye movement desensitization and reprocessing into their approach to psychotherapy. *Journal of Psychotherapy Integration*, 14(3), 227–252.

Donovan, D. (1996). Assessment issues and domains in the prediction of relapse. *Addiction, 91*, S29–S36.

Donovan, F. (Producer), & Nalepinski, B. (Director). (1999). *EMDR: Looking through hemispheres* [Documentary]. United States: Fran Donovan Productions.

Duncan, B., Hubble, M., & Miller, S. (1997). *Psychotherapy with "impossible" cases: Effective treatment of therapy veterans*. New York: W. W. Norton & Company.

Duncan, B. L., Miller, S. D., Wampold, B. E., & Hubble, M. A. (Eds.) (2009). *The heart and soul of change: Delivering what works in therapy*. 2nd ed. Washington, D. C.: American Psychological Association.

Dworkin, M. (2005). *EMDR and the relational imperative: The therapeutic relationship in EMDR treatment*. New York: Brunner-Routledge.

Edmond, T., Rubin, A., & Wambach, K. (1999). The effectiveness of EMDR with adult female survivors of childhood sexual abuse. *Social Work Research*, 23, 103–116.

Edmond, T., Sloan, L., & McCarty, D. (2004). Sexual abuse survivors' perceptions of the effectiveness of EMDR and eclectic therapy. *Research on Social Work Practice*, 14(4), 259–272.

Ehlers, A., Bisson, J., Clark, D.M., Creamer, M., Pilling, S., Richards, D., Schnurr, P., Turner, S., & Yule, W. (2010). Do all psychological treatments really work the same for post-traumatic stress disorder? *Clinical Psychology Review*, 30, 269-276.

El-Sheikh, S., & Bashir, T. (2004). High-risk relapse situations and self-efficacy: Comparison between alcoholics and heroin addicts. *Addictive Behaviors*, 29(2004), 753–758.

The EMDR Institute. (n.d.). History of EMDR. Retrieved April 17, 2010, from http://www.emdr.com/history.html.

The EMDR Institute. (n.d.). Theory: The adaptive information processing model. In *EMDR Institute, Inc.* Retrieved April 23, 2010, from http://www.emdr.com/theory.htm.

The EMDR International Association. (2009). Definition of EMDR. In *What is EMDR?* Retrieved April 18, 2010, from http://www.emdria.org/displaycommon.cfm?an=1&subarticlenbr=56.

Evans, K., & Sullivan, J. M. (1995). *Treating addicted survivors of trauma.* New York: The Guilford Press.

Farrell, D., Dworkin, M., Keenan, P., & Spierings, J. (2010). Using EMDR with survivors of sexual abuse perpetrated by Roman Catholic priests. *Journal of EMDR Practice and Research, 4*(3), 124–133.

Fletcher, A. (2001). *Sober for good: New solutions for drinking problems—advice from those who have succeeded.* New York: Houghton Mifflin.

Fletcher, K. E. (1996). Childhood posttraumatic stress disorder. In E. Mash & R. Barkley (Eds.), *Child psychopathology*, pp. 242–276. New York: Guilford Press.

Foa, E. B., Keane, T. M., & Friedman, M. J. (2000). *Effective treatments for PTSD: Practice Guidelines of the International Society for Traumatic Stress Studies.* New York: Guilford Press.

Forgash, C. & Copeley, M. (2008). *Healing the heart of trauma and dissociation with EMDR and ego state therapy.* New York: Springer Publishing.

Fosha, D. (2000). *The transforming power of affect: A model for accelerated change.* New York: Basic Books.

Fosha, D., & Slowiaczek, M. I. (1997). Techniques to accelerate dynamic psychotherapy. *American Journal of Psychotherapy, 51*(2), 229–251.

Foster, S., & Lendl, J. (1996). Eye movement desensitization and reprocessing: Four case studies of a new tool for executive coaching and restoring employee performance after setbacks. *Consulting Psychology Journal: Practice & Research, 48*(3), 155–161.

Gaunt, K. D. (2006). *The games black girls play: Learning the ropes from double-dutch to hop-hop*. New York: New York University Press.

Gelinas, D. (2003). Integrating EMDR into a phase-oriented treatment for trauma. *Journal of Trauma and Dissociation*, 4(3), 91–135.

Grand, D. (2010). *Brainspotting BSP*. Accessed April 21, 2010, from http://www.brainspotting.pro.

Granfield, R. & Cloud, W. (1999). *Coming clean: Overcoming addiction without treatment*. New York: New York University Press.

Grant, M. (2009). *Change your brain, change your pain*. Wyong, NSW, Australia: Mark Grant.

Grant, M., & Threlfo, C. (2002). EMDR in the treatment of chronic pain. *Journal of Clinical Psychology*, 58(12), 1505–1520.

Greenwald, R. (2006). The peanut butter and jelly problem: In search of a better EMDR training model. *EMDR Practitioner*. Retrieved April 7, 2008 from http://www.emdr-practitioner.net.

Greenwald, R. (2007). *EMDR within a phase model of trauma-informed treatment*. New York: The Haworth Press.

Grenough, M. (2005). *Oasis in the overwhelm: 60-second strategies for balance in a busy world*. New Haven, CT: Beaver Hill Press.

Grey, E. (2008, September). *EMDR: It's more than eye movement*. Poster presented at the annual meeting of the EMDR International Association, Phoenix, AZ

Grey, E. (2008, September). *EMDR theory exists: An explanation of neuro-physiological underpinnings.* Workshop presentation at the Annual EMDR International Association Conference, Phoenix, AZ.

Grey, E. (2010, April). *Gaining clarity ... Driving your EMDR practice with the adaptive information processing model.* Workshop presented at the annual meeting of EMDR Canada, Toronto, Ontario.

Grey, E. (n.d.). Your Brain. In *Chrysalis Mental Health and Wellness, Inc.* Retrieved April 25, 2010, from http://www.rtpgh.com/YourBrain.html.

Grey, E. (2010). *Unify your mind: Connecting the feelers, thinkers, & doers of your brain.* Pittsburgh, PA: CMH&W, Inc.

Groeschel, B. (1984). *Spiritual passages: The psychology of spiritual development.* Chestnut Ridge, NY: Crossroads Publishing Company.

GWC, Inc. (1993). *Human addiction* [DVD]. Cahookia, IL: GWC, Inc.

Haggis, P. (Director & Producer). (2007). *In the Valley of Elah.* [Motion Picture]. United States: Warner Independent Pictures.

Hase, M. (2010). CraveEx: An EMDR approach to treat substance abuse and addiction. In M. Luber (Ed.), *EMDR scripted protocols: Special populations* (pp. 467–488). New York: Springer Publishing Company.

Hase, M., Schallmayer, S., & Sack, M. (2008). EMDR reprocessing of the addiction memory: Pretreatment, posttreatment, and 1-month follow-up. *Journal of EMDR Practice and Research, 2* (3), 170–179.

Henry, S. L. (1995). Pathological gambling: Etiologic considerations and treatment efficacy of eye movement desensitization/ reprocessing. *Journal of Gambling Studies*, 12(4), 395–405.

Hensley, B. J. (2009). *An EMDR primer: From practicum to practice.* New York: Springer Publishing Company.

Herman, J. L. (1992). *Trauma and recovery.* New York: Basic Books.

Herschell, A. D., Kolko, D. J., Baumann, B. L., & Davis, A. C. (2010). The role of therapist training in implementation of psychosocial treatments: A review and critique with recommendations. *Clinical Psychology Review*, 30(2010), 448–466.

Howell, E. (2008). *The dissociative mind.* New York: Routledge.

Institute of Medicine of the National Academies. (2008). *Treatment of posttraumatic stress disorder: An assessment of the evidence.* Washington, D. C.: The National Academies Press.

Johnson, D., & Vanvonderen, J. (2005). *The subtle power of spiritual abuse: Recognizing and escaping spiritual manipulation and false spiritual authority within the church.* Grand Rapids, MI: Bethany House Publishing.

Joplin, L. (2005). *Love, Janis.* New York: Harper Collins.

Kaftal, E. (2008, November). *Post-traumatic stress disorder.* Workshop session presented at the All-Ohio Counselor's Conference, Columbus, OH.

Keenan, P. S., & Farrell, D. P. (2000). Treating morbid jealousy with eye movement desensitization and reprocessing utilizing a cognitive-interweave—a case report. *Counselling Psychology Quarterly*, 13(2), 175–189.

Kim, D., & Choi, J. (2004). Eye movement desensitization and reprocessing for disorder of extreme stress: A case report. *Journal of the Korean Neuropsychiatric Association*, 43(6), 760–763.

Korn, D. (2009). EMDR and the treatment of complex PTSD: A review. *Journal of EMDR Practice and Research*, 3(4), 264–278.

Korn, D., & Leeds, A. (2002). Preliminary evidence of efficacy for EMDR resource development and installation in the stabilization phase of treatment of complex post traumatic stress disorder. *Journal of Clinical Psychology*, 58, 1465–1487.

Kotlowitz, A. (1991). *There are no children here.* New York: Anchor Books.

Lee, C. (2008). *A summary of errors and omissions: A response to the Institute of Medicine report commissioned by the DVA to assess the scientific evidence on the treatment modalities for PTSD.* Austin, TX: EMDR International Association.

Leeds, A. (2009). *A guide to the standard EMDR protocols for clinicians, supervisors, and consultants.* New York: Springer Publishing Company.

Levine, P. (1997). *Waking the tiger—Healing trauma.* Berkeley, CA: North Atlantic Books.

Levitin, D. (2006). *This is your brain on music: The science of a human obsession.* New York: Plume/Penguin Books.

Lipke, H. (2000). *EMDR and psychotherapy integration: Theoretical and clinical suggestions with focus on traumatic stress.* Boca Raton, FL: CRC Press.

Lipke, H. (2004). *A four-activity model of psychotherapy and its relationship to eye movement desensitization and reprocessing (EMDR) and other methods of psychotherapy.* (Revised). Retrieved May 1, 2009, from http://www.howardlipke.com/articles/ Four_Activity.pdf.

Lipke, H. (2009). On science, orthodoxy, EMDR, and the AIP. *Journal of EMDR Practice and Research,* 3(2), 109–112.

Luber, M. (2009). *Eye movement desensitization and reprocessing (EMDR) scripted protocols: Basics and special situations.* New York: Springer Publishing Company.

Luber, M. (2010). *Eye movement desensitization and reprocessing (EMDR) scripted protocols: Basics and special populations.* New York: Springer Publishing Company.

Luber, M., & Shapiro, F. (2009). Interview with Francine Shapiro: Historical overview, present issues, and future directions of EMDR. *Journal of EMDR Practice and Research,* 3(4), 217–231.

Lusk, J. T. (Ed.) (1992). *30 scripts for relaxation and healing imagery.* Duluth, MN: Whole Person Associates.

MacLean, P. D. (1990). *The triune brain in evolution: Role in paleocerebral functions.* New York: Plenum Press.

Manfield, P. (2003). *EMDR casebook: Expanded second edition.* New York: W. W. Norton & Company.

Mangold, J. (Director), Keach, J. (Producer), & Conrad, K. (Producer). (2005). *Walk the line.* [Motion Picture]. United States: 20th Century Fox.

Marich, J. (2009a). EMDR in addiction continuing care: Case study of a cross-addicted female's treatment and recovery. *Journal of EMDR Practice and Research,* 3(2), 98–106.

Marich, J. (2009b). *EMDR in addiction continuing care: A phenomenological study of women treated in early recovery.* ProQuest Dissertations & Theses: Full Text. (UMI No. 3355347).

Marich, J. (2010). Letter to the editor. *Journal of EMDR Practice & Research, 4*(2), 100–103.

Marich, J. (2010). EMDR in addiction continuing care: A phenomenological study of women in early recovery. *Psychology of Addictive Behaviors, 24*(3), 498-507.

Marlatt, G., & George, W. (1984). Relapse prevention: Introduction and overview of the model. *British Journal of Addiction, 79*, 261–273.

Maxfield, L. (2007). Current status and future directions for EMDR research. *Journal of EMDR Practice and Research, 1*(1), 6–14.

Maxfield, L., & Hyer, L. (2002). The relationship between efficacy and methodology in studies investigating EMDR treatment of PTSD. *Journal of Clinical Psychology, 58*, 23–41.

McGoldrick, T., Begum, M., & Brown, K. W. (2008). EMDR and olfactory reference syndrome: A case series. *Journal of EMDR Practice and Research, 2*(1), 63–68.

Miller, A. (2005). *The body never lies: The lingering effects of hurtful parenting.* New York: W. W. Norton & Company.

Miller, D., & Guidry, L. (2001). *Addictions and trauma recovery: Healing the body, mind, and spirit.* New York: W. W. Norton & Company.

Moos, R., & Moos, B. (2006). Rates and predictors of relapse after natural and treated remission from alcohol use disorders. *Addiction, 101*, 212–222.

Moskovitz, A. (2001). *Lost in the mirror: An inside look at borderline personality disorder*, 2nd ed. Latham, MD: Taylor Trade Publishing.

Najavits, L. (2001). *Seeking safety: A treatment manual for PTSD and substance abuse*. New York: The Guilford Press.

Naparstek, B. R. (1994). *Staying well with guided imagery*. New York: Warner Books/Grand Central Publishing.

Naparstek, B. R. (2004). *Invisible heroes: Survivors of trauma and how they heal*. New York: Bantam Books.

Norcross, J. (2002). *Psychotherapy relationships that work: Therapist contributions and responsiveness to patients*. New York: Oxford University Press.

Parnell, L. (2007). *A therapist's guide to EMDR: Tools and techniques for successful treatment*. New York: W. W. Norton & Company.

Parnell, L. (2008). *Tapping in: A step-by-step guide to activating your healing resources through bilateral stimulation*. Boulder, CO: Sounds True Books.

Pearlman, L. A., & Courtois, C. A. (2005). Clinical applications of the attachment framework: Relational treatment of complex trauma. *Journal of Traumatic Stress*, 18(5), 449–459.

Popky, A. J. (2005). DeTUR, an urge reduction protocol for addictions and dysfunctional behaviors. In R. Shapiro (Ed.), *EMDR solutions: Pathways to healing* (pp. 167–188). New York: W. W. Norton & Company.

Popky, A. J. (2010). The desensitization of triggers and urge reprocessing (DeTUR) protocol. In M. Luber (Ed.), *EMDR scripted protocols: Special populations* (pp. 489–516). New York: Springer Publishing Company.

Prochaska, J., Norcross, J., & DiClemente, C. (1994). *Changing for good: The revolutionary program that explains the six stages of change and teaches you how to free yourself from bad habits.* New York: William Morrow.

Ricci, R. J., & Clayton, C. A. (2008). Trauma resolution treatment as an adjunct to standard treatment for child molesters. *Journal of EMDR Practice and Research*, 2(1), 41–50.

Ricci, R. J., Clayton, C. A., & Shapiro, F. (2006). Some effects of EMDR treatment with previously abused child molesters: Theoretical reviews and preliminary findings. *Journal of Forensic Psychiatry and Psychology*, 17, 538–562.

Rothschild, B. (2000). *The body remembers: The psychophysiology of trauma treatment.* New York: W. W. Norton & Company.

Santoro, R., & Cohen, R. J. (1997). *The angry heart: Overcoming borderline and addictive disorders.* Oakland, CA: New Harbinger Publications.

Scaer, R. (2005). *The trauma spectrum: Hidden wounds and human resiliency.* New York: W. W. Norton & Company.

Schurmans, K. (2007). EMDR treatment of choking phobia. *Journal of EMDR Practice & Research*, 1(2), 118–121.

Scott, W. J. (1993). *The politics of readjustment: Vietnam veterans since the war.* New York: Walter de Gruyter, Inc.

Shapiro, F. (1991/1995). *Light stream relaxation CD.* Retrieved June 28, 2010, from http://www.emdrhap.org/store/product_info.php?cPath=21&products_id=83.

Shapiro, F. (1999) Eye movement desensitization and reprocessing (EMDR): Clinical and research implications of an integrated psychotherapy treatment. *Journal of Anxiety Disorders*, 13, 35–67.

Shapiro, F. (2001). *Eye Movement Desensitization and Reprocessing: Basic principles, protocols, and procedures*, 2nd ed. New York: The Guilford Press.

Shapiro, F. (2006). *EMDR: Part I training manual, revised.* Watsonville, CA: EMDR Institute.

Shapiro, F. (2008). *The EMDR approach to psychotherapy: EMDR humanitarian assistance program basic training course.* Watsonville, CA: The EMDR Institute.

Shapiro, F., & Forrest, M. (1997). *EMDR: The breakthrough "eye movement" therapy for overcoming stress, anxiety, and trauma.* New York: Basic Books.

Shapiro, F., & Maxfield, L. (2002). Eye movement desensitization and reprocessing (EMDR): Information processing in the treatment of trauma. *Journal of Clinical Psychology/In Session: Psychotherapy in Practice*, 58(8), 933–946.

Shapiro, F., & Solomon, R. (2008). EMDR and the adaptive information processing model: Potential mechanisms of change. *Journal of EMDR Practice and Research*, 2(4), 315–325.

Shapiro, F., Vogelmann-Sine, S., & Sine, L. (1994). Eye movement desensitization and reprocessing: Treating trauma and substance abuse. *Journal of Psychoactive Drugs*, 26(4), 379–391.

Shapiro, R. (2005). *EMDR solutions: Pathways to healing.* New York: W. W. Norton & Company.

Shapiro, R. (2009). *EMDR solutions II: For depression, eating disorders, performance, & more.* New York: W. W. Norton & Company.

Shortridge, J. (2009). *When she flew.* New York: NAL Accent.

Singer, I. B. (1972). *Enemies: A love story.* New York: Farrar, Straus, & Giroux.

Solomon, M. F., & Siegel, D. (2003). *Healing trauma: Attachment, mind, body, and brain.* New York: W. W. Norton & Company.

Stewart-Grey, E. (2008). *De-stress: A qualitative investigation of EMDR treatment.* ProQuest Dissertations & Theses: Full Text. (UMI No. 3329984).

Stickgold, R. (2002). EMDR: A putative neurobiological mechanism of action. *Journal of Clinical Psychology*, 58(1), 61–75.

Tapert, S., Ozyurt, S., Myers, M., & Brown, S. (2004). Neurocognitive ability in adults coping with alcohol and drug relapse temptations. *The American Journal of Drug and Alcohol Abuse*, 30(2), 445–460.

Terr, L. (1991). Childhood traumas: An outline and overview. *American Journal of Psychiatry*, 148, 10–20.

van der Kolk, B. (2003). Post-traumatic stress disorder and the nature of trauma. In M. F. Solomon & D. Siegel (Eds.), *Healing trauma: Attachment, mind, body, and brain* (pp. 168–195). New York: W. W. Norton & Company.

van der Kolk, B., McFarlane, A., & Weisaeth, L. (Eds.). (1996). *Traumatic stress: The effects of overwhelming experience on mind, body, and society.* New York: The Guilford Press.

van der Kolk, B. A., Spinazzola, J., Blaustein, M. E., Hopper, J. W., Hopper, E. K., Korn, D. L., & Simpson, W. B. (2007). A randomized clinical trial of eye movement desensitization and reprocessing (EMDR), fluoxetine, and pill placebo in the treatment of posttraumatic stress disorder: Treatment effects and long-term maintenance. *Journal of Clinical Psychiatry*, 68(1), 37–46.

Van Sant, G. (Director), & Bender, L. (Producer). (1997). *Good Will Hunting*. [Motion Picture]. United States: Miramax.

VandenBos, G.R. (Ed.) (2007). *APA dictionary of psychology*. Washington, DC: The American Psychological Association.

Vesely, A. (Producer & Director). (2009). *Viktor & I* [Documentary film]. Austria: Alexander Vesely Productions.

Walitzer, K., & Dearing, R. (2006). Gender differences in alcohol and substance use relapse. *Clinical Psychology Review*, 26, 128–148.

Walton, M., Blow, F., Bingham, R., & Chermack, S. (2003). Individual and social/environmental predictors of alcohol and drug use 2 years following substance abuse treatment. *Addictive Behaviors*, 28, 627–642.

Weil, A. (2010). Breathing: Three exercises. In *Weil*. Retrieved February 14, 2010, from http://www.drweil.com/ drw/u/ART00521/three-breathing-exercises.html.

Weintraub, A. (2004). *Yoga for depression: A compassionate guide to relieve suffering through yoga*. New York: Broadway Books.

White, W., & Kurtz, E. (2006). *Recovery-Linking addiction treatment & communities of recovery: A primer for addiction counselors and recovery coaches*. Pittsburgh, PA: The Addiction Technology Transfer Center Network.

Winterbottom, M. (Director), Broadbent, G. (Producer), & Jones, D. (Producer). (1997). *Welcome to Sarajevo*. [Motion Picture]. Channel 4/Miramax.

Worden, J. (2002). *Grief counseling and grief therapy*, 2nd ed. New York: Springer Publishing Company.

Yalom, I. (2001). *The gift of therapy: Reflections on being a therapist*. London, England: Piatkus.

Yalom, I., & Elkin, G. (1974). *Each day gets a little closer: A twice-told therapy*. New York: Basic Books.

Zweben, J., & Yeary, J. (2006). EMDR in the treatment of addiction. *Journal of Chemical Dependency Treatment*, 8(2), 115–127.

Index